Image Pattern
Recognition

V. A. Kovalevsky

Image Pattern Recognition

Translated from the Russian by Arthur Brown

Springer-Verlag
New York   Heidelberg   Berlin

V. A. Kovalevsky

Institute of Cybernetics
Academy of Sciences of the Ukranian SSR
Kiev, USSR

Arthur Brown

10709 Weymouth St.
Garret Park, MD 20766
USA

AMS Classification (1980): 68G10
CR Classification (1980): 3063

With 54 illustrations.

Library of Congress Cataloging in Publication Data

Kovalevskiĭ, V A
  Image pattern recognition

  Bibliography: p.
  Includes index.
  1. Optical pattern recognition. 2. Image processing. I. Title.
TA1650.K67   621.3819'598   79-25286

Title of the original Russian edition: Metody Optimal'nyh Rešeniĭ v Raspoznavanii Izobrazeniĭ. Publisher: Nauka, Moscow, 1977.

9 8 7 6 5 4 3 2 1

ISBN-13:978-1-4612-6035-6   e-ISBN-13:978-1-4612-6033-2
DOI: 10.1007/978-1-4612-6033-2

Preface

During the last twenty years the problem of pattern recognition (specifically, image recognition) has been studied intensively by many investigators, yet it is far from being solved. The number of publications increases yearly, but all the experimental results—with the possible exception of some dealing with recognition of printed characters—report a probability of error significantly higher than that reported for the same images by humans.

It is widely agreed that ideally the recognition problem could be thought of as a problem in testing statistical hypotheses. However, in most applications the immediate use of even the simplest statistical device runs head on into grave computational difficulties, which cannot be eliminated by recourse to general theory.

We must accept the fact that it is impossible to build a universal machine which can learn an arbitrary classification of multidimensional signals. Therefore the solution of the recognition problem must be based on *a priori* postulates (concerning the sets of signals to be recognized) that will narrow the set of possible classifications, i.e., the set of decision functions. This notion can be taken as the methodological basis for the approach adopted in this book.

To specify a set of concrete *a priori* postulates we propose first to define the process that generates the images to be recognized by means of parametric models—i.e., we define the stochastic dependence of the images on various parameters, of which some are essential and others are nuisance parameters. The recognition problem can then be seen as that of adopting an optimal decision as to the values of the essential parameters. The concept of the parametric model allows us to adopt a single point of view with regard to various recognition methods and various formulations of the problems of learning and self-learning. In particular, it allows us to develop an approach to the problem of structural analysis of composite images as a generalization of the linguistic approach to the problem of recognizing images distorted by noise. We propose an optimization approach to the problem of structural analysis, and offer a method for solving the problem.

In all of the cases that we shall consider, the criterion of optimality is either the probability of making a wrong decision or the likelihood function. The latter is usually easier to compute than the former. It is well known that under certain conditions the maximization of the likelihood function is equivalent to minimizing the probability of making a wrong decision. This is usually the goal of pattern recognition in practical applications. The methods we describe in this book are based on the solution of optimization problems, and the optimality criterion is justified from the point of view of the applications.

The methods we describe are mainly oriented toward the recognition of graphic images in the presence of noise. They have been applied to the development of character readers and to systems for the automatic processing of photographs of particle tracks resulting from physical experiments. Together with modern methods for preprocessing halftone images, they can be used to solve problems in the analysis of aerial and satellite photographs of the earth's surface, images of micro-objects found in biological and medical research, etc.

Most of the chapters of this book are based on the unifying idea of parametrizing the process that generates the images to be recognized, and obtaining the maximum-likelihood estimates for the parameters.

There are nine chapters. The first is devoted to a survey of the literature on both theory and technique of image recognition. The material cited is classified according to the approach used for formulating the problem. The first section of the chapter defines the basic concepts and terms for the field of image processing. After analysis of the results obtained by various authors, it is concluded that effective algorithms for image recognition should be constructed on the basis of a study of the specific features of concrete problems.

In the second chapter we describe a parametric model of a pattern-generating process and show how, using this model, we formulate the problems of recognition, learning and self-learning under various circumstances. We first analyze the obstacles that hinder the successful application of the known general theoretical methods and of several empirical approaches to the image recognition problem. In essence, the second chapter contains a general formulation of the problem, which comprehends most of the special cases and marks out a way to surmount the obstacles that have to be met.

The third chapter is devoted to the problem of teaching a machine to recognize patterns, or learning pattern recognition. We consider a new and more general formulation of the parametric learning problem, taking into account the mutual dependence among realizations of the training sample and the influence of nuisance parameters. It is shown that in the presence of nuisance parameters the statistical problem of learning becomes one of estimating parameters from a mixed sample. The well-known statistical formulation of the self-learning problem is a special case of the formulation given here. We also present a formulation that has undeservedly escaped the attention of research workers in this field—namely one based on minimization of the posterior Bayesian risk. This formulation is the most adequate to meet practical demands and leads to a new class of decision rules, distinct from the traditional ones.

In Chapter IV we consider questions connected with the choice of a system of features, i.e., a means for describing a pattern. We introduce the concept of the insufficiency of a description; this concept, as a criterion, provides a quantitative estimate of the distance between the description and a sufficient statistic. We also indicate the role of entropy as a measure of insufficiency, and we prove some theorems on the quantitative relationship between the conditional entropy and the minimum probability of recognition error. These theorems may be useful in solving problems connected with the choice of optimal systems of features.

The remaining chapters of the book are devoted to the solution of several image recognition problems, using the parametric models defined in Chapter II.

In Chapter V we consider a strategy for solving the recognition problem in the presence of nuisance parameters, which we call the *method of admissible transformations*. We use the method of maximum likelihood to obtain an estimate of the parameters. Using two formally defined notions —prototype image and similarity—we formulate the recognition problem as a search for those values of the parameters yielding a prototype that is most similar to the given signal. We also examine the case for which the set of admissible prototype images is a linear subspace of the signal space, of small dimensionality, and we develop the so-called correlation method, which is optimal in this case. Some experimental results are adduced.

In Chapter VI we solve the recognition problem for the case in which the number of values assumed by nuisance parameters is large and maximization of the likelihood function by an exhaustive search is very cumbersome. We consider a piecewise linear function of bounded complexity, and seek the values of its parameters that will minimize an upper bound of the probability of a recognition error. This task reduces to the search for the minimax of a function of very many variables, and can be implemented by a generalized gradient method. We describe an application to the computation of optimal templates for a character reader.

In Chapter VII we describe a method for recognizing composite images, called the *reference sequence method*. Like the correlation method, it derives from a system of admissible transformations. It is much more powerful, however; that is, it is applicable in cases where the images in one class may differ from one another by their dimensions and other geometric features. Each of the recognition classes is defined by describing a sequential image-generating process. The process consists of building an image from elementary pieces, according to established rules, and then subjecting it to distortion by random noise. It is shown that under given circumstances, the maximum-likelihood sequence of elementary pieces can be found by dynamic programming. The method yields not only a classification of composite images but also a structural analysis of them. Some algorithms are given for the solution of concrete problems.

In Chapter VIII the reference sequence method is used to solve the recognition problem for a one-dimensional sequence of images. We consider the important problem of recognizing a typewritten line of characters that are not separated by blanks and that are distorted by noise and random injuries. We prove a theorem on the necessary and sufficient conditions for indicating a portion of the optimal sequence before the analysis of the whole sequence is completed.

Chapter IX is devoted to a description of a character reader that implements the concepts, methods, and algorithms described in this book. We describe a technological implementation of the algorithms substantiated in Chapters V and VI. We also discuss the operational characteristics of the reader and the results of experiments in reading a large mass of documents.

It is clear from the foregoing remarks that the book deals with problems of both theory and application in image recognition. It is useful for readers at several levels of preparation. For an overview of the problems one may limit one's reading to the first and second chapters, to Section 3.5 of Chapter III, to Chapter V, and to the first three sections of Chapter VII. Those who are interested primarily in the theory and methodology may omit Chapter V (but not Section 5.1) and Chapter IX, as well as Sections 7.5 and 7.6 and the greater part of Chapter VIII (but not Section 8.4). Those readers who are already familiar with the problem and who are interested in applications should first familiarize themselves with the basic ideas presented in Chapters II and V (Sections 5.1 and 5.2) and then go to Chapter VI and the following chapters.

The author wishes to thank M. I. Šlezinger most warmly for many fruitful discussions.

V. Kovalevsky

Contents

CHAPTER I

The Current State of the Recognition Problem

Although papers dealing with pattern recognition have been appearing in the literature for more than twenty years, and in ever increasing numbers, the subject itself cannot as yet be said to be clearly outlined as a scientific discipline. Most of the papers represent either projects for some electronic circuitry or *ad hoc* algorithms for solving concrete applied problems. The value of such studies depends primarily on the experimental results that have been obtained.

Theoretical papers generally contain a formal statement of the problem to be solved, which allows us to envision the scope of the results obtained in the paper, and this is often important, since it lets us see what position the algorithms derived there should assume in the whole field. Furthermore, formal theoretical schemes usually embrace most of the algorithms that have been empirically derived, and so allow us to judge their potential and scope.

We regard it as expedient to review here the principal papers on recognition, in approximately chronological order, and classify them according to their formulation of the problem and their method of solution. Since this book is mainly devoted to the problem of recognizing image patterns, our review will be confined to those papers dealing with the recognition problem in general and with methods for image recognition in particular. Papers on speech recognition, medical diagnosis, geological exploration, etc. will not be considered.

We divide the papers into three classes, depending on how they formulate the problem:

1.   papers of a heuristic nature, characterized by an attempt to find practically useful algorithms for recognition or learning, on the basis of intuitive considerations;
2.   those founded on assumptions about the decision functions used for recognition;
3.   those founded on stated assumptions about the signals to be recognized, i.e., papers containing a model of the input signals.

The following survey does not pretend to be exhaustive, and cannot be, because the number of publications in the field of pattern recognition is very large. Priority has been given to those that either offer a well-defined formulation of the problem or contain results that are essential for the applications.

Before we begin the survey, it is worthwhile to recall the basic concepts and terminology in the field of image recognition, and to introduce some notation.

1.1 Basic Concepts and Terminology

A *monochrome* or *black and white image* is a plane region in which a *brightness* is defined at every point as a function of the coordinates of the point. Since the brightness of an image on paper or on a transparent film depends on the illumination produced by the light source, it is often useful to consider the *coefficient of absorption a* at each point of the image, rather than the brightness: $a = (b_m - b)/b_m$, where b is the brightness and b_m the maximum brightness. The coefficient of absorption may also be called the *blackness*, although this is not properly a term of optics. [*Translator's Note.* In the English literature the term "gray shade" (cf. R. M. Haralick, "Glossary and index to remotely sensed image pattern recognition concepts," *Pattern Recognition*, 5, pp. 391–403, 1973) is used to refer to a variety of concepts related to the brightness function. We shall use this term everywhere instead of "brightness or blackness".] We shall denote the gray shade at the point whose coordinates are (x, y) by the function $v(x, y)$, and we will specify, when necessary, which of the two physical quantities we are considering.

Image recognition is generally taken to mean the assignment of a given image to one of a set of *image classes* that are predefined by some definite means. We shall use the letter k to denote the class index. (A summary of the notation is given in the appendix.) Classes of images characterized by a common essential property or group of properties will be called *abstract images*. For instance all of the shapes shown in Figure 1.1 correspond to the single abstract image of a "triangle". Thus the terms "class", "abstract image", and sometimes "pattern" will be taken as synonymous. Pattern recognition is a process of abstraction, discarding the details of a given image that from some stated point of view are inessential, and singling out the principal property (from the same viewpoint), which is considered as the defining characteristic of the image class.

Figure 1.1 Some shapes corresponding to the abstract image of a triangle.

We often need to define not one, but several characteristics of a given image—for example to designate various predefined elementary images of which the given image consists, and to specify their dimensions, relative positions, etc. We shall then speak of a *structural analysis*.

The term "image description" has also been used in this case [50, 51]; however, it has also been used in a broader sense, and we therefore prefer the term "structural analysis" or we speak about the "structural description" of an image. The more general term *image processing* (or *picture processing*) refers not only to recognition and structural analysis, but also to various transformations of an image with the aim of enhancing its quality: e.g., filtering out random perturbations (noise), restoring the sharpness of defocused images, increasing the contrast, delineating contours, etc.

By its very definition, an image is fully characterized by a function $v(x, y)$ specifying the spatial distribution of its gray shade. The wave nature of light prevents an image from having arbitrarily fine details. Therefore the function $v(x, y)$ can be defined with a prescribed precision by its *digital representation*, i.e., by an array of integers approximating the average gray shades in each of a finite number of small pieces of the plane that cover the image. In most cases the images to be recognized are given in such digitized form.

To obtain a digital representation of an image we must first use a *sampling* process to measure the gray shades in many discrete points of the plane. Then a *quantization* process must be applied to each result of these measurements to convert it into a corresponding integer.

During the sampling we construct in the region of the plane containing the given image, or *field of view*, an array of regularly spaced points. The spacing between the points is called the *sampling step*. Each point is surrounded by a small neighborhood called a *cell*, or *resolution cell*. The cells may or may not overlap. In most cases the cells are formed by a network of vertical and horizontal lines, and then they are rectangular.

For each cell we are to measure its average gray shade. This measurement may be always thought of as projecting the image on an array of small light-sensitive devices in such a way that each cell is exactly projected on the aperture of a single device. We shall call such an array of light-sensitive devices a *retina* by analogy with the retina of the eye. The sampling procedure will be considered in the sequel as projecting the image onto a retina. Therefore each resolution cell of an image will be considered as a back-projection of the aperture of a single light-sensitive device onto the image plane and will be called a *retina cell*.

During the sampling we measure for every retina cell its average gray shade:

$$v_i = \int \int_{\Omega_i} v(x, y)\omega_i(x - x_i, y - y_i)\,dx\,dy,$$

where Ω_i is the domain of the ith cell and x_i, y_i are the coordinates of its center, and ω_i is a weighting function that characterizes the planar distribution of the illumination and/or the photosensitivity of the measuring device—for instance a photocell. The results of such a measurement are called the *samples* of the given image, and are denoted by v_i, where i is the index number of the cell, $i = 1, 2, \ldots, N$; and N is the number of cells in the retina. When we measure blackness, the value of v_i lies in the range $[0, 1]$. The results of sampling are usually *quantized* to a set of equally spaced gray shade values. For this purpose we divide the range of gray shade into intervals and assign to each interval a discrete value called its *quantum level*, e.g., an integer or a binary code. Then we replace each sample v_i by the discrete value corresponding to the interval containing v_i. The array of the quantized samples is called the *digital image* or *picture array*. The reader will find some more details on the image digitization in [91]. We shall denote the quantized gray shade by the same symbol v_i if it will cause no misunderstanding. An example of digitization is shown in Figure 1.2. The image in Figure 1.2b displays 10 quantum levels.

The input data for all image processing, including image recognition, consist of some measurements carried out on the original image. The results of these measurements are called the *initial features* on which the recognition process works. The components of a digitized representation form a particular case of the notion of the initial features. Initial features of a different nature can be obtained, for instance, by projecting an image through a transparency and measuring the integrated transmitted light. (Here a transparency is taken to mean a semitransparent film with a predefined distribution of optical density.)

In image recognition theory the set $\{v_i\}$ of all measured initial features is called a *signal*. We shall assume that the signal is an N-dimensional vector; we denote it by v. A digitized representation of an image is also a signal. Therefore, we shall use the terms "signal" and "image" as synonyms.

For recognition, it is necessary to decide for each image presented whether or not it belongs to one of the predetermined classes. We shall denote the *decision* by the variable d, and we remark that the set D of all

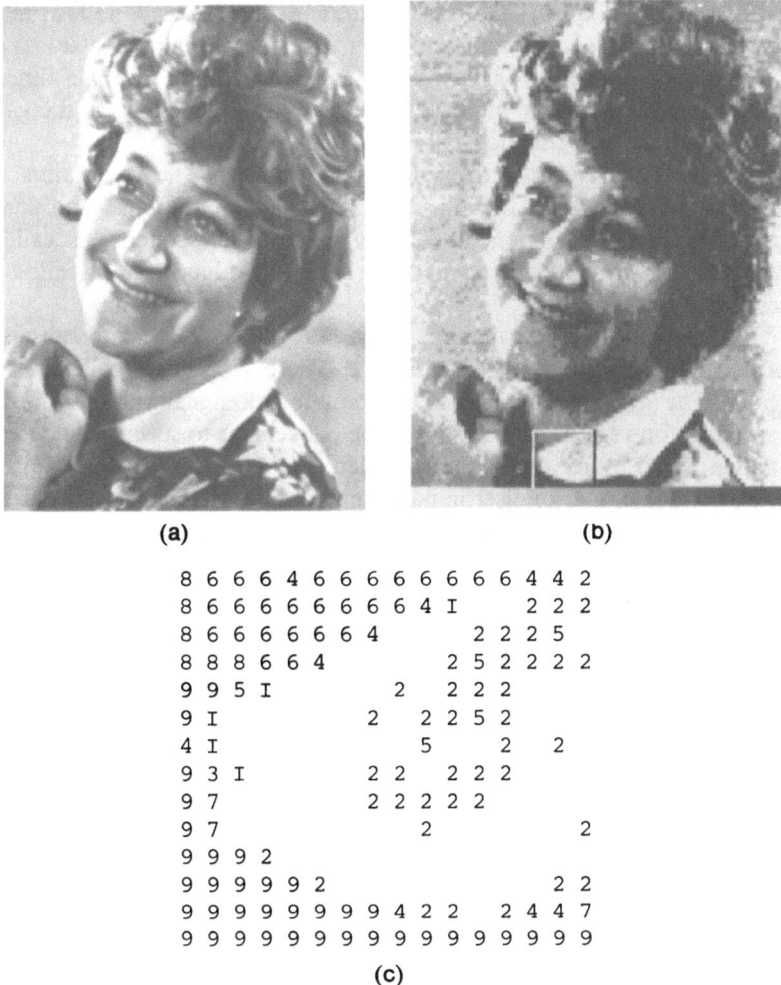

(a)   (b)

```
8 6 6 6 4 6 6 6 6 6 6 6 6 4 4 2
8 6 6 6 6 6 6 6 6 4 I     2 2 2
8 6 6 6 6 6 6 4       2 2 2 5
8 8 8 6 6 4           2 5 2 2 2 2
9 9 5 I           2     2 2 2
9 I               2     2 2 5 2
4 I                   5       2     2
9 3 I             2 2     2 2 2
9 7               2 2 2 2 2
9 7                     2               2
9 9 9 2
9 9 9 9 9 2                           2 2
9 9 9 9 9 9 9 9 4 2 2     2 4 4 7
9 9 9 9 9 9 9 9 9 9 9 9 9 9 9 9
```

(c)

Figure 1.2 Digitization of an image: (a) original image; (b) digital image; (c) digitized gray shades for the square region indicated in (b).

values of d does not necessarily coincide with the set K of classes. The decisions must satisfy certain constraints arising from the available information about the image classes. This information, however, is usually given not in the form of measurements made on real images, but in some abstract form. We say, for instance, that the class corresponding to the letter "Π" consists of images containing two vertical lines capped by a single horizontal line. However, if we want to determine whether the gray shades measured over all the cells of a retina satisfy the class membership criterion, we have to go from the class description in terms of lines to a *decision rule* which assigns every image (or signal) to one of the designated classes. The recognition problem consists in the determination of such decision rules on the basis of descriptions of the classes. One also makes use of optimality requirements and other data, as we shall see later.

The decision depends on the image being recognized, and is a function of the components of the digitized image, or, more generally, of the values of the features. This function is called the *decision function*.

In order to arrive at a decision satisfying all of the constraints it is necessary to execute a certain sequence of computational and logical operations on the components of the image. This sequence' is called a *recognition algorithm*. The idea underlying the algorithm is called the *recognition method*.

The decision function partitions the set V of all signals v into subsets U_d corresponding to the several decisions d. These subsets are called *decision regions*. The decision function is constant for all signal values lying in a single decision region. At times it will be convenient to specify the decision function $\mathcal{F}(v)$ by means of the so-called *discriminant functions* $\tilde{f}_d(v)$, one for each value of d. The discriminant functions are defined so that for all v in the decision region indexed by d,

$$\tilde{f}_d(v) > \tilde{f}_k(v) \quad \text{for } k \neq d.$$

That is, the decision is defined by the index of the discriminant function assuming the largest value at a given point v.

In order to write out an explicit expression for a decision function defined by means of discriminant functions, it is useful to introduce a notation that we will often employ. We shall denote by $\arg\max_{x \in X} f(x)$ the value of the argument x for which the function $f(x)$ attains its maximum value over the set X. The set X will not be specified whenever misunderstandings will not arise on that account. When the maximum is attained on a set of values of x, the set will be denoted by $\mathrm{Arg}\max_x f(x)$. Then $\arg\max_x f(x)$ will denote some one value of x contained in the set $\mathrm{Arg}\max_x f(x)$. The notations $\mathrm{Arg}\min_x f(x)$ and $\arg\min_x f(x)$ are similarly defined.

In this notation the decision d adopted via the discriminant functions $\tilde{f}_k(v)$ can be written as

$$d = \arg\max_k \tilde{f}_k(v).$$

Another useful notation was introduced in [48]. We denote by $\ulcorner Pr \urcorner$ the mapping of the truth values of the predicate Pr that assigns the value 1 for truth and 0 for falsehood. Thus

$$\ulcorner 7 > 5 \urcorner = 1, \qquad \ulcorner 2 > 10 \urcorner = 0.$$

The enclosing marks $\ulcorner$ and $\urcorner$ are called *corners*. They are convenient for writing out functionals of predicates; for example the probability that $x > a$ for a random variable x with the density function $p(x)$ can be written as

$$\mathbf{P}(x > a) = \int \ulcorner x > a \urcorner p(x)\,dx.$$

The set V of values assumed by the signal v is also known as the *signal space*. When every component of the signal assumes an infinite (and uncountable) number of values, the signal space is taken as the N-dimensional Euclidean space, and the components of the signal v are taken as Cartesian coordinates. The generally accepted symbol for N-dimensional Euclidean space is R^N.

If the discriminant functions are continuous, the subsets of signals corresponding to the several decisions (classes) are separated by the partitioning hypersurfaces whose equations are of the form

$$\tilde{f}_d(v) = \tilde{f}_k(v).$$

Points in the hypersurfaces are excluded from the decision regions, and no decision is defined for them. If the discriminant functions are linear, the hypersurfaces are linear manifolds, and are called *separating hyperplanes*.

The recognition process begins with the initial measurements. Usually the set of such measurements, or initial features—for instance the set of components of a digitized representation of an image—is very large. Thus the image of a character which is digitized in the process of automatic character recognition will be decomposed into several hundred components. Quite naturally we wish to replace these by another set of characteristics that have more content; these are the *secondary features*. They must have less volume, but must characterize the image to be recognized as completely as do the initial features.

Sometimes we do not possess all the necessary data for constructing a definitive decision rule. The missing data on the images and the desired classification can be derived by experiment. This phenomenon gives rise to the *learning problem*, which consists in the following:

We are given a *training sample*, or *training sequence* representing a set of observed images—or, more generally, signals—with a decision corresponding to each observation, e.g., a statement of the correct class to which the observed image belongs. A training sample has the form

$$\mathcal{L} = \left\{ (v^1, k^1), (v^2, k^2), \ldots, (v^l, k^l) \right\},$$

where v^j is the jth observation and k^j is the class to which it belongs. Our aim is to find a decision rule that will provide proper classification not only for the observed samples but also for samples to be observed in the future. We note that this definition leaves open the question of what is meant by a *proper classification*; a precise answer will be given below.

A rather interesting learning problem arises when the signals in the training sample are not accompanied by an indication of the corresponding class to which they belong. Then the decision rule we seek must divide the observations into similarity classes, i.e., into classes containing observations that in some well-defined sense are close to each other. This represents the *self-learning* problem, or the problem of *nonsupervised learning*, or the problem of cluster analysis. In the early days of pattern recognition theory, this problem had an aura of mystery about it, but is now quite well formulated and has a down-to-earth character, provided there exists a criterion that permits the evaluation of the quality of any given classification. Given these, the self-learning problem reduces to the search for optimal classifications.

Most of the images that have to be recognized have been subjected to various distortions, and they exhibit many minor defects or departures from the ideal form (Figure 1.3). It is impossible to take into account the causes of all these defects, and they are to be thought of as *random perturbations*, or *noise*. The components v_i of the signal are to be thought of then as random variables, and the set of components, or the signal as a whole, is to be regarded as a multidimensional random variable v. A decision, being a deterministic function of the value of a random variable, is itself a random variable.

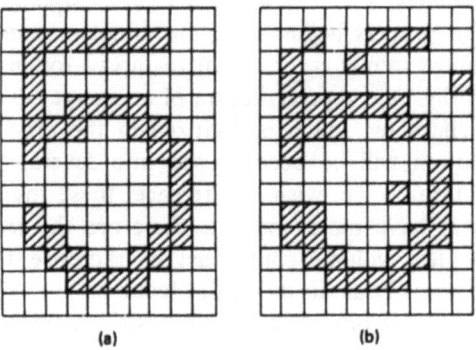

(a)   (b)

Figure 1.3   Ideal and perturbed images.

Along with the classification of images accomplished by the pattern recognition procedure, there exists in most cases some true or objective classification—so that, in principle at least, it is possible to know the true class to which any image belongs. For instance, when we are trying to recognize the image of a typewritten letter, the true class is defined by the name of the key that produced the letter. There are, of course, recognition problems for which no such "true" classes are defined—for instance the class of "beautiful" images. No true classes exist also in several areas of cluster analysis, where the formation of classes takes place during the analysis of the images. An example arises in the study of living cells, if we must classify microphotographic images of such cells according to their form, into the classes "normal" and "abnormal". Here we can hardly speak of a true or objective classification.

When there exists a true classification, and the decision rule yields for the given image a result different from the true class of that image we speak of a *misclassification*, or a *classification error*. The number of errors can be decreased if we allow the decision rule to deal with difficult, doubtful images by giving an undefined decision, i.e., by refusing to decide. We call such a decision a *rejection*.

Since the decision in the presence of noise is a random variable, we may speak of the *probability of error* and the *probability of rejection*. These two quantities are the most important characteristics of a recognition system or recognition algorithm.

In place of the clumsy expression "probability of correct recognition" there are other terms in occasional use, such as "recognition performance", or "reliability", or "quality of recognition". However, the quantities corresponding to these expressions are less useful than the error probability, since their numerical values are close to unity, e.g., of the order of $1 - 2 \times 10^{-4}$. Moreover, some of the expressions in question are used in other senses, and cannot be assumed to have universal acceptability. We will therefore not use them, and will instead use the more precise concepts of the probability (or frequency) of errors and rejections.

The error probability is a fundamental criterion by which we can judge the suitability of a recognition system whenever there exists an objective basis for correct classification. The recognition problem is therefore often formulated as a search for the optimal decision rule under this criterion. When there is no objective classification, as for instance in problems of cluster analysis, we have to develop another criterion that will be useful in dealing with the applications.

In an overwhelming majority of the practically important cases of pattern recognition, the classification must not depend on changes in the image that might arise from changes in the observational conditions rather than in the observed object itself. Therefore we normally demand of the decision rule that it should at least be invariant under *translations* of the image, i.e., it must be independent of the position of the image within the field of view. In many cases we also want the decision rule to be invariant under projective or affine transformations.

Given a noise-free image, the pattern recognition rule can be made independent of the position of the image by a *centering process*, in which some easily identified characteristic point of the image is brought by displacement to a fixed point in the field of view. After such a centering, all images that differ only by their position become identical, and the classification can be made without respect to their initial positions. In a similar fashion we can eliminate the effects of size, rotation, etc. However, in the presence of noise such normalization can hardly be done *before the recognition*; as we shall see, the development of an invariant decision rule presents a rather complex problem.

Often the images in a given class have a fairly constant size and shape. Then the classification can be done by comparing the images with models. These models are called *masks, stencils, templates,* or *prototypes*. The term *prototype* is also used to denote an ideal preimage which is the archetype of the images in a given class—that is, an idealized image from which the observed images are generated by various transformations and perturbations. We will use it primarily to denote such an archetype, and the models used for comparison will be called *templates*. We will use this term even in

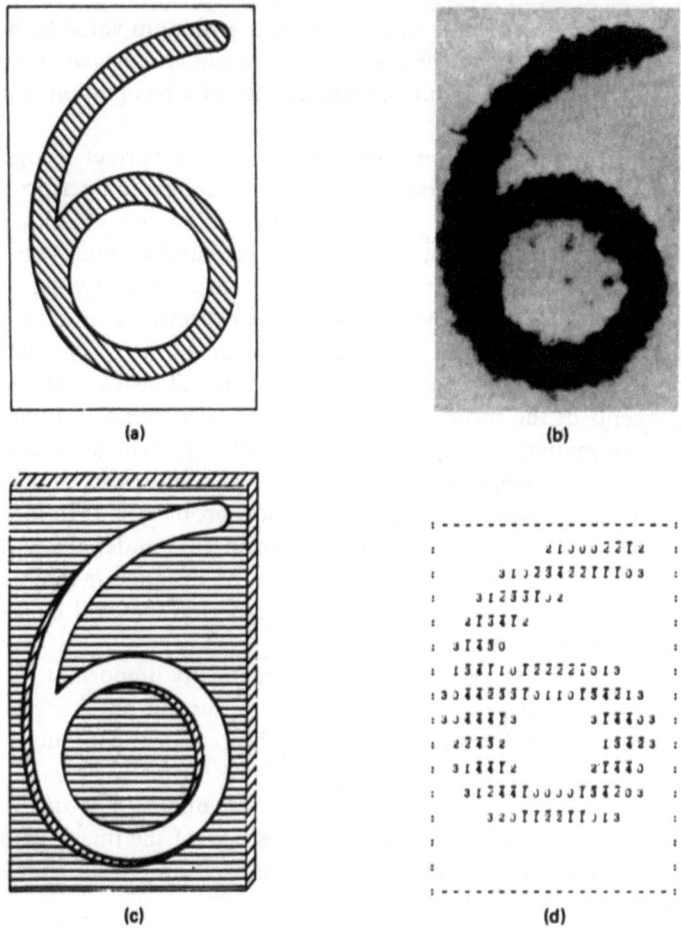

Figure 1.4   Prototype image, and template: (a) prototype; (b) observed image; (c) optical template; (d) template as produced by a computer.

those cases when the image is not directly compared with a template image but is compared by some indirect process (Figure 1.4). Sometimes, however, the prototype provides the best template, and then, as for instance when we use the correlation method (Chapter V), the difference between template and prototype disappears.

One of the most important practical recognition problems is that of the so-called *reading machine*, or *character reader*, a machine dedicated to the input of documents into a computer, using either typescript or handwritten characters. The character reader works on a stack of documents, taking them one by one. It recognizes the characters one by one, codes the decisions and delivers a numeric code, in the form of a standard signal, to the computer (or other machine for which the contents of the documents are destined).

Other problems in the recognition and processing of images are almost always solved by general-purpose computers equipped with *scanners* that can digitize the input images. The gray shades as measured by the scanner are quantized and converted to binary codes before they are fed to a computer. Further processing of the image is done by the computer according to the stored program that implements the recognition or processing algorithm.

The terms we have defined appear in much of the pattern-recognition literature, and may be taken as generally acceptable. The accompanying remarks, however, do not necessarily constitute a definition; any attempt to provide such definitions would render the exposition clumsy and would scarcely contribute to a better understanding of the concepts. The foregoing material is primarily aimed at helping a reader who is unfamiliar with the field to get a grasp on the basic concepts that are dealt with in Chapter I. The concepts needed for the later development are defined and explained below, as they are introduced.

1.2 Heuristic Paths

The early work in image recognition consisted in general of attempts to invent "good" methods, and many highly ingenious processes were proposed.

One of the first, for the recognition of printed characters, was the so-called *template-matching method*, in which a prepositioned character image was compared with a series of template masks, or stencils, by which all the characters in the given alphabet were represented. The prepositioning was done by locating the edges of the character, say the left edge and top edge. Various criteria were proposed for assessing the degree of correspondence between the image and the template: the amount of light transmitted or reflected; the difference in the total light obtained with "positive" and "negative" masks; the current flowing in an electrical circuit containing analogues of the image and template; and other such quantities. Although all these were realized by different technical devices, they all had much in common, since they can be represented by linear functionals of the images. The decision as to which character class corresponds to the image usually amounts to choosing the template whose linear functional has the largest (or in some methods the smallest) value.

The *method of fragments* is a variant of the template-matching method. Instead of comparing an entire template with the whole of the image, only selected portions of the image are examined. Each such portion will exhibit either black or white, depending on which character is represented by the image; a logical function uses this information to decide which character is being represented.

Clearly, the template-matching and fragment methods are unusable if the characters come from different type fonts, and more so for hand-written characters. Therefore attempts have been made to develop more flexible methods. The projection method amounts to summing the "amount of black" or the number of intersections of the image with each of several horizontal strips placed across it. The order in which the maxima and minima of this sum succeed one another from strip to strip is observed. A second projection of the same image is obtained by the use of vertical strips. These data on the alternation of maxima and minima in both projections allow us to recognize an image without regard to its size or position, and, to some extent, without regard to change of shape. This method does not guarantee reliable recognition, since some figures that are distinct nevertheless yield identical, or very nearly identical, projections— for instance an oblique cross and the outline of a rhombus whose diagonals are parallel to the axes of projection. Moreover, through deformations of the image and through random perturbations, the projections can suffer significant changes. Therefore, projection analysis is in itself a difficult task.

A more popular method is the so-called *method of stroke analysis*. This consists in the detection of vertical and horizontal segments and of arcs in various orientations, together with the measurement of their lengths and the analysis of their mutual relative positions. In the opinion of its authors this method should permit the recognition of characters from different fonts.

Quite different from those described above are the methods founded on edge tracking. They are normally implemented by flying-spot scanners; the bright spot on the screen of a cathode-ray tube (CRT) is projected onto the image of the character, and the reflected light is detected by a photomultiplier. A simple feedback circuit forces the electron beam of the CRT to move so that the projected light spot falling on the image moves along the boundaries between light and dark regions, i.e., along the contours of the image. An analysis of the sequence of directions in which the light spot moves will provide a description of the image which is independent of the size and position of the representation of the character.

Most of these methods have been or are being used in the optical character-reading machines. Most such machines require the use of special stylized type fonts; the machines that can read text printed in different fonts have a complete set of templates in their memories for all the admissible fonts, and are therefore as complex and costly as a big computer.

All the existing machines demand very high quality in the preparation of the documents submitted to them. Imperfections in the quality of the print —defects, dirt, broken lines, shape deviation from the standard—all result in recognition errors or rejections. The latter occur when the image appears not to correspond to any of the templates. In the face of low-quality print the machines have much higher error and rejection probabilities than humans do.

The relatively high error probabilities do not stem from shortcomings peculiar to specific systems; rather they arise from a general cause, namely that the decision as to whether a given image belongs to one character class or another depends on a set of many intermediate, local, and (most importantly) independent decisions. Each such intermediate decision deals with only a portion of the image; it is taken without reference to decisions made about other portions. These independent decisions relate to:

whether an individual elementary portion of the image is black or white; the location of the boundary of the character when the image is pre-positioned;

the presence or absence of one or other stroke or fragment;

the orientation of boundary segments; maxima and minima in the projected image;

or other similar characteristics.

In the presence of random noise, dirt, defective type, etc. a local decision cannot be completely reliable. Its reliability might be improved by taking into account the information contained in some other image portions statistically interrelated with the portion under consideration. If a decision on an image portion is made without reference to other portions, some of the information about the whole image is irretrievably lost, just as it is by the independent recognition of single letters in an illegibly written word. Correct decisions about the letters can only be made by utilizing the context, i.e., by recognizing whole words or phrases.

Similarly, in the recognition of complex images we must take into account the corresponding geometric context—that is, we must consider limitations on the admissible combinations of elements of the images.

To a greater or lesser extent all of the heuristic methods for character recognition make decisions about separate portions of the image without taking into account their interdependence. We need only note that most of these methods center an image by reference to its edges. The decision as to where the character is in the field of view of the reader is made by finding two neighboring rows or columns for which the gray level is below some threshold in one and above in the other. Such a decision is extremely unreliable in the presence of ink spots or type flaws, and an erroneous centering of the image generally leads to recognition errors.

The simplest methods for character recognition are therefore usable only when the printed matter satisfies very stringent conditions on the shape of the type and the quality of the print. To yield an acceptably high probability of correct recognition, the print quality must be so high that the local decisions have a very low error probability. In other words, no essential element of any character may be distorted or damaged.

The next stage in the development of heuristic (intuitive) methods is marked by the appearance of the notion of the *perceptron*. In an effort to find a practical solution of the recognition problem, and even more, to understand how humans solve this problem and learn to solve new problems, Frank Rosenblatt put forward the perceptron model in 1958 [87]. In his earliest papers, Rosenblatt did not base the model on either theoretical grounds or sharply formulated hypotheses. Later on, however, the perceptron model served as a starting point for the construction of a substantial and fruitful theory of nonparametric learning, which we describe below. We shall present the principles of the perceptron in terms that are in common use, which differ from Rosenblatt's.

A digitized image v is transformed into a set of secondary features $\psi_j(v)$, $j = 1, 2, \ldots$ which are linear threshold functions of the components v_i:

$$\psi_j(v) = \ulcorner \sum_i a_{ji} v_i > \vartheta_j \urcorner. \tag{1.1}$$

Here v_i is the ith component of the digitized image, a_{ji} and ϑ_j are the parameters of the jth transformation. The meaning of the corners $\ulcorner$ and $\urcorner$ has already been explained, on p. 6.

The value of $\psi_j(v)$ will be 1 if $\sum a_{ji} v_i > \vartheta_j$ and 0 otherwise. Rosenblatt uses the term A-element for the transducers that implement the functions (1.1). He proposed that the parameters a_{ji} and ϑ_j characterizing the relations between the A-elements and the retina be specified by a random process under certain contraints.

The decision rule is constructed with the help of discriminant functions linear in the $\psi_j(v)$,

$$\tilde{f}_k(v) = \sum_j c_{kj} \psi_j(v), \tag{1.2}$$

where c_{kj} is a coefficient called the *weight* of the jth secondary feature or the jth A-element in the kth discriminant function. The decision as to whether the image v belongs to a specified class of images is made by assigning v to the class for which the corresponding discriminant function has the highest value.

A perceptron learns in the following way: It is shown a sequence of images—i.e., they are projected onto its retina—which together form a training sample. For every image, a human teacher specifies the class to which it belongs, i.e., inputs to the perceptron the correct index number k of the class. If the decision d produced by the perceptron is wrong ($d \neq k$), the weights c_{kj} of the kth discriminant function are incremented by amounts proportional to the values of the $\psi_j(v)$ and the weights c_{dj} are incremented by amounts proportional to $-\psi_j(v)$. If the decision is correct, all weights are left unchanged.

Experimental studies of the perceptron have been carried out by simulation on computers and by the construction of specialized models. These studies have shown that if the images of a given class are projected onto approximately the same group of retina cells, the perceptron can achieve a recognition probability of 70–95% after a sufficiently long learning period, provided that all the images are roughly centered and are of roughly the same size.

These results, of course, do not always satisfy the needs of practical applications. Nevertheless, it is very noteworthy that we can teach a machine to recognize signals, using such simple methods and imparting no information about the sets of signals themselves. On this account the concept of the perceptron has aroused great interest and has been the subject of many theoretical and experimental studies.

Aside from the experimental studies, much work has been done on further developments of the concept. Rosenblatt would appear to have been the first to propose the notion of the self-learning recognizer. However, he did not point out clearly enough the substantive meaning of this problem, nor the possibility of stating it formally so as to permit the determination of precisely what kind of classification should be implemented by a self-learning system, i.e., how such a classification is to be distinguished from an arbitrary one. Rosenblatt also introduced a series of improvements in the structure of the perceptron. Some variants in the perceptron scheme were put forward by A. G. Ivahnenko, B. Widrow, K. Steinbuch and others. A compact summary of the basic results of work along these lines is given in a book by N. J. Nilson [56], which contains a compact and intelligible exposition of the learning problem as a whole.

A number of authors have made important contributions by studies of the mathematical problem that the perceptron solves. Most of these were devoted to the problem of convergence of the perceptron learning process when the set of secondary features is prespecified and the target decision rule is known to exist. We discuss a few of them below.

It is also important to know what recognition problems can in principle be solved by decision rules that can be realized in the form of perceptrons. Some interesting arguments in this connection have been advanced by M. M. Bongard [9]. Marvin Minsky and S. Papert have published a profound and original study of this problem in their monograph [48]. They consider a class of perceptrons that is somewhat wider than the one we have just described, and succeed in showing that many recognition problems that can be very simply formulated are in principle insoluble by a preceptron. On the other hand, their analysis of the perceptron learning algorithm shows that for certain values of its parameters that algorithm has great merit: (1) it is very simple; (2) it allows us to find a solution to the problem of separating the training sample by a finite number of steps (of course, if the decision rule exists); it is in fact a very simple variant of the algorithm for the iterative solution of a system of linear inequalities. Minsky and Papert also state many other interesting results in recognition and learning and in collateral problems.

The most interesting property of any learning system is its ability to extrapolate, i.e., to recognize images not presented in the training sample. The perceptron, like most recognizers, implements in the space V of the primary features a set of piecewise continuous discriminant functions [piecewise continuous because of the discontinuity of the threshold functions $\psi_j(v)$]. It therefore has a "natural" ability to extrapolate by continuity: it puts into the same class both a signal and the neighboring signals. The real interest, however, is in its ability to make distant extrapolations. From this point of view, the perceptron's ability to extrapolate depends on the transformation implemented by its i-elements. Therefore, for a perceptron with random coefficients a_{ji}, its ability to extrapolate may be only accidentally adequate for any concrete recognition problem, and that with vanishingly small probability.

In fact, many authors, including Rosenblatt, have shown that the perceptron we have described—the so-called three-layer perceptron— cannot extrapolate in the practically important case when the images of a given class may differ by affine transformations. Minsky and Papert have shown that a three-layer perceptron cannot do this, since the extrapolation requires that the weights generated in the learning process must be unbounded. The memory space required, as a result of this unbounded- ness, for the storage of the weights with the necessary precision would exceed the space required for the straightforward storage of all the images presented in the training samples. For this reason the perceptron is not efficient in practical use for image recognition, and the great hopes pinned to it have been only partially realized. Today we can describe a quite clearly defined class of non-parametric learning problems for which the perceptron is adequate, and we shall say more about these problems in the next section.

Despite the shortcomings we have cited, the perceptron has played an extremely important role in the development of the science of recognition. The idea of creating a simple universal machine that is able to learn for various recognition tasks inspired many investigators to further search. On the other hand, mathematical studies of the perceptron have served as the basis for an entire branch of recognition theory, which we shall now consider.

1.3 Methods Based on Assumptions about the Family of Decision Functions

In a formal statement of the learning problem, prior knowledge about the classes of signals can be expressed either in the form of assumptions about the sets of signals corresponding to the various classes, or in the form of assumptions about the family of suitable decision functions. In the first case, the information about the signals can be expressed by parameter- dependent conditional probability distributions. If the values of the parameters are unknown, they can be estimated from experimental data. This is the *parametric* approach; we shall discuss it in the next section.

In the second case we suppose given a fairly wide family of decision functions, and we do not explicitly use the information about the signals. In the *nonparametric* learning problem, the aim is to choose a decision function from the given family. This is equivalent to the approximation of an unknown function by means of functions belonging to a given family.

In recognition problems the decision functions usually take on discrete values, which are constant over each of the sets of signals to be separated.

Therefore the approximation of the decision functions sometimes reduces to a covering of the different subsets by some standard regions in the space, e.g., hyperspheres [20] or intersections of half spaces. Methods of learning founded on these covering techniques are intuitively transparent. For the hyperspheres, they consist in storing certain "representative" or "essential" points from the training sample and in surrounding them with neighborhoods containing "nearby" or "similar" points. In the case when there is reason to suppose that each of the sets of signals to be recognized can be covered by a relatively small number of standard regions, the approximation algorithm will work. An example is the classification of a small number of standard signals distorted by Gaussian noise. In this case each class can be represented by a small number of hyperspheres.

Another and similar approach, known as the *method of potential functions* [2], consists in using for approximation the union of certain fuzzy sets defined by a *potential function*. In this case we approximate the discriminant function rather than the decision function, by adding the potentials, which decrease with increasing distance from various centers chosen during the learning process. This approach has been found to be equivalent to the approximation of the discriminant functions by series expansions.

We consider the following problem: The set of input signals v must be divided into two classes. Then we need only one discriminant function, $\tilde{f}(v)$, which is equal to the difference of two customary discriminant functions (cf. Section 1.1). In this case the decision is dictated by the sign of $\tilde{f}(v)$. Suppose it is known that a discriminant function having positive values on the first class and negative values on the second can be represented in the form of a finite or infinite sum

$$\tilde{f}(v) = \sum_j c_j^* \psi_j(v). \tag{1.3}$$

If the sum is an infinite series, the coefficients c_j^* and the set of functions $\{\psi_j(v)\}$ must satisfy the conditions

$$\sum_j (c_j^*)^2 < \infty \tag{1.4a}$$

and

$$\sum_j \psi_j^2(v) < \infty. \tag{1.4b}$$

We may impose the weaker condition $|\psi_j(v)| < m$ in place of (1.4b), but then the coefficients c_j^* must satisfy the stronger condition

$$\sum_j (c_j^*/\lambda_j)^2 < \infty,$$

where the λ_j form an absolutely convergent series. Then, instead of $\{\psi_j(v)\}$ we can use the set of functions $\{\lambda_j \psi_j(v)\}$, and this system satisfies both of the conditions (1.4), since the weights in the discriminant functions $\tilde{f}(v)$ are equal to c_j^*/λ_j.

Suppose we are given a training sample $\mathcal{L}$, which consists of a sequence of values v' of the signal v together with the teacher's assignment of the sign of the function $\tilde{f}(v')$, i.e., the assignment of each signal value to one or other of the two classes. We wish to find an algorithm that provides an increasingly better approximation to the discriminant function as new values v' appear. In other words, we wish to construct a function $f(v)$ which approximates $\tilde{f}(v)$ so that it agrees with it as to sign on the training sample.

One variant of such an algorithm is the following: We are to construct a potential function

$$\sum_j \psi_j(w)\psi_j(v) = \mathcal{K}(w,v). \tag{1.5}$$

Given (1.4), it is easy to see that the potential function is bounded even when the sum on the left is an infinite series. It is positive for $v = w$ and is generally nonzero for $v \neq w$. The function $f'(v)$ approximating the discriminant function $\tilde{f}(v)$, given the input v' from the training sample $\mathcal{L}$, is defined by the recursion formula

$$f'^{+1}(v) = f'(v) + \gamma'\mathcal{K}(v'^{+1},v). \tag{1.6}$$

Here the coefficient γ' is defined by the equation

$$\gamma' = \tfrac{1}{2}\left[\operatorname{sign}\tilde{f}(v'^{+1}) - \operatorname{sign}f'(v'^{+1})\right].$$

When the sign of the discriminant function $\tilde{f}(v'^{+1})$ as assigned by the teacher agrees with the sign of the tth approximation $f'(v'^{+1})$, we have $\gamma' = 0$ and $f'^{+1}(v) = f'(v)$. Otherwise, the appropriate correction increment is applied to the value $f'(v'^{+1})$, and at the same time a correction is applied to the approximating function at all those points v not in the training sample and for which $\mathcal{K}(v'^{+1},v) \neq 0$. This procedure defines the extrapolation of the function $f'(v)$ for points not in the training sample. For subsequent recognitions it is necessary to store in memory all the sample points at which a correction was made, and the corresponding values of γ'.

Another version of this algorithm defines the function $f'(v)$ by the set of coefficients c_j' in its expansion via the system of functions $\{\psi_j(v)\}$ similar to the expansion (1.3). According to (1.3) the discriminant function is linear in the $\psi_j(v)$; in a space where the coordinates are the $\psi_j(v)$ $(j = 1,2,3,\ldots)$, the separating surfaces are defined by the equations

$$\sum c_j\psi_j(v) = 0$$

and so are hyperplanes. This space is therefore called the *rectifying space*. Every signal v maps into a corresponding point of the rectifying space. Our task is to find the hyperplane that divides the given sample into two subsamples; we accomplish it via the recursion formula

$$c^{t+1} = c^t + \gamma^t \psi(v^{t+1}), \tag{1.7}$$

where c^t is a vector with the components c_j^t and $\psi(v)$ a vector with the components $\psi_j(v)$, and γ^t has the same meaning as before.

The formula (1.7) corresponds to one of the variants of the perceptron learning algorithm, and it is therefore commonly understood that the method of potential functions is a generalization of perceptron theory.

Much work has been done on the convergence of different variants of this learning algorithm. An early and very significant paper is due to A. Novikoff [86], in which the following result is obtained: If there exists a vector c^* such that all the vectors ψ corresponding to the sample $\mathcal{L}$ satisfy the conditions

$$[c^*, \psi] \geqslant a > 0 \quad \text{and} \quad \|\psi\| \leqslant b,$$

then the correction according to (1.7) to the vector c^t is produced only a finite number m of times, and $m \leqslant b^2/a^2$.

Novikoff's theorem has later been proved in different ways by many other authors, for instance in [48]. A number of important results pertaining to the convergence of algorithms of this class have also been obtained by the developers of the potential-function method [2].

It has been shown further that the procedure (1.7) and the equivalent procedure (1.6) both extremalize some functional of the form

$$\mathbf{M}(f(v)[\operatorname{sign} f(v) - \operatorname{sign} \tilde{f}(v)]),$$

where $\mathbf{M}$ denotes the mathematical expectation, or mean value, v is a random variable, $\tilde{f}(v)$ is the true discriminant function, and $f(v) = \sum_j c_j \psi_j(v)$ is the approximating function.

It is known that the extremum of the mean value of a random variable depending on a parameter can be found by the method of stochastic approximation [46], which leads to an iterative procedure like that in (1.7) but differing in the form of the coefficients γ^t. Thus, the algorithms for the method of potential functions and for the learning of perceptrons can be seen as particular cases of stochastic approximation. Ja. Z. Cypkin [66] drew attention to this fact, and showed that the same is true of many other proposed learning algorithms.

In particular, the method of stochastic approximation solves certain problems of nonsupervised learning, or self-learning. The first formal statement of the problem of nonparametric self-learning as a problem of maximizing a given functional appeared in a paper by M. I. Šlezinger [69]. In this formulation, the signals v^t appearing in the training sample are to be distributed into n classes in such a way that the sum of the quadratic distances among the pairs of signals of the same class is to be minimized.

The problem was solved by an iterative stochastic approximation algorithm.

Problems of this type, in which one looks for a classification that minimizes a given functional, have recently come to be known as *variational* or *nonparametric self-learning* problems. They have been solved by many authors, in several variants. Ja. Z. Cypkin and G. K. Kel'mans [67] showed that the iteration methods used by most authors of papers on nonparametric self-learning can be seen as particular cases of stochastic approximation. (Parametric methods will be discussed in the next section.)

The state of the art of the statistical theory of learning is described in a monograph by V. N. Vapnik and A. Ja. Červonenkis [10]. It contains a complete analysis of the known approaches, together with a number of original results. The most important of the latter are discussed below. In particular, the authors propose the method of the *generalized portrait*, a very effective algorithm for the construction of an optimal separating hyperplane in the rectifying space. Optimality means, for instance, "lying at the greatest distance from the sample points". A characteristic of this method is the multiple use of the training sample. The generalized portrait method has given rise to a number of concrete algorithms which have been successfully used in medical diagnosis, geological exploration, etc.

An algorithm due to B. N. Kozinec [41] is worth noting among the many developed for the construction of optimal separating hyperplanes. It converges more slowly than the generalized portrait algorithm, but is attractive because of its simplicity.

M. I. Šlezinger and L. A. Svjatogor have described a steepest-descent algorithm [71], which gives an exact solution. This virtue, however, is expensive; on each iteration one must solve a system of linear equations whose order does not exceed the number of points in the sample. For small samples in a many-dimensional space the method is highly effective.

It must be noted that the solution of a learning problem by constructing a linear discriminant function in the rectifying space is successful only if the rectifying space is constructed in accordance with whatever prior information we have about the class to which the approximated function is known to belong. In most cases this prior information must define a fairly narrow class of functions, for instance, the class of functions definable as a finite segment of a series in a given system of basis functions $\{\psi_j(v)\}$.

The approximation methods we have described are in principle universal, that is, they allow us to approximate a very broad class of functions. This universality, however, conflicts with the ability to extrapolate, and with practical feasibility [83]. This conflict becomes more acute as the dimensionality of the signal space increases.

The essence of this conflict is simple and transparent; if we want a learning algorithm to extrapolate the teacher's instructions to points of the image space (or more generally the signal space) not contained in the training sample, then the values of the discriminant function at these points must depend on its value at other points, lying within the training sample. Therefore the values of the discriminant function at various points must be related to some *a priori* dependence, given prior to the training sample. Thus we must impose on the discriminant function conditions that are stringent enough to allow us to express the value of the function at some points in terms of its value at other points which are not necessarily nearby. Such conditions, for example, might be the prescription of a finite, and in fact small, set of functions in terms of which the desired function must be expanded in a series. Less stringent conditions, such as continuity, smoothness, "nonfloridity" [2], do not allow us to escape the curse of dimensionality.

In fact, the class of functions of an N-dimensional variable v, satisfying all the conditions mentioned just above, necessarily contains functions taking on arbitrarily prescribed values on the vertices of the unit N-dimensional cube.*

It follows that the rectifying space has dimensionality not less than 2^N, and our function must be prescribed at 2^N points during learning. But this number grows very rapidly compared to N; if N is only a few tens in magnitude, such a prescription is already impossible in principle. We conclude that the definition of a function of many variables by prescribing its values at different given points is feasible only when we are given in advance a sufficiently narrow family of functions known in advance to contain the function we are seeking to define.

In the past it has been difficult to apply these arguments in concrete cases, for lack of a precise notion of what is meant by a "sufficiently narrow family of functions". However, V. N. Vapnik and A. Ja. Červonenkis have given a precise definition in their work on the minimization of empirical risk. The results of this work are summarized in the monograph [10] mentioned earlier. Their basic idea is as follows: Let us suppose that decision functions or decision rules $\mathscr{F}(v, C)$, belonging to some family S, are tested on a training sample of length l with the aim of finding a rule for which the recognition error probability $p(C)$ is at a minimum. Each rule $\mathscr{F}(v, C)$ is characterized by the number $n(C)$ of errors made on the training sample, or by the error frequency

$$\nu(C) = n(C)/l.$$

---

* These functions may, for instance, be Nth-degree polynomials

$$f(v) = \sum_{j=1}^{2^N} f_j \prod_{i=1}^{N} \left(\alpha_{ij} v_i + (1 - \alpha_{ij})(1 - v_i) \right),$$

where α_{ij} is the ith coordinate of the jth vertex of the cube, and may take on the values 0, 1; v_i is the ith coordinate of the variable point v; and f_j is the value of the function f at the jth vertex of the cube. This is a specialized interpolation polynomial: if the argument v coincides with the kth vertex of the cube, i.e.,

$$v_i = \alpha_{ik} \quad \text{for all } i = 1, 2, \ldots, N,$$

then all terms vanish except the kth, which equals f_k.

If we choose the rule giving the lowest empirical frequency of error, say $\mathcal{F}(v, \hat{C})$, it is possible that a small number of errors may have been due to chance, and that the best rule is in fact some other rule belonging to S. If the number of rules in S is finite, say N_S, we may apply the law of large numbers to estimate the probability that all of the empirical frequencies differ from the true probability $p(C)$ by an amount not greater than ε. With this as our fiducial probability we may assert that the error probability for the rule chosen on the basis of minimum empirical error frequency differs from the true probability by an amount not greater than 2ε.

The same authors have shown that a family containing an infinite number of rules can be characterized by a quantity which they call its *capacity*; for instance, the capacity of the family of linear threshold functions in N-dimensional space is $N + 1$. A study of other families of functions used in learning shows that in all the cases studied the capacity of the family is equal to the number of adjustable parameters. For classes with finite capacity one can, in the same way as for finite N, establish the relationship among the length l of the training sample, the deviation ε of the frequency $v(C)$ from the true error probability $p(C)$, and the fiducial probability. For families with infinite capacity the deviation of the empirical error frequency from the true error probability is not bounded; therefore in this case the error frequency tells us nothing useful about the error probability. In other words, learning is meaningless in this case. And we are in precisely this situation when we attempt to find a "universal" family of decision rules, i.e., a family allowing us to approximate an arbitrary decision rule. Such a family necessarily has infinite capacity.

These results allow us to solve a nonparametric learning problem and to estimate the error probability without reference to any information about the signal probability distribution. The estimate depends on the capacity of the family, the fiducial probability, and the length of the training sample. Using the estimates we have obtained, we may solve not only the problem of choosing an optimal rule belonging to the family, but also the problem of the best choice of the decision-rule family. For this, we consider a sequence of families $S_1, S_2, S_3, \ldots$ with increasing capacity, in which each family contains its predecessor. For each rule $\mathcal{F}(v, C)$ in S_j we may write the following inequality:

$$p(C) < v(C, S_j) + \varepsilon(S_j) \tag{1.8}$$

for the recognition error probability. For any given length l of the training sequence, this inequality holds with the given fiducial probability. There remains the task of optimizing the estimate of error probability, i.e., of optimizing the right-hand side of the inequality (1.8). For optimization within a family we choose the rule that minimizes $v(C, S)$. When we pass to a family with greater capacity, the quantity $v(C, S)$ cannot increase, since each family contains all the rules in its predecessors, i.e., S_{j+1} contains every rule in S_j. On the other hand, the second term increases because the capacity of the family increases. It follows that there exists a family for which the right-hand side of (1.8) is at a minimum.

This approach, called the *well-ordered minimization of risk*, allows us to solve new problems, connected with the selection of a set of features, the choice of the signal space, etc. In particular, it allows us to resolve a known paradox connected with the choice of the degree of a regression polynomial: namely, if we wish to make a polynomial approximation of a continuous function which is represented by l readings, and the degree of the polynomial is not specified in advance, we find that the best approximation is given by a polynomial of degree l, which is absurd. The use of well-ordered minimization allows us to find a reasonable solution of this problem.

It is difficult to overestimate the value of these results. Nevertheless it would be wrong to suppose that the need for studying the probability distribution of the signals has disappeared. The fact is that for an unknown signal probability distribution we cannot be sure that a given class of decision functions, or sequence of classes with increasing capacity, contains a rule good enough to ensure a small error probability. We can of course try out some sequence of families, and if we succeed the problem is solved. If, however, we do not succeed, the pathways leading to the discovery of usable families of decision rules remain completely unknown.

Another difficulty lies in the fact that the estimates of the sample sizes adequate for learning are far from consoling. For instance, when using the family of linear discriminant functions and assuming very modest requirements, say $N = 100$ and $\varepsilon = 0.01$, with a fiducial proability of 0.95, equation (13.7) of [10] yields the estimate $l \simeq 2 \times 10^7$. Given the current technology of computer learning, the use of samples of such size for the development of a single discriminant function is hardly practical. Taking both kinds of difficulty into account, we must conclude that a successful solution of the recognition problem requires the use of *a priori* knowledge about the set of signals corresponding to the classes to be recognized.

1.4 Methods Based on Assumptions about the Properties of the Signals

If we know certain properties of the classes of images to be recognized, we can choose a family of decision functions having not too large a capacity, or even choose a wholly defined function, yielding a satisfactory probability of correct recognition. These properties should be stated in the form of a model of the image classes which will—at least in principle—allow us to generate images identical to the real images in the classes considered.

Even in the early stages of image recognition theory one finds models defining image classes by means of characteristic functions invariant under a certain group of plane transformations representing admissible motions of the image in its plane. According to these models images that differ by a translation, rotation, and scaling belong to the same class. Therefore the decision function must be also invariant under the same group. Various methods for constructing such functions were proposed; one consisted in calculating functionals of the images, called "moment invariants" [76]. For instance, a functional invariant under translations has the form

$$M^{mn} = \iint v(x, y)(x - \xi)^m (y - \eta)^n \, dx \, dy,$$

where $v(x, y)$ is the distribution of gray shade for the given image, x and y are Cartesian coordinates in the plane of the image, and ξ and η are functionals of $v(x, y)$ locating the centroid of the given image. They are computed by setting M^{10} and M^{01} equal to zero. It is easily seen that the functionals M^{mn} with different m and n are unchanged by a translation of the image, i.e., when $v(x, y)$ is replaced by $v(x - a, y - b)$. Similarly, one can construct more complex expressions invariant under scaling, rotation, etc.

Moment invariants have been used as secondary features, and the classes in a space of features having modest dimensionality are separated by hyperplanes. The latter can be found by one or other learning algorithm. Moment invariants up to and including the sixth order were employed in [76]. In experiments on the recognition of handwritten symbols, the error frequency reached several percentage points, which is of course unacceptable in practice.*

Similar recognition methods have been used by many other authors. Two which are very close to the method of moment invariants are based one on computation of the *autocorrelation function* of the image

$$f(\xi, \eta) = \iint v(x, y)v(x - \xi, y - \eta) \, dx \, dy$$

and another on the two-dimensional spectrum of the image. Both of these are based on the calculation of a functional which is invariant under translation, scaling, and sometimes rotation. These functionals play the role of secondary features.

V. S. Faĭn [63] studied a rather richer class of transformations, by considering the parameters of a topological mapping that will convert one of a fixed set of prototypes into the image as given. Thus, Faĭn's model of the set of images belonging to a given class is not equivalent to a region in an N-dimensional space (as assumed by most of the other authors) but to a manifold of few dimensions representing the trajectory of a vector

---

* We should note that the recognition of alphanumeric characters differs from other recognition problems in that it demands a very high probability of correct recognition. Its aim is to provide computer input, or to transmit data via communication channels. These processes require high reliability: it is customary to require error probabilities not exceeding 10^{-4}, and sometimes as low as 10^{-6}. Therefore, recognition methods yielding error probabilities of the order of 10^{-2} are generally regarded as unsatisfactory for recognition of alphabetic characters, and *a fortiori* unsatisfactory for numeric characters.

depending on a few variable parameters. (In this respect, his model resembles the prototype domain introduced by Kovalevsky in 1962 [32].)

Fain proposes to recognize an image by defining the number and coordinates (x, y) of what he calls its characteristic points. Given these data one must choose one or more prototypes having similar characteristic points and evaluate the parameters of the topological transformation which would make the given image identical or almost identical with one of the prototypes. This done, he compares the transformed image with the prototypes by computing linear discriminant functions. Unfortunately, the concept of the characteristic points and the method for finding them needs to be defined more precisely.

In essence, all the methods we have been looking at normalize the image before recognizing it. So do the autocorrelation and two-dimensional spectrum methods, since the translation invariants they generate do not completely define the image, and the auxiliary specifications they need are equivalent to normalizations. Before these methods can recognize an image they need to estimate the parameters of the transformation—translation, scaling, or some more general topological transformation. Then either the image itself or its representation in the secondary feature space is subjected to an inverse mapping which in principle brings it into a suitably normalized form. Then the recognition process is carried out by means of linear discriminant functions.

Many experiments have shown that such methods do not work well in the presence of noise, because the normalization procedure often maps two different classes of noisy images into sets that are not separable by hyperplanes, that is, sets with overlapping convex hulls. At first glance this statement seems paradoxical, but it is not hard to see that it is true. To see this no computation is needed. In fact, when a noisy image is normalized the normalization parameters are subject to error; for instance the coordinates of the centroid are perturbed by the noise. On this account the normalized images belonging to a single class do not coincide perfectly. The convex combinations of these, which can be found by averaging the gray shades at each point of the field of view, tend to appear as diffuse gray spots. Two classes of images that are close to each other in shape may, if the noise is sufficiently intense, give rise to identical gray spots. But this means that the convex hulls of the corresponding classes intersect at the point of the image space corresponding to the gray spot, and are therefore not linearly separable.

The unsatisfactory experimental results obtained by preliminary normalization, and the foregoing remarks on the reasons for the lack of success, lead us to think that the model for image classes ought to deal with the inevitable noise as well as with the set of admissible transformations. For this, we need the machinery of probability theory, which enables us to translate the problem of character recognition into a problem of optimal statistical decision theory.

A very large number of papers have been written in the field of statistical recognition theory. The conceptual basis of these papers, and the ABC of statistical recognition theory, is the classical problem of minimizing a Bayesian risk. The essence is as follows:

We look on an image (or more generally an input signal) as a random variable v, and we suppose that a probability distribution over the space of values of v is given, together with its dependence on the value of a parameter k, which for concreteness we shall suppose is discrete. The parameter k induces a certain objective classification of the signals, and we may use it as a class index. In the Bayesian formulation of the recognition problem the index k is taken to be a random variable with the known probability distribution $p(k)$. Given an input signal v we must make a decision d belonging to some discrete decision set which may or may not coincide with the set of values of k. We can make a quantitative estimate of the correctness of the decision d: if the parameter of the distribution is k and we make the decision d, we encounter a loss, or punishment, $w(k,d)$. The mean loss is known as the *recognition risk*. What we want is to find a rule for making decisions on the basis of the input signals v, i.e., a decision function $d = \mathcal{F}(v)$, which leads to a minimum mean loss, or minimum risk.

An example may serve to make the meaning clearer. Suppose that the input signal represents the image of an alphabetic character on some retina. The values of k correspond to the various letters of the alphabet. For every k there exists a conditional probability distribution with density function $p(v|k)$. The *a priori* distribution $p(k)$ corresponds to the frequency of the occurrence of the letter with index k in the source language. The decision consists in choosing a letter of the alphabet. One other decision is also customarily allowed—namely the rejection decision —when the image cannot be successfully analyzed. In this case, the set of decisions does not coincide with the set of values of the parameter k.

The following definition provides an example of the loss matrix: the loss for a correct decision is zero, the loss for an erroneous decision is unity, and the loss for a rejection is some positive fraction $\alpha < 1$. The decision function for this task will implement a method of recognition that results in minimum mean loss.

If we are given the probability distributions $p(v|k)$ and $p(k)$, we may construct the general solution of the Bayesian problem. To simplify the presentation, we shall confine ourselves to the case of a discrete set of signals v. If v is continuous, summations must be replaced by the corresponding integrals. The risk will be defined by the equation

$$\mathcal{R} = \sum_{v} \sum_{k} p(v,k)w(k, \mathcal{F}(v)), \qquad (1.9)$$

where $p(v,k)$ is the joint distribution of the random variables v and k.

Then the laws of compound probability yield the joint distribution $p(v,k)$ in terms of the known distributions:

$$p(v,k) = p(v|k)p(k),$$

or in terms of the *posterior distribution* $p(k|v)$ of the class k given the input signal v

$$p(v,k) = p(k|v)p(v). \qquad (1.10)$$

The latter expression is more convenient to use, and the posterior distribution $p(k|v)$ on the right hand side of it can also be expressed in terms of known distributions by the use of Bayes' formula

$$p(k|v) = \frac{p(v|k)p(k)}{p(v)},$$

where $p(v) = \sum_k p(v|k)p(k)$. Substituting (1.10) in (1.9) we find

$$\mathcal{R} = \sum_v p(v) \sum_k p(k|v)w(k, \mathcal{F}(v)).$$

It is clear that the risk $\mathcal{R}$ represents a sum over the space of signals v. Therefore the value of the optimal decision function can be prescribed for each signal v without reference to its value for other signals. We define it so that we minimize the *conditional risk for given* v:

$$\mathcal{R}_v = \sum_k p(k|v)w(k, \mathcal{F}(v)). \qquad (1.11)$$

According to (1.11) the value of the optimal decision function $\mathcal{F}_{opt}(v)$ for a given v is the index d corresponding to the column of the loss matrix $w(k,d)$ which minimizes the scalar product of the column with the posterior distribution vector $\{p(k|v): k = 1, 2, \ldots, n\}$:

$$\hat{d} = \mathcal{F}_{opt}(v) = \arg\min_d \sum_k p(k|v)w(k,d).$$

Let us consider an important particular case, the square antidiagonal matrix

$$w(k,d) = \lceil k \neq d \rceil = 1 - \delta_{kd},$$

where $\delta_{kd} = \lceil k = d \rceil$ is the Kronecker delta, equal to 1 when $k = d$ and to 0 otherwise. In our present case the loss is constant and equal to 1 for any error, and the risk turns out to equal the error probability. The conditional risk $\mathcal{R}_v$ is equal to the *conditional error probability*:

$$\mathcal{R}_v = p_e(v) = \sum_k p(k|v)(1 - \delta_{kd})$$

$$= \sum_k p(k|v) - p(d|v) = 1 - p(d|v).$$

To minimize the conditional risk R_v and therefore also the total risk R, we must choose a value of d for which the posterior probability $p(d|v)$ is maximized:

$$\hat{d} = \mathcal{F}_{opt}(v) = \arg\max_d p(d|v).$$

Thus, given an antidiagonal loss matrix the optimal decision is the one that maximizes the posterior probability.

The Bayesian solution of the recognition problem is applicable in the great majority of the practically important problems. There are exceptions, notably in those cases where it makes no sense to speak of the prior distribution $p(k)$, for instance when we are to diagnose a rare and dangerous illness of a specific single patient. In such cases, we can hardly want to minimize the mean risk; rather we should want to minimize the maximum loss, i.e., consider the worst case. Then we would use the *minimax decision* [8, 44].

It is commonly supposed that the principal difficulty in the use of Bayesian decisions lies in the fact that the conditional distributions $p(v|k)$ are unknown. In fact, these distributions for real signals are usually so complicated that analytical expressions for them are very difficult to write down. Even when we are dealing with the relatively simple task of recognizing typed characters from a single type font, the conditional distribution $p(v|k)$ must take into account a host of random factors besides the shape of the kth letter of the alphabet and the noise introduced in the printing process. We must include variations in the position of the image with respect to the retina (translations), variations in line width, contrast, background gray shade, and many others. A distribution taking account of all these factors can be represented as a multiple integral over the space of the corresponding parameters. We may even suppose that we can write out the integral in advance, without special investigation or experiment, and yet obtain enough precision to yield satisfactory recognition. The integral will have the form

$$p(v|k)$$
$$= \int \int \ldots \int p(v|k, b_1, b_2, \ldots, b_m) p(b_1, b_2, \ldots, b_m) \, db_1 \, db_2 \ldots db_m.$$

Here $b_1, b_2, \ldots, b_m$ are parameters of the transformation, $p(v|k, b_1, b_2, \ldots, b_m)$ is the conditional distribution which we can represent to a first approximation by the normal distribution with mean value dependent on the parameters, and $p(b_1, b_2, \ldots, b_m)$ is the joint distribution of the parameters. We can suppose the latter to be constant in an m-dimensional parallelepiped which defines the intervals of possible values of each of the parameters.

This approximation of the true distribution $p(v|k)$, rough though it is, nevertheless comes far closer to it than any of the models used up to now. The principal difficulty is that we cannot immediately use it for recognition purposes, since the calculation of the multiple integrals would present colossal computational difficulties. For instance, the number of parameters b_j is not less than 5; in computing the integrals by summation we need at least 20 to 40 discrete values for each parameter. Then the integrand must be calculated at least $20^5 = 10^{6.5}$ times. For a dimension $N = 300$, each calculation involves about 1000 arithmetic operations. So we need $10^{9.5}$ operations to evaluate one discriminant function. It is impossible to do this in real time in the reading machine. Neither is it feasible to calculate the decision functions in advance and store their values in a table, simply because of the great volume of memory required to store the values of a function of a multidimensional argument.

Because of all these difficulties a Bayesian recognizer can be implemented only in relatively simple cases. It has been shown, for instance, that in recognizing two classes described by multivariate normal distributions having covariance matrices which are the same for both classes but are otherwise arbitrary, the optimal discriminant function is linear. If the covariance matrices are not identical, the discriminant function is quadratic. Explicit expressions for the optimal functions are given in [56].

The statistical recognition problem can also be formulated and solved when the classes of decision functions are given in advance. The general Bayesian solution described above is of course not applicable, since it presupposes the decision functions to be free of constraint. If the functions are confined to a given class, we must use some device for maximization under constraint. A problem of this kind arises in connection with the above mentioned example of discrimination between two normal distributions with different covariance matrices, if we seek the best among all linear discriminant functions. A minimax formulation of this problem was solved by T. W. Anderson and R. P. Bahadur [77], who obtained an analytic expression for the solution.

Let us look at a more complicated problem. Let us suppose that each of the two classes $k = 1, 2$ is defined by a set of multivariate normal distributions with the distribution functions $P_j(v)$, where the parameter $j = 1, 2, \ldots, m_1$ for the first class and $j = m_1 + 1, m_1 + 2, \ldots, m$ for the second. Given a parameter value and a decision function $\mathcal{F}(v)$, we can compute the risk

$$\mathcal{R}_j = \int \ulcorner \mathcal{F}(v) \neq k(j) \urcorner \, dP_j(v), \qquad (1.12)$$

where $k(j)$ denotes the class to which the jth distribution refers. We recall that the corner function represents the binary truth value of the predicate appearing as its argument, i.e., it has the value 1 if the predicate is true and 0 if false. We shall look for the decision function in the class of linear threshold functions.

If the parameter j is a random variable with a known distribution function, we can obtain the mean or Bayesian risk by averaging (1.12) over j. It is difficult, however, to obtain the minimum value of the risk when $\mathcal{F}(v)$ is constrained to belong to a definite class of functions. We shall instead minimize the maximum of the individual risks (1.12) over j.

If all the distributions P_j are normal, with means μ_j and unit covariance matrix, it is not difficult to see that the particular risk (1.12) depends monotonically on the Euclidean distance from the point μ_j to the separating hyperplane defined by the function $\mathcal{F}(v)$. The maximum risk is attained at that value of j for which the corresponding μ_j lies closest to the hyperplane. To minimize the maximum risk, we must find the hyperplane properly dividing the points μ_j into two classes and lying at the greatest distance from these points. The algorithms given in [10] and [41] may be used for this purpose (cf. Section 1.3).

In the more general case there are more than two classes, each defined by distributions $P_j(v)$ with differing means μ_j and differing covariance matrices. A method for solving the problem in this case has been proposed by M. I. Šlezinger [73, 74] and has been used for the construction of a reading machine [13]. It is described in Chapter VI.

In the formulations we have given so far, the distributions $p(v|k)$ have been assumed to be known. When they are partially known, i.e., known to belong to some parametrized family, we have the *parametric learning problem*. This is the problem of recreating a distribution by sampling.

There are two basic ways to solve this problem. In the first, learning is seen as the establishment of statistical estimates of the unknown parameters of a distribution by use of the sample; these estimates are then substituted for the parameters in the expression for the distribution function. This approach has been applied principally in evaluating multivariate normal distributions [56]. Its use for image recognition is hampered by the fact that in this case the distributions depend on the nuisance parameters, and the estimation problem becomes really complicated. The problem of learning in the presence of nuisance parameters has been considered by Kovalevsky and is discussed in Chapter III. The reconstruction of distributions by the substitution of estimates has a shortcoming, namely that the decision rules so obtained are not, strictly speaking, optimal, i.e., they do not minimize the risk. A correct formulation of the problem of minimizing the conditional Bayesian risk for a given training sample leads to a different method for reconstructing distributions. This method consists in finding the posterior distribution of a parameter and computing the posterior distribution of the recognition parameter k by convolution of the given prior distribution with the posterior parameter distribution found. The approach is also set forth in Chapter III.

Many papers have been devoted to the statistical or parametric problems of self-learning. The formulation of these problems is quite different from the variational formulations discussed above. The basic difference is that it is based on a model of the signals, that is, on assumptions about their distributions. These assumptions imply criteria which in the variational case are merely postulated. Briefly, the statistical problem of self-learning amounts to the estimation of the parameters of two or more distributions on the basis of a composite sample.

The first purely statistical studies of this nature were published long before the appearance of the term "self-learning". Later, D. B. Cooper and P. W. Cooper [78] proposed the above formulation of the self-learning problem and solved it for the normal distribution, using the method of moments. They also obtained the following interesting result: Suppose that the signal distribution is given and is known to be a mixture of two distributions differing only in their means. Then the two distributions can be determined uniquely by means of the given mixed distribution.

The necessity of a maximum-likelihood estimate has been pointed out many times. This problem was solved by M. I. Šlezinger [72]. The idea underlying his iteration algorithm is very simple. Suppose that the distributions $p(v|a_k)$ for each of the classes ($k = 1, 2, \ldots, n$) are known except for the values of the parameters a_k, which are to be estimated. Suppose that we have a learning algorithm A_{lr} that allows us to estimate these values and also the prior probabilities p_k of the classes, if we are given a sample $(v^1, v^2, \ldots, v^l)$ and if we know for each v^j the probabilities p_{jk} that it belongs to the class k. On the other hand, if we knew the values of the parameters a_k and the probabilities p_k, we could use a recognition algorithm A_{rec} to infer from an arbitrary v^j the posterior probabilities of the classes. Slezinger showed that if we begin with arbitrary values of the parameters (a_k, p_k) and use them in A_{rec} to obtain the posterior distributions of the v^j in the training sample, then use these as the p_{jk} in A_{lr} to get new values for (a_k, p_k) and repeat the whole process many times, the resulting sequence of approximations will converge to the maximum-likelihood estimate of the parameters a_k and p_k. He also proposed a stochastic approximation algorithm yielding an improvement in the estimates of the parameters with the appearance of each current v^j in the training sample.* Computer experiments have been made for the one-dimensional normal distribution and for actual recognition of typed characters [22].

A monograph by A. V. Milen'kii [47] is the only one of its kind; it presents a deep and many-sided study of the problem of self-learning.

The methods for solving the parametric problems of learning and self-learning are rarely used for pattern-recognition purposes, because the fundamental difficulty in image recognition is not the lack of knowledge of the necessary probability distributions but the inability of currently available methods and machinery to compute the corresponding densities. This difficulty is connected with the fact that image recognition is not much affected by noise but much more by variability in the structure and geometric characteristics of the images. This aspect of the problem has received ever increasing attention since the mid sixties.

During this time several papers have been concerned with the problem of *structural analysis*, which is related to the problem of pattern recognition. Among the several authors we may cite the following: R. A.

---

* Šlezinger, M. I. Teoretičeskie voprosy i algoritmy obučenija i samoobučenija raspoznavaniju obrazov (Avtoreferat dissertacii), Institut kibernetiki AN USSR, Kiev, 1968. [Theoretical questions and algorithms for learning and self-learning in pattern recognition (author's review of his dissertation)], Institute of Cybernetics of the Ukrainian Academy of Sciences, Kiev, 1968.

Kirsch [82], R. Narasimhan [50, 51], and V. P. Romanov [59, 60]. This work was in part motivated by the need to automate the processing of photographs of particle tracks obtained from spark or bubble chambers. It is not useful to regard this task as a signal classification problem. The problem is to distinguish particle tracks against a noisy background and determine the values of such parameters as direction, curvature, length, branching angles, etc. It has been suggested that character recognition could be accomplished by similar methods: given a geometric description of an image, one would use this description for recognition.

The rules for constructing complex images out of elementary segments, as considered in these papers, are of considerable interest. These rules represent species of formal grammars and put specific limitations on the image descriptions that can be obtained by solving the problem. The formal language for describing images is in this way connected with the structure of the images belonging to a given class. This has been called the *linguistic* or *structural* approach to the image recognition problem.

R. Narasimhan [50, 51] proposes to compose images by using such elements as straight line segments or pieces of circular arcs. Each element has two or three distinguished points, to which the distinguished points of other elements are to be attached. The image of an arbitrary character can be formed in this way by the use of definite rules. The description of an input character image then consists of a list of its constituent elements and of a specification of the way in which they are interconnected.

V. P. Romanov [60] considers the problem of describing an image consisting of several nonintersecting black polygons. The elements he considers when analyzing the image are squares, each occupying a 7×7-cell portion of the retina. These squares are divided into 2, 4, or 8 sectors by lines radiating from the center of the square with an angular separation of $45°$ or a multiple of $45°$. Some of the sectors are black, the rest white. The figures thus formed are used as templates for the analysis of the elements of images. The centers of the templates are placed, in turn, in the various cells of the retina; maximum correlation is used to determine which template is most like the corresponding input square. Each retina cell is marked with a symbol corresponding to the selected template. Next, sequences of identical symbols are isolated, corresponding to the sides of the polygon; their mutual dispositions define the type of the polygon. Next the number and mutual dispositions of all the polygons in the field of view are determined. Then the computer implementing the algorithm reports the number of figures, their designations, dispositions, etc.

T. G. Evans [79] has described a very general scheme for representing an image-generating grammar, written in the algorithmic language LISP. According to Evans, this scheme allows us to analyze compound images represented as collections of elements, for instance as a polygon is represented by its vertices. These elements are to be described in a standard form admitted by the analysis program. For example, the program requires a list of the vertices, their coordinates, and their connecting edges. The lists are processed by a method analogous to syntactic analysis.

The earlier papers on the linguistic approach were for the most part characterized by the following shortcomings:

1. It is assumed that the initial description of the images is given in the form of a sequence of designated elementary images. However, these designations cannot be obtained immediately from physical measurements performed on the image. To find them, one must solve the problem of recognizing the elementary images. This task is in itself very difficult.
2. The presence of noise is not taken into account in either the recognition of elementary images or the analysis of the whole image.
3. The rules for synthesis of an image from elementary images are given, but not the rules for analysis.

These deficiencies have been overcome by the reference sequence method [38–40, 84]. The underlying idea is as follows: A formal grammar is used only for the definition of the set of admissible prototypes, or reference images, represented as sequences of predefined elementary parts. The actual image is looked on as a random variable, for which one of the reference images represents the mean value. For a given actual image, we look for the reference image that maximizes the likelihood function. The maximum is found by the use of dynamic programming. This method is described, in detail, in Chapter VII.

Later, K. S. Fu and his co-authors published a number of papers (see, for instance, [81]) in which a somewhat different method was put forward for taking random distortions into account. They introduced the notion of a *statistical grammar*, in accordance with which the elementary images making up a compound image appear with specified probabilities. A given actual image can appear as a result of the realization of one of several possible sequences of application of the rules of the grammar. The probability of appearance of a given image is taken as the sum of the probabilities of all possible methods of generating it. The computational difficulties incidental to the large number of possible sequences were overcome by an idea close to the concepts of dynamic programming.

A highly interesting approach to the problem of structural analysis of images is to be found in some papers by A. Martelli and U. Montanari (see, for instance, [85]), who use the so-called nonsequential dynamic programming method. They propose to overcome the computational difficulties connected with the very large number of states by a method based on the approximation of a function of many variables by the sum of several functions each involving fewer variables.

The work of I. B. Mučnik [49] holds a special position in this area, because of his attempt to automate the creation of the set of the structural elements by which the description of images is to be carried out.

The linguistic approach to recognition is far from being exhausted and would appear to offer one of the best prospects. Papers on two-dimensional grammars are now appearing (cf. [88–90]) which deal with the specifics of image structures that are different from the structure of one-dimensional sequences. Two-dimensional grammars are being used for the analysis of halftone images in the presence of noise, and there is every reason to expect significant progress in image recognition from this approach.

1.5 Applications and Results

At the moment, the practical success of image recognition methods must be regarded as rather modest. The achievements are primarily in the construction of devices for reading alphanumeric characters—the so-called *reading machines* or *character readers*. However, both in the Soviet Union and abroad, these machines require the input characters to have fixed outlines, i.e., prescribed type fonts or, if handwritten, to be traced within rigidly prescribed constraints, else the reliability of the readers is unsatisfactory. Attempts to build readers that will accept arbitrary handwritten characters are to be considered as not satisfactory.

Among the devices worked out in the USSR, those most nearly meeting the practical requirements are the ČARS described in Chapter IX, plus the R711 and RUTA-701 (designed by the Vilnius SKB VM) [3], and the machine described by V. S. Katinskii and B. D. Tihomirov [31]. The RUTA-701 is dedicated to preparing computer input from multiline documents, i.e., it is a "page reader". It reads 10 numerals and 4 ancillary characters. These symbols can be written on an "Optima" typewriter or they may be hand-drawn. Handwritten numerals must be written in small rectangles that are previously printed on special forms, using inks that are not perceived by the scanner. There are also some constraints on the configuration of the symbols. The maximum reading rate is 220 characters per second. The error probability, according to some preliminary data, is of the order of 10^{-4}.

The RUTA-701 uses two different recognizers: one for typescript and the other for handwritten characters. Typed characters are recognized by comparing them with a set of templates. Handwritten characters are recognized by use of quasitopological features indicating the presence of closed loops in different parts of the character. Also some geometrical characteristics are used. Both recognizers center the image of the character by reference to its edges. Fifteen of these machines have been produced; they are installed in various cities in the USSR.

The R711 was designed by the Vilnius SKB VM in collaboration with the Centronic combine of the German Democratic Republic. It is a document reader, devoted to reading small-format documents, containing no more than four lines which are read in one pass. It reads 10 numerals and 8 ancillary symbols, which can be printed by a typographical process or written on a special typewriter equipped with the special type fonts

ROS-A or ROS-B. These are Russian versions of OCR-A and OCR-B fonts, especially designed for use with reading machines. The reader also accepts handwritten characters under the same restrictions as those imposed by the RUTA-701.

The R711 has held up in trials. In these, documents not conforming to standard were rejected by hand (about 10%). The rejection and error rates for the remainder were both of the order of 10^{-6}. For the hand-rejected documents the error rate was an order of magnitude higher, and the rejection rate two orders. Two of these machines were built.

The reader described by Katinskiĭ and Tihomirov [31] was designed for use on typeset text. Because of the wide variety of fonts used in printing, it is designed to accept several fonts. The templates for all the characters in each font are stored on magnetic tape, and are called out as needed into the operating memory, a magnetic core store. The collection of templates that will be needed for a given piece of text is prescribed during the manual editing process, prior to input to the machine. Images and templates are both stored in binary code, i.e., there are two gray levels.

The recognizer compares the image with the template; the criterion of agreement is the Hamming distance. The image is centered before the comparison is made, and undergoes a preliminary classification according to the presence and position of the basic strokes of the character.

The reader is a complex and specialized high-speed digital computer. It reads about 100 characters per second, with an error rate of the order of 10^{-2}.

Outside the Soviet Union, primarily in the USA, character readers have been manufactured for the last 15 years, by a number of different firms. A review of these can be found in [15].

The machines developed up to now can be classified into four groups, depending on the kinds of character they will accept:

1. machines for reading marks made by hand on special forms;
2. for characters printed with magnetic inks;
3. for optically sensed stylized characters, i.e., type fonts especially designed for machine reading;
4. for the customary fonts.

Among the mark-reading machines of a few years ago were the well-known "Lector" and "Autolector" readers made by the British firm Leo (later combined with ICL). These were applied to the automatic processing of orders in commercial establishments, reading statistical data, etc. In the USSR, a similar machine, the "Blank-2", was built in Minsk by the NIIEVM.

Magnetic ink readers have been constructed in Europe and the USA. Despite the inconvenience of having to use special printers and typewriters, and despite the high rejection rate of these machines, due to the unrecognizability of single characters, they have found widespread use in banks and other financial and commercial establishments.

Most of the development work on optical readers has been devoted to those accepting stylized fonts. Machines of this type have been built by many American firms. The maximum reading speed ranges from 70 to 2000 characters per second; the cost, from $50,000 to $200,000. These machines center the image by reference to its edges, and either compare it with templates or perform a logical analysis of its elements. As a rule, no detailed description of the recognition method is published, nor are there data on the error rate under operational conditions. It is known only that the requirements for accuracy of printing and for homogeneity of the paper are very high. Apparently the error rate of the machines did not meet the users' demands, since most of the machines were withdrawn from production within a year or two after they were announced, either because of low performance or because their requirements on the print quality were too strict.

The International Standards Organization (ISO) has recently established a standardization of type fonts for optical readers, and some work has also been done in the USSR on the establishment of such fonts. An All-Union standard has been issued for two fonts: ROS-A and ROS-B (GOST 16330-70).

A great deal of interest attaches to the multifont readers produced by Philco and Recognition Equipment, designed to read multiline documents printed in nonstylized type. Both machines are based on template matching. The Philco reader has a relatively high error rate—of the order of 0.3–1%. The Recognition Equipment reader is a complex and costly machine, incorporating a CDC-910 computer with a memory of 8 to 10 thousand words, with a cycle time of 8 microseconds. It significantly increases the potential capabilities of reading machines and simplifies the management of them, since it can read mixed documents of different dimensions and with differing fonts. The alphabet of acceptable characters is determined by a set of 360 templates, including numerals, letters, other typewritten symbols, computer printer characters, etc. It is capable of speeds up to 2400 characters per second and costs in the range of $550,000 to $750,000. Two models are known to have been put into service—one in an airline and the other in a Swedish bank—but no details on their operational effectiveness and error rates are available.

The automatic processing of photographs of particle tracks is also an area of great importance, and significant studies have been made on the processing of bubble-chamber tracks. In view of the very large number of such photographs, both stored and newly produced in physical experiments, the effectiveness of the exploration depends to a great extent on the ability to process them by means of high-speed computers. Until recently, the computers were used only for following tracks after preliminary human guidance. The main process used the *histogram method*, which consists in selecting a rectangular portion of the image and summing the gray shade values along narrow parallel strips. This process is repeated for different directions of the system of strips; an analysis of the output yields a determination of the position and the direction of the axial lines of the selected portion of the track.

Recently, the method described in Chapter VII—the reference sequence method—has been used to develop a highly noise-resistant algorithm with a broader potential. This algorithm determines the coordinates of a point from which several tracks radiate, follows all the tracks, and defines for each a narrow corridor within which the bubble events related to that track occur. It does this without regard to breaks in the track or to the presence of extraneous lines in the photograph.

Another intensively studied subject is the recognition of biological objects: cancer cells, blood cells, chromosomes, etc. Many institutions in the USSR, the USA, and other countries have attained good practical results in this field.

Many other interesting results in image processing and image recognition are regularly published in the international journal *Computer Graphics and Image Processing* (Academic Press, New York).

More and more attention is being paid to the computer processing of photographs and video images of the earth's surface received from satellites. The aim of the processing is to enhance the images, i.e., to increase the contrast, sharpen the image, and remove noise. The recognition of objects in such images is very difficult, and only the first approaches are being cleared up. The same can be said of the problem known as *three-dimensional scene analysis*.

It is interesting to compare progress in image recognition with progress in recognizing signals of different physical characteristics. Many applications in the fields of medicine, geology, weather prediction, industrial quality control, etc., have used the method of nonparametric learning [25, 26, 53], and primarily by means of linear discriminant functions. The essential difference between these applications and the recognition of alphanumeric characters lies in the much higher error rates admissible in the former; normally, error rates of a few percentage points are acceptable. Results of this kind can be achieved whenever the sets of input signals are approximately convex. Examples, and a bibliography, can be found in [10].

Significant results have been recently achieved in speech recognition. The use of skillfully selected secondary features has allowed the construction of relatively simple machines that will recognize the speech of different speakers. By limiting the vocabulary to a few tens of words, and by using information about the admissible word associations, the error rate for word recognition has been reduced to a few percentage points.

Another approach to speech recognition is based on a parametric model of speech signals and on the application of dynamic programming to maximize the agreement between the prototype signal and the input signal [11, 26]. This approach allows the use of a large vocabulary (several hundred or even several thousand words) and achieves a higher reliability —for a 200-word vocabulary the error rate does not exceed 0.5%, with a rejection rate of about 2.5% [11]. In this case, however, the machine must be attuned to the individual speaker. The development prospects for this approach appear to be favorable, and we can expect very shortly to see practical applications of speech recognizers.

In addition to [11], see also: Vintsiuk, T. K., Generative Grammars and Dynamic Programming in Speech Recognition with Learning. Conference Record of IEEE Int. Conf. on Acoustics, Speech, and Signal Processing, Philadelphia, 1976, pp. 446–452.

1.6 Conclusions

In a retrospective look at the path marked out by whole armies of workers in the field of image recognition, we must conclude that the many attempts to find a practical solution, on the basis of intuition and without the support of deep mathematical analysis of the problem, have in most cases been unsuccessful. The only exceptions are those methods that have been used in character readers. The optimistic hopes for the development of bionic models, like the perceptron, which would be capable of independent self-learning for recognition, without the implant of *a priori* information by humans concerning the concrete problem, have also not been realized.

The difficulties they encountered have led research workers to increase their efforts to study the specifics of the problem, and this has been fruitful. When the conditions were found for the uniform convergence of the empirical risk to the true risk, they not only provided a basis for a practically useful solution of the nonparametric learning problem—they also provided a basis for a rational compromise in the war between two methodologically opposite points of view regarding nonparametric learning. The partisans of one side believed that with a sufficiently large training sample one could approximate any "good" classification, without making the slightest use of *a priori* information about the probability distribution of the input signals. The opposite view held that the nonparametric learning problem is completely meaningless, since if one knows only the empirical risk and knows nothing about the prior distributions, then nothing can be said about the true risk. However, it turns out that if one adopts for the learning process a family of decision rules having finite capacity, a meaningful estimate of the true risk can be obtained. If, moreover, the family has been successfully divined, the results of the learning can be applied and will be wholly reliable.

Nevertheless, nonparametric learning has not been successful for image recognition, because the classes of input images do not form convex sets and the use of linear discriminant functions in the primary feature space cannot be successful. No adequate rectifying spaces have been discovered.

In this connection, the way to the discovery of suitable families of decision rules lies in the study of the specific properties of sets of images belonging to the same class, i.e., in the development of mathematical models of image classes. A number of important problems regarding the choice of optimal decision rules have been formulated and solved on this basis.

A number of new problems have been solved in the course of the development of the linguistic or structural approach to the problem of recognition—in particular, thanks to the development of models that take account of noise as well as of the structure of the image.

The following chapters deal with the results obtained by parametric models of sets of images.

CHAPTER II

A Parametric Model of the Image-Generating Process

As may be seen from the foregoing review, there is no common approach to the problem of pattern recognition that would allow us to place the many individual contributions precisely. In this chapter we attempt to formulate the general problem in such a way as to include most of the particular problems of recognition and to let us regard them from a single point of view.

Essentially, we propose an approach to the recognition problem that not only unites the earlier points of view but also sketches the way to overcome the difficulties encountered in earlier investigations. On the basis of this approach, a number of practical problems in recognition and learning have been solved. These problems and their solutions are described in our later chapters.

2.1 Difficulties in Image Recognition

The basic conclusion emerging from a study of the problems of image recognition is that recognition is very difficult, and that the difficulty arises from the complex structure of the set of signals to be recognized, as they occur in the majority of application problems. Consider, for instance, the signal arising from a light-sensitive mosaic, or retina, when it is illuminated by the projected image of a character. We shall regard such a signal as a multidimensional vector. The set of signals generated when the image of a single character is translated so that it occupies all possible positions on the retina, cannot be described by a simple and well-studied probability distribution, nor as a convex set suitable for discriminating it.

If we analyze the properties of this set, we find that, in geometric language, it represents a polyhedron, fantastically twisted in the multidimensional space. We can corroborate this statement by noting that in this space no three points defined by three translations of the same character lie on a straight line. In fact, if we average the gray shades corresponding to two translations (Figure 2.1) of a character, we do not obtain an image corresponding to some third translation of the original. The distance between two points corresponding to two translations of a character depends on the parameter of the relative translation in a nonmonotone way. For instance, if we give a digitized image of the letter **E** a vertical displacement, and compare it with the undisplaced image, we find that the number of retina cells having equivalent blackness goes down at first and then suddenly increases. This nonmonotonicity is the reason for representing the set of signals as a "spirally" twisted surface.

Thus the sets of signals cannot be thought of as even approximately convex, and therefore the illustrations accompanying many papers on recognition—which portray either convex sets or unions of a few convex sets—fail completely to represent even the simplest problem of recognizing images of characters, namely recognizing the images of standard shape (fonts) placed in arbitrary positions on the retina. In reality, the set of such images can only be satisfactorily approximated by the union of as many convex sets as the number of different retina cells that can be reached by a fixed point of an image under all possible translations. Some considerations in support of this assertion are given in [71].

If we take into account the influence of factors other than translations, the number of convex sets required in our ensemble becomes even larger. In a practical case, the number may be very great, comparable with the estimated number of operations needed for calculating a probability density as described in Section 1.4.

The complexity of the structure of the sets of images belonging to a single class is responsible for the major difficulties. Most of the heuristic methods make use of separating hyperplanes, which are mainly useful for separating convex sets; as a result of the complexity of the image structure,

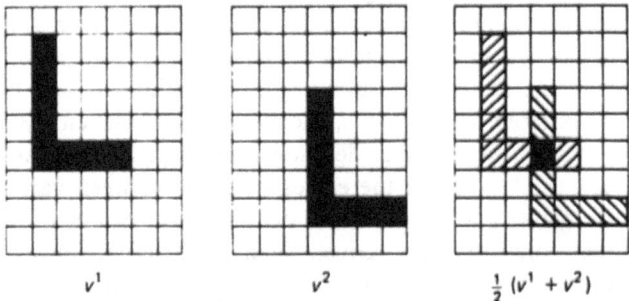

v^1 $\qquad\qquad$ v^2 $\qquad\qquad$ $\frac{1}{2}(v^1 + v^2)$

Figure 2.1   Linear combination of two images.

neither heuristic methods nor Bayesian optimization can yield a satisfactory error rate. In all the known experiments, the error rate is many times greater than that which is achievable by humans with respect to the same images.

Most of the approaches to image recognition listed in Chapter I also fail in the face of these difficulties. As was pointed out in Section 1.4, a preliminary normalization of the image should yield a notable decrease in the variety for images that have undergone an affine transformation. It does not, however, bring good results, because in the presence of noise the sets of normalized images are not convex, and their convex hulls intersect one another.

Another possible approach consists in solving the nonparametric learning problem. However, as was indicated in Section 1.3, there is no universal family of decision rules that can be used for recognizing arbitrary image classes. Such a family would have infinite capacity, and learning would be impracticable. The chosen class of decision rules must have finite capacity, and for a satisfactorily small error rate it must be adequate to deal with the properties of the image classes to be recognized. In other words, we must find a finite set of "good" or "informative" features, such that in the space of those features the discriminant functions are sufficiently simple, say linear. The role of such secondary features might be assumed, for instance, by certain functionals of the input signal, which would remain relatively constant over the signals of a single class, and would change significantly in passing from one class to another. One feels intuitively that such functionals exist, and that human beings could profitably use something of this sort for recognition. However, there are no known methods for finding them; moreover, as will be shown at the beginning of Chapter IV, most of the known attempts to formulate the problem of an optimal set of secondary features have been unsuccessful, since the optimal sets arising from these statements of the problem invariably turn out to be sets consisting of a single functional corresponding to the optimal decision rule.

To solve the problem of image recognition, which is characterized by the complex structure of the sets of images and the high dimensionality of the signal space, it would seem useful to study the properties of these sets. The result would be a mathematical model of the process that generates all the images belonging to all the classes under consideration. Such a model must describe the changes in the image in passing from class to class, as well as the changes in the image corresponding to a single class and induced by translations, variable stroke width, inconstant contrast, etc. With such a model, one can find an optimal decision rule, or at least a class to which that rule belongs. A study of the correspondence between various models of the sets of images and the classes of decision rules can be profitable also from another point of view. Given such a correspondence, we could determine the scope of old or new recognition algorithms, that is, we could show what properties an image class must have if it is to be correctly recognized by a given algorithm.

It may seem that if we try to build an adequate model of the sets of images we are asking too much. For, in order to separate two classes of multidimensional signals, we do not need a detailed knowledge of their distribution functions; it is often sufficient to know the projections of these functions on the normal to the optimal separating hyperplane. However, to separate many classes we need many such projections, i.e., one per pair of classes. Moreover, in practical problems we have to separate each class from arbitrary alien images, and in this case we need as detailed a description of the image class as we can get, i.e., a detailed knowledge of the probability distribution is desirable. Studies of the models of image classes are therefore justified.

2.2 A Parametric Model with Additive Noise

Most, and perhaps all, of the problems of recognition, learning and self-learning can be formulated in terms of the general scheme we are about to describe.

The input signals v, which are in general multidimensional vectors, arise from some physical process which is influenced by a number of factors. Each factor is characterized by a parameter. Among all the parameters there is one that interests us—the *recognition parameter* k, whose value we obtain in solving the recognition problem. In particular, this parameter may serve as the symbol standing for a class or abstract image (cf. p. 2); it may be multidimensional, discrete, or continuous. In addition there may be other parameters whose values are unknown but are of no immediate interest. They do, however, influence the process giving rise to signals, just as does the parameter k. Some among them may be constant during the course of a given problem; we denote them by the single character a, and we think of a as a single multidimensional *constant parameter*.

The signal v may depend on factors that change from one realization of it to another. There are usually many of these, and they are usually independent of one another; some of them can be represented by a simple and well-known multivariate probability distribution, for instance the normal distribution. We shall refer to these as *random perturbations*, or *noise* (cf. p. 8) and denote them by a multidimensional random variable r. The components of the noise vector act more or less independently on the components of the signal v.

Other nonconstant factors act rather on the signal as a whole than on its components. The action of these can be characterized by some parameters, but the values of these parameters are unknown at each realization of the input signal. They should not be thought of as random variables, since their probability distribution is either undefined or unknown. The fact that they change their values from one input signal to another is the source of an essential difficulty in the recognition process. We shall refer to them as *nuisance parameters*, in the sense in which this term is used in mathematical statistics [23, 44]. We shall denote the ensemble of the nuisance parameters by the character b, and think of it as a multidimensional quantity. Then the signal v can be represented as a multidimensional function of the parameters

$$v = f(k, a, b, r), \qquad (2.1)$$

where k, a, and b are respectively the recognition parameter, the constant parameter, and the nuisance parameter; r is the noise.

The dependence (2.1) and the noise distribution $p_{noise}(r)$ essentially define the distribution of the signal v considered as a function of the parameters k, a, and b. We shall write this distribution in the form $p(v|k, a, b)$, using the bar character to denote dependence of the probability function not only on k, as a conditional distribution, but also on the parameters a and b (for this usage see, for example the book by M. deGroot [23]). (Of course, k may not be a random variable, but a parameter and then one cannot speak of a conditional probability distribution. Nevertheless, we use this notation.)

In the absence of the nuisance parameter the distribution has the form $p(v|k, a)$, which has been considered in studies of the parametric learning problem (cf. Section 1.4). In those studies the parameter a was estimated on the basis of a training sample [56] or its posterior distribution was derived from the training sample [34, 56, 57]. Then, either by substitution of the estimate for a in $p(v|k, a)$ or by convolution of the posterior distribution with $p(v|k, a)$, the distribution $p(v|k)$ is established as a function dependent only on the recognition parameter k. The problem of recognizing input signals v after learning can now be thought of as the discovery of a decision rule based on the given distribution $p(v|k)$ that will optimally estimate k in some definite (usually Bayesian) sense, for each input signal v.

In such a formulation the postlearning recognition task reduces to the verification of simple statistical hypotheses about the recognition parameter k, and is applicable only to the cases, rarely met in practice, when the only influence on the signal is that of the parameter k. In reality, many nuisance factors are usually also at work on the signal.

For a fixed value of a the model (2.1) defines for each value of k not one, but many, probability distributions. A different distribution corresponds to each different value of b; therefore the estimation of k on the basis of an input signal represents the testing of composite statistical hypotheses [44].

To solve this problem we need to know the distribution function $p(v|k, a, b)$ or know the function (2.1) together with the distribution of the noise r. In actual recognition problems the signal v normally has very high dimensionality, with several hundred components. The number of components of all the parameters is normally much lower. Therefore, it is much easier to investigate the dependence of the signal on the parameters than to investigate an unknown multivariable signal distribution.

To avoid the necessity for a detailed study of the latter distribution we must assume that the variance of the random perturbations is not very great and that therefore their influence on the signal-generating process is much weaker than that of the parameters k, a, b. In a more exact formulation, this stipulation means that the elementary recognition problem—the separation of two classes with the distribution functions $p(v \mid k^1, a^1, b^1)$ and $p(v \mid k^2, a^2, b^2)$ having two arbitrary fixed values of k, a, and b—is soluble with a small error probability if the chosen values of the parameters are essentially distinct. The terms "essentially distinct" and "small error probability" must be defined with regard to the concrete circumstances of each actual recognition problem.

Our stipulation on the function $p(v \mid k, a, b)$ amounts to saying that variations in the signal due to essential variations in the parameters are not lost behind the noise. It is a quite natural stipulation, else the recognition problem would be extremely difficult, and would not admit solutions with small error rates. But we know from practice that in the majority of cases such good solutions exist: the recognition problems that we are acquainted with are almost always correctly solved by humans.

Our stipulation as to the small variance of the noise allows us to assume that an exact knowledge of the noise distribution is less important than an adequate knowledge of the way in which the signal depends on its parameters.

These reasonings can be made explicit in the particular case of additive noise. Suppose that the model (2.1) has the form

$$v = E(k, a, b) + r. \tag{2.2}$$

Here $E(k, a, b)$ is a multidimensional function of its parameters, and defines the way in which the signal is generated in the absence of noise, and r is a multidimensional random variable with a known probability distribution $p_{\text{noise}}(r)$.

The values of $E(k, a, b)$ may be naturally interpreted as *reference signals*, or *prototypes*, which would be observed if there were no noise. The function $E(k, a, b)$, evaluated at all points of its parameter space, yields a set of prototypes which may be very large and may contain an extremely varied collection of images.

If $p_{\text{noise}}(r)$ has zero mean value, a prototype appears as the mean value of a random image v for fixed values of the parameters. Provided that the variances of the individual components of $p_{\text{noise}}(r)$ are small, then no matter what its particular form may be, the observed signals v will lie close to the value of the prototype $E(k, a, b)$. If two values $E(k^1, a^1, b^1)$ and $E(k^2, a^2, b^2)$ are far enough apart, the corresponding sets of observed signals are also far apart and can be separated with an error probability that decreases with increasing separation of the prototypes and with

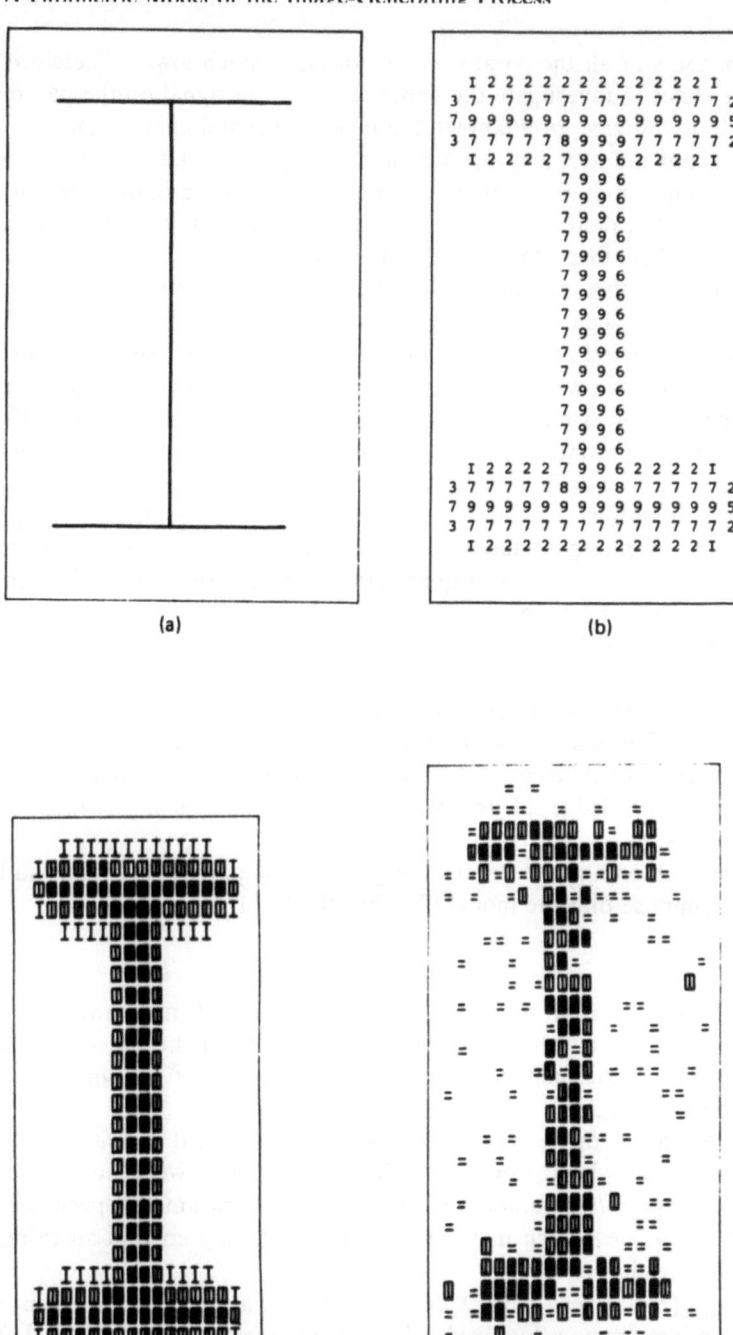

Figure 2.2 The generation of an image by the use of a parametric model: (a) the archetype; (b) the transformed prototype (components of digitized image); (c) the transformed prototype (regenerated image); (d) the model noisy image.

decreasing variance of the noise. Therefore an exact knowledge of the noise distribution $p_{\text{noise}}(r)$ is less valuable the greater the distance between the prototypes and the smaller the variance of the noise.

Let us consider an example illustrating the meaning of the model (2.2). Let the image of a selected typewritten character from a fixed font be situated in the plane xOy, and let it be dissected by a scanning device into many small cells; these will define the image as a multidimensional vector v. The components of v are the quantities v_i representing the gray shade of the ith cell, so that $0 \leqslant v_i \leqslant 1$.

To express the dependence of E on its parameters, we introduce the notion of the *archetype* $e^{(k)}$, which represents either an ideal image of the kth class in a fixed position on the plane xOy and with maximum contrast, or a schematic image of the kind depicted in Figure 2.2(a).

The prototype E represents a digitized image of the character and, as opposed to the schematic image $e^{(k)}$, has a given line width. The various values of E can be obtained by applying to $e^{(k)}$ an operator $\mathfrak{T}_{\xi,\eta}$ depending on the horizontal and vertical translation parameters ξ and η. Such an operator converts the archetype $e^{(k)}$ into an image of the sort depicted in Figure 2.2(b) and (c). If we introduce the effect of the contrast parameter α and the background-darkening parameter β, the components E_i of the prototype E can be represented in the form

$$E_i = \alpha\left(\mathfrak{T}_{\xi,\eta}\, e^{(k)}\right)_i + \beta.$$

The corresponding model of the image v is expressed, in accordance with (2.2), as the sum of the prototype E and the noise r. Its components are

$$v_i = \alpha \times \left(\mathfrak{T}_{\xi,\eta}\, e^{(k)}\right)_i + \beta + r_i. \tag{2.3}$$

An example of the model image is shown in Fig. 2.2(d).

In the case under consideration the index k of the archetype plays the role of the recognition parameter. The identifier of the type font from which the characters are drawn should be regarded as a constant parameter. In the model (2.3) the ensemble of the parameters k and a is represented by the set of components $e_i^{(k)}$ of the archetype. The quantities α, β, ξ, η are nuisance parameters, and r is the noise, to which we assign a multivariate normal distribution. The normality assumption is not crucial provided the variances are small enough, i.e., it plays no role in establishing the structure of the set defined by the equations (2.3); this structure is primarily defined by the form of the archetypes $e_i^{(k)}$ and the dependence of the signal v on the parameters α, β, ξ, η.

In keeping with the above, we now suggest the following formulation of the recognition and learning problems; it is applicable not only to images, but also to other kinds of signals.

Suppose it is known that the input signals can be represented as noisy values of a given multidimensional function $E(k, a, b)$, which itself depends on the recognition parameter k, an unknown constant a, and the nuisance parameter b, say in the fashion of (2.2). Suppose that the noise distribution is also known. We are given a training sample $\{v^j\}$, and we are required to estimate the constant parameter a and then to find a rule for estimating the recognition parameter k for an arbitrary input signal v.

It may seem that this formulation has the same deficiencies as the formulation of the nonparametric learning problem given in Section 1.3, in which the family of decision functions is prescribed. For, the lack of knowledge of the functions (2.1) or (2.2) and of the noise distribution $p_{\text{noise}}(r)$ seems to give precisely the same difficulty as the lack of knowledge of the family of decision functions. This would be true if we were to try to estimate the unknown function purely on the basis of the empirical material contained in the training sample. The same reasons that make it impracticable to reconstruct a decision function of a many-variable argument without prior information also make it impracticable to reconstruct a multivariate distribution function. Even for a very rough approximation we need 2^N values for an arbitrary N-dimensional distribution, and even when N is as small as 50 this number is impracticable.

However, our proposed formulation assumes the use of our whole stock of information on the nature and properties of the signals to be recognized. The application of the model (2.2) allows us to avoid the difficulties inherent in the empirical study of an arbitrary multivariate distribution, since the introduction of the nuisance parameters allows us to assume that the components of the noise are independent. The argument justifying this assumption is as follows.

As we showed earlier, the dependence of the prototype $E(k,a,b)$ on the nuisance parameter should take into account all the factors that act simultaneously on most or all of the components of the signal. These are the factors that make the components of the signal mutually dependent. Once all such factors have been absorbed in $E(k,a,b)$, the remaining noise can be taken as a random variable with independent components. The distribution of such a variable can be evaluated empirically with satisfactory precision. In most applications it suffices to construct a histogram for each component.

We can also get acceptable results if we assume that the noise is described by a normal distribution, for most of the discriminant functions are linear or piecewise linear. But a linear function of a multidimensional random variable v, having the form

$$f(v) = \sum_{i=1}^{N} c_i v_i,$$

is a random variable which has an approximately normal distribution if the components v_i are independent (and if certain auxiliary conditions are satisfied), even though the distributions of the components are far from being normal. Thus the model with normally distributed noise and the model with arbitrary independently distributed noise components lead to the same class of distributions of the value of a linear discriminant function. It is precisely these distributions that define the basic characteristic of the recognition algorithm—namely its error probability. Therefore the results obtained with a model presupposing a normal distribution can be applied to the more general class of signals in which the components are independently distributed. Thus, the whole complexity of the structure of the set of signals is contained in the parametric dependence of $E(k, a, b)$ rather than in the noise distribution $p_{\text{noise}}(r)$.

The parameters k, a, and b characterize the conditions under which the signal is generated. Therefore, to understand the model (2.2) of the signals we need to study the signal-generating process on the basis of the knowledge that has been built up in that branch of natural science to which the recognition problem belongs. Although such a study does not lend itself to formalization, it is a natural feature of all scientific and technical research.

The difference between the two formulations under consideration is that in the first (nonparametric learning) the information we have about the properties of the signal is to be expressed by means of a family of hypersurfaces which separate the pairs of signal sets representing pairs of classes. These surfaces are described by functions defined on the space of the input signals. When the sets to be separated are complex and nonconvex, it is difficult to define the separating surfaces.

In the second formulation (the parametric model) the same sets are described in terms of some small-dimensional skeletons, or regression surfaces, on which these sets are, so to speak, threaded. The regression surface is given in parametric form, and the parameters are substantively related to the factors influencing the process that generates the signals.

The methodological distinction between the two formulations is even more significant: the second immediately shows the way to solve concrete application problems—namely to study the process that generates the signals. To solve problems given in the first formulation we ought to do the same thing, but we arrive at this conclusion only after considering all the arguments we have just put forward. Having arrived there, we must essentially abandon the first formulation and replace it by the second, because the construction of a family of suitable decision functions on the basis of a model of the signals amounts to solving the problem in the second formulation.

2.3 The General Parametric Model

In practical applications we often have to consider nonadditive noise. For instance, when we consider noisy signals quantized into two levels, we cannot describe the noise as a random summand. The following formulation describes a more general model for taking the noise into account; it conserves the concept of the prototype and thus allows us to deal with sets of signals having a complex spatial configuration. Let $p(v|E)$ be a multivariate distribution defined on the N-space V of the signals v and dependent on the N-dimensional parameter E which takes values in the same space. Let E be the mean value or the mode (the most probable value) of the distribution $p(v|E)$. Then, just as in the case of the model (2.2), we shall refer to E as the *prototype* for the signals v generated in accordance with $p(v|E)$. By varying the prototype E we can, figuratively speaking, move the distribution cloud $p(v|E)$ to any part of the space V. If we suppose, as before, that E depends on the parameters k, a, and b, then the signals generated for fixed values of these parameters will be distributed according to the function

$$p(v|E(k,a,b)). \tag{2.4}$$

Writing the distribution in the form (2.4) instead of the more general form $p(v|k,a,b)$ allows us to use standard analytical means for describing the very complicated cloud-form sets surrounding the trajectory of the vector $E(k,a,b)$ traced out as a consequence of variation in the parameter b. If b is multidimensional, the trajectory is a multidimensional manifold in the signal space V, usually of much lower dimensionality than V itself.

The model (2.2) is a particular case of (2.4) and corresponds to the case

$$p(v|E(k,a,b)) = p_{\text{noise}}(v - E(k,a,b)).$$

If (2.4) is a multivariate normal distribution with mean $E(k,a,b)$ and unit covariance matrix, the model (2.2) corresponds to the case of normal additive noise

$$p(v|E(k,a,b)) = C \exp\left[-\frac{(v - E(k,a,b))^2}{2\sigma^2} \right]. \tag{2.5}$$

Then the probability density is a function of the Euclidean distance between the points v and E, and it is useful to introduce the Euclidean metric into the space V.

We get another example by assuming that V is a binary space, i.e., each component of v and E has only two values: $v_i, E_i \in \{0, 1\}$ ($i = 1, 2, 3, \ldots, N$) and that the components v_i are mutually independent random values (with fixed E). Then (2.4) can be written as the product of the distributions of the components:

$$p(v|E(k,a,b)) = \prod_{i=1}^{N} p^*(v_i|E_i(k,a,b)). \tag{2.6}$$

The distribution p^* is specified for each component by two quantities

$$p^*(1|0) = \psi_0 \quad \text{and} \quad p^*(0|1) = \psi_1 \tag{2.7}$$

where ψ_0 and ψ_1 are the conditional probabilities that a binary component of the signal is not equal to the corresponding binary component of the prototype [the remaining two quantities are defined by the normalization conditions:

$$p^*(0|0) + p^*(1|0) = p^*(0|1) + p^*(1|1) = 1].$$

When ψ_0 and ψ_1 are equal, (2.4) can be expressed by means of the Hamming distance:

$$p(v|E(k,a,b)) = (1 - \psi)^{N - \mathcal{K}} \psi^{\mathcal{K}}, \tag{2.8}$$

where N is the number of components, $\mathcal{K}$ is the Hamming distance between the binary vectors v and $E(k,a,b)$, i.e., the number of discordant components of these vectors.

The model (2.4), which was introduced to deal with nonadditive noise, allows us to formulate the general learning and recognition problem for arbitrary noise in the same terms as those used above. The formulation given on p. 45 can be retained unchanged. One must only keep in mind the fact that the noise distribution has the form (2.4) in the general case.

2.4 Recognition and Learning Viewed as Problems of Optimal Decision with Respect to Parameter Values

In following out our general scheme, we now propose to consider various recognition tasks as the making of decisions on the values of the parameters of the signal-generating process. We represent the process in the parametric form $E(k,a,b)$, displaying the prototype signal as a function of its parameters, and we write the conditional distribution $p(v|E)$ to display the effect of noise.

We use maximum likelihood as our decision criterion, in the following way: Let the probability density $p_\theta(x)$ of the random variable x depend on the unknown value of the parameter θ, which is, however, known to belong to some set Ω. We are to estimate the value of θ on the basis of experimental data yielding the value x_1 for x. The *likelihood function* for the given value x_1 is defined as the value of $p_\theta(x_1)$, treated as a function of θ. The value $\theta = \hat{\theta}$ for which this function assumes its maximum value is known as the *maximum-likelihood estimate* of θ.

It is not difficult to see that when θ is itself a random variable, uniformly distributed on the set Ω, the maximum-likelihood estimate coincides with the optimal Bayesian decision.

In the parametric learning problem in which we must estimate the parameter values from a sample with many observations, the *asymptotic efficiency* of the maximum-likelihood estimate is highly important. An *efficient estimate* is one having the least variance among all admissible estimates, and an asymptotically efficient estimate is one that becomes efficient as the training-sample size increases.

In the general case the maximum-likelihood estimate is not based on explicit arguments for optimality [44]. However, taking into account its nearness to the Bayesian optimal estimate in some cases, and its simplicity, it is very frequently used, and we shall use it widely in the rest of our exposition. It allows us to make a uniform and systematic approach to the multiform problems of recognition and learning, and its comparative simplicity allows us to solve a number of highly complex problems.

Several particular cases are treated below.

2.5 Recognition in the Absence of Nuisance Parameters

Suppose that the signal-generating process is unaffected by the nuisance parameter b, and that the constant parameter a is known. Then the prototype depends only on the recognition parameter k, and for every k we have a single known distribution

$$p(v \mid E(k)). \tag{2.9}$$

Then if the prior distribution $p(k)$ is known, we can solve the minimum-Bayesian-risk problem (cf. Section 1.4). If $p(k)$ is not known, we can either solve the minimax problem [8] or estimate k by maximum likelihood. We estimate k by inserting the observed value of the signal v in the expression (2.9) for the probability density and finding the maximum of the resulting likelihood function with respect to k. The recognition methods based directly or indirectly on the model (2.9), and their applicability for image recognition, were discussed in Section 1.4.

2.6 Recognition with Nuisance Parameters

We now introduce the nuisance parameter b, and as before we take a to be known. Then for every k there exists a set of distributions $p(v \mid E(k,b))$. The distribution of b is unknown, or even nonexistent. This gives rise to the problem of discriminating among compound hypotheses [44]. The Bayesian decision method is inapplicable. One method of solution consists in finding the maximum-likelihood estimate for the pair of parameters b and k [23]; in other words, given v, we must find the pair of values k and b for which the likelihood function $p(v \mid E(k,b))$ assumes its maximum value. The value of k is then the one we are seeking for class identification.

This approach to the recognition problem is the basis for the method of admissible transformations, described in Chapter V. Concrete implementations of this method are given in Chapters V, VII, and VIII; they differ among themselves in the number of nuisance parameters and in the way the prototype depends on them. The parametric model also provides a basis for a formal statement of the problem of the structural analysis of images; this question is taken up in Chapter VII.

2.7 Optimization of the Decision Rule over a Prescribed Class

In some applied problems of image recognition, the maximum-likelihood method requires scanning over an excessive number of values of the nuisance parameter and is therefore too complex for practical implementation. It is then useful to limit the complexity by prescribing some parametrized class of decision rules and, using the model of the images to be recognized, choosing an optimal rule from the prescribed class. The estimated error probability can be usefully chosen as the optimality criterion, since it is normally used as a measure of the reliability of the recognition process in practical applications.

The following problem statement is a generalization of the search for the minimax of the specific risk (1.14), as discussed in Section 1.4. We consider a model of the form $p(v \mid E(k,b))$ with a nuisance parameter b that has among its components the translation parameters (and perhaps some others). Given a class of piecewise linear decision rules of the form

$$d = \arg\max_{k} \max_{\zeta} \left[v, c(k,\zeta) \right]$$

(the square brackets [ ] here denote scalar multiplication) where the N-dimensional vectors $c(k,\zeta)$ are templates with which the signals v are to be compared, and ζ is a parameter specifying the translation of the template relative to the field of view. The expression

$$\max_{\zeta} \left[v, c(k,\zeta) \right]$$

is a random variable whose distribution for the various classes k must be studied in order to find the upper bound of the probability of assigning the images with the distribution $p(v \mid E(k,b))$ to some class $l \neq k$. Then, varying the components of $c(k,\zeta)$, we obtain the least of these bounds. This problem must be solved by numerical methods; therefore we must construct a concrete model of the set of images that will allow us to obtain numerical values of all the parameters necessary to specify the distribution $p(v \mid E(k,b))$ for the several values of k and b. The task is examined in some detail in Chapter VI.

2.8 Learning and Self-Learning

Suppose now that the distribution of the signal v depends on the unknown value of the constant parameter a but does not depend on the nuisance parameter, i.e., that it has the form $p(v \mid E(k,a))$. We are given a training sample $\mathcal{L}$ consisting of l pairs $(v^j, k^j)\, j = 1, 2, \ldots, l$, where k^j denotes the class to which the signal v^j belongs. As was noted in Section 1.4, the reconstruction of the distribution of the signal on the basis of these data is the parametric learning problem.

Both of the known formulations of this problem can be stated in the language of parametric models. Suppose that we require a maximum-likelihood estimate of the parameter a. We compute the likelihood function for the given sample $\mathcal{L}$. The probability density for the pair (v^j, k^j) is

$$p(v^j, k^j \mid a) = p(v \mid E(k^j, a)) p(k^j), \qquad (2.10)$$

where $p(k)$ is the prior probability assigned to the kth class. The method for computing the probability density for the whole sample consisting of l such pairs depends on whether or not the pairs are mutually independent. It is generally assumed that they are independent, and we shall assume so also. Then, by the definition of mutual independence among random variables, the probability density for the whole sample is obtained by multiplying the probability densities for the individual pairs:

$$p(\mathcal{L} \mid a) = \prod_j p(v^j \mid E(k^j, a)) p(k^j). \qquad (2.11)$$

This expression, viewed as a function of the parameter a, is a likelihood function. The maximum-likelihood estimate for a is obtained by finding the value of a that maximizes (2.11). If the prior probabilities do not depend on a, it is sufficient to find the maximum of the simpler expression

$$\prod_j p(v^j \mid E(k^j, a)) \qquad (2.12)$$

with respect to a.

The maximum likelihood estimate of a as found by this process represents the result of the learning program. When we substitute it into the expression $p(v \mid E(k, a))$, we shall have obtained a concrete distribution usable as the basis for selection of an optimal decision rule. Learning problems of this kind have often been discussed in the literature [10, 56].

As we have already noted, in the great majority of the papers dealing with the parametric learning problem the sample pairs (v^j, k^j) are assumed to be mutually independent random variables. This assumption is not always realistic; we shall discuss the case of nonindependence below, in Section 3.1.

In the general case the prototype signal depends on the nuisance parameter b as well as on the parameters k and a; in fact, it does so in all applied image-recognition problems. It is impossible to imagine a practical case in which the nuisance parameter is absent, since it characterizes among other things the translations, changes in line width, contrast, etc. Nevertheless, most of the studies of parametric learning have omitted the effect of the nuisance parameter. Taking it into account makes the problem substantially more complicated; we shall investigate the general problem, together with the effect of the assumption that the sample pairs are mutually dependent, in Sections 3.1 and 3.2.

The second formulation of the parametric learning problem is as follows: We are given, as in the first formulation, the distribution $p(v \mid E(k,a))$ and the sample $\mathcal{L}$. We are to find a decision rule $F(v, \mathcal{L})$, as a function of the training sample, that will minimize the conditional risk (for a given sample). The solution of this problem is taken up in Section 3.3.

Using the parametric model and the maximum-likelihood estimate, we can also formulate the self-learning problem. It differs from the learning problem in that the training sample consists of only the values v^j $(j = 1, 2, \ldots, l)$. The probability density for v^j is obtained by summing (2.10) over the k^j, and the likelihood function has the form

$$\prod_j \sum_k p(v^j \mid E(k,a)) p(k) \tag{2.13}$$

If the prior probabilities $p(k)$ are not given, we must find the maximum of (2.13) not only with respect to a but also with respect to $p(k)$, $k = 1, 2, \ldots, n$. Then we have the estimates of a and of the $p(k)$ as well. This problem, which has been studied by M. I. Šlezinger [72], was considered in Section 1.4.

2.9 Problems with Nonstatistical Criteria

There are formulations of the recognition problem in which the statistical characteristics of the signal play no role; these may be called the *deterministic* formulations. This term has also been used to designate the recognition problems with nonintersecting classes, i.e., those problems in which the conditional probability (or probability density) of each of the possible signals may be greater than zero on a single class only. This use of the term is unfortunate, however (cf. [10], for instance), since the recognition problem with nonintersecting classes is a special case of the statistical recognition problem, and the term "deterministic" ought to be used as the opposite of the term "statistical". We shall use it to mean that in our deterministic formulations there is no trace of statistical or probabilistic concepts.

For instance, suppose that each of two classes to be recognized is defined by some number of prototype signals $E(k,b)$, where $k = 1, 2$ is the class index and $b \in B_k$ is the index of the prototype signal in the class. We are to find the hyperplane separating the subsets of prototype signals corresponding to $k = 1$ and $k = 2$, and yielding the maximum distance from the nearest prototype signal.

It is not difficult to see that the probabilistic minimax problem considered in Section 1.4 reduces to this formulation. The parametric model (2.5), with known a, also corresponds to this problem, with the distribution $p(v \mid E(k,b))$ chosen to be normal with mean $E(k,b)$ and unit covariance matrix.

In many other cases also, the statistical formulation derives the functional to be optimized from the probabilistic character of the noise, while the deterministic formulation takes this functional as given; this makes the difference between the two approaches. Thus any deterministic recognition problem can be viewed as a statistical problem already partially solved.

The nonparametric learning problem, in which we are seeking the parameters of the decision function, can also be viewed as a special case of the decision problem with a statistical model of the signals, in which the class of decision functions has already been deduced from the model. For instance, if the sets defined by the condition $\max_{b \in B_k} p(v \mid E(k,a,b)) > \theta$ for fixed k and a are such that their convex hulls corresponding to different values of k do not intersect for any value of a, we may conclude that the decision rules will be linear. In the deterministic case, the class of decision functions is prescribed as linear from the outset.

It follows from what we have said that at the root of every deterministic problem, just as in the statistical case, there lies a (possibly nonunique) parametric model of the signal, which is not given in explicit form. If we know this model, we can judge the usefulness of our optimization criteria and define the scope of the algorithms we obtain.

2.10 Conclusions

The recognition of images is difficult because the set of signals to be recognized has a complex structure. For this reason, neither the many heuristic devices nor the simple statistical models have given satisfactory results in the majority of the applications.

An attack on the recognition, learning, and self-learning problems should be begun with the construction of a parametric model defining the effect of the several factors on the process that generates the observed images, or, more generally, signals. The model should be constructed on the basis both of what we know about the process and of some further study of it. Such study, even though it does not lend itself to formalization, is characteristic and usual in scientific and technological research.

The parametric model suffices for the formulation of all the known and newly emerging problems of recognition, learning, self-learning and structural analysis. The statement and solution of some of these problems will be given below.

CHAPTER III

The Parametric Learning Problem

As we noted in Chapter I, learning methods—whether parametric or nonparametric—are rarely applied in the recognition of images. For nonparametric methods the reason is that it is difficult to find a suitable class of decision rules with finite capacity when the structure of the sets is as complex as it is in visual images (cf. Section 1.3).

When the distributions of the image classes are known to within the parameter values, it is in principle possible to formulate the parametric learning problem, as we did in Section 2.8, in terms of a parametric model; we showed there how it reduces to optimization by finding the maximum-likelihood estimate of the unknown parameter. This formulation occurs often in the literature [10, 56]. It is not immediately applicable, however, to the recognition of images, since the probability distributions of images usually depend on a nuisance parameter, and this fact is not taken into account in the formulations referred to. Moreover, the images in the learning sample are usually assumed to be independent, while there exist many practical applications in which this assumption is invalid. The characters serving as input to a reading machine, for instance, are generally interdependent because of the context, i.e., the redundancy of text material. Another kind of dependence exists because the type font is normally constant throughout a single line, or even throughout an entire document, and because the state of the ink ribbon in the printer changes slowly in time.

For these reasons the study of the parametric learning problem in the presence of a nuisance parameter and interdependence in the training sample is of great practical as well as theoretical interest. We shall consider this problem in Sections 3.1 and 3.2, using the maximum-likelihood method.

This method is simple and clear, but we must remember that it does not minimize the risk. [We recall that we said in Section 1.4 that a learning process founded on an estimate of the unknown parameter a in the distribution $p(v|E(k,a))$ fails to minimize the risk.] The learning problem formulated as the minimization of the conditional risk, with a given sample, has already been studied in the literature [34, 57].

In view of the great importance of the optimality approach, this problem is considered below, in Section 3.3.

3.1 Learning with a Sample of Mutually Dependent Signals in the Presence of a Nuisance Parameter

We shall consider the following approach to the problem of finding an optimal decision rule: Suppose it is known that the conditional distribution of the signal for each class to be recognized depends on a nuisance parameter b and belongs to a known family parametrized by a. We are given a training sample $\mathcal{L}$ consisting of l realizations v^j of the signal v (note that the upper index j denotes the jth realization of the vector v; a subscript is used to denote the index of a component of a given vector). For each v^j we are also given the true value k^j of the classification parameter k. Using the training sample $\mathcal{L}$, we are to find the maximum-likelihood estimate $\hat{a}$ of the parameter a and choose the corresponding distribution from the parametric family by setting $a = \hat{a}$. When this is done the learning is finished; the result is a probability distribution to be used in the solution of the recognition problem.

The first step is the computation of the likelihood function. The specific difficulty imposed by the interdependence of the observed signals arises from the fact that we can no longer compute the likelihood function by multiplying the likelihood functions of the individual input pairs (v^j, k^j).

In keeping with the model (2.4) developed in Chapter II, we shall suppose that the signals are distributed with probability density

$$p(v|E(k,a,b)), \qquad (3.1)$$

where $E(k,a,b)$ is a prototype depending on the recognition parameter k, the unknown constant parameter a, which is to be estimated from the training sample, and the nuisance parameter b.

If the signals v are distributed in accordance with (3.1), the distribution for a fixed E depends on no other factors. Consequently the jth signal v^j in some learning sequence with a fixed prototype $E(k^j,a,b^j)$ is independent of a preceding signal v^i, $i < j$. This means that the influence of v^i on v^j can be exercised only via the prototype $E(k^j,a,b^j)$, and if the prototype is fixed there is no influence. For fixed a, the influence goes via k^j and b^j, i.e., k^j and b^j depend on v^i or on k^i and b^i, and then (for nonfixed E) v^j depends on v^i.

Such dependence is altogether natural if the realizations of the noise for successive appearances of the signal do not influence one another. In the case of machine-written symbols this means, for instance, that the occurrence of random defects in the successive characters does not depend on the occurrence of these defects in the preceding characters. On the other hand, the stroke width of the successive characters, being a component of the nuisance parameter, can depend on the stroke width of the preceding characters, since both stroke widths depend on the inkiness of the ribbon.

The dependence between successive values of k^j can be described by a conditional distribution $p(k^j|s^{j-1})$, depending on the state s^{j-1} of the process generating the sequence. The state s^j is defined by the recursive relation

$$s^j = S(s^{j-1}, k^j). \tag{3.2}$$

Thus, s^j depends on all the preceding values of k and on some initial state s^0.

We can write down a similar relationship for the joint distribution of the parameters k and b. The conditional probability of the pair (k, b) will be denoted by $p(k^j, b^j|s^{j-1})$, where the state s^j is defined by the relation

$$s^j = S(s^{j-1}, k^j, b^j). \tag{3.3}$$

Now let us consider the training sample $\mathcal{L}_{1,l}$ consisting of the l pairs (v, k):

$$\mathcal{L}_{1,l} = \{(v^1, k^1), (v^2, k^2), \ldots, (v^l, k^l)\}. \tag{3.4}$$

The probability density for this sample, and therefore also the likelihood function, can be expressed in terms of the conditional probability $p(k^j, b^j|s^{j-1})$ defined above, together with the relation (3.3). We denote by $\mathcal{L}_{j,l}$ the following finite segment of the training sample:

$$\mathcal{L}_{j,l} = \{(v^j, k^j), (v^{j+1}, k^{j+1}), \ldots, (v^l, k^l)\}. \tag{3.5}$$

The density $p(\mathcal{L}_{j,l}|a, s^{j-1})$ for this segment depends on a and on the state s^{j-1}, which exists after the appearance of the first $j-1$ pairs. We can compute it by means of the obvious recursion

$$p(\mathcal{L}_{j,l}|a, s^{j-1}) = \sum_{b^j} p(v^j|E(k^j, a, b^j))p(k^j, b^j|s^{j-1})p(\mathcal{L}_{j+1,l}|a, s^j), \tag{3.6}$$

where, in agreement with (3.3),

$$s^j = S(s^{j-1}, k^j, b^j).$$

The symbol $\sum_{b^j}$ denotes summation over the set of values of the parameter b^j, which set is assumed to be discrete. For a continuous set, the summation should be replaced by integration.

We are now able to write down the most general form of the likelihood function for the training sample, by using (3.6):

$$p\left(\mathcal{L}_{j,l}\,|\,a,s^0\right) = \sum_{b^1} p\left(v^1|E(k^1,a,b^1)\right)p\left(k^1,b^1|s^0\right)$$

$$\times \sum_{b^2} p\left(v^2|E(k^2,a,b^2)\right)p\left(k^2,b^2|s^1\right)\sum_{b^3}\ \cdots$$

$$\times \cdots \times \sum_{b^l} p\left(v^l|E(k^l,a,b^l)\right)p\left(k^l,b^l|s^{l-1}\right). \quad (3.7)$$

Computation of the value (3.7) should be carried out by a technique similar to that of dynamic programming [6]: we first compute the quantities $p(\mathcal{L}_{l-1,l}\,|\,a,s^{l-2})$ for all values of s^{l-2}, as functions of a. Then, using (3.6), we compute $p(\mathcal{L}_{l-2,l}\,|\,a,s^{l-3})$ for all s^{l-3}, and so on until we reach $p(\mathcal{L}_{1,l}\,|\,a,s^0)$.

If the conditional probability $p(k^j,b^j|\ s^{j-1})$ and the relations (3.3) are known only to within the parameter values, then in principle one can estimate the values of these parameters by maximizing (3.7).

When the nuisance parameter is absent (3.6) is substantially simplified:

$$p\left(\mathcal{L}_{j,l}\,|\,a,s^{j-1}\right) = p\left(v^j|E(k^j,a)\right)p\left(k^j|s^{j-1}\right)p\left(\mathcal{L}_{j+1,l}\,|\,a,s^j\right). \quad (3.8)$$

It is then easy to find a simple expression for the likelihood function:

$$p\left(\mathcal{L}_{1,l}\,|\,a,s^0\right) = \prod_{j=1}^{l} p\left(v^j|E(k^j,a)\right)p\left(k^j|s^{j-1}\right). \quad (3.9)$$

The sequence of values s^{j-1} which must be inserted in (3.9) is completely defined by the sequence k^j and thus can be found by using (3.2), starting with s^0, which is assumed to be known.

If the probabilities $p(k^j|s^{j-1})$ do not depend on a, then a can be estimated by maximizing only the product of the first factors in (3.9). Then the function to be maximized has the same form as in the case of independent signals [cf. (2.12)].

Thus we arrive at an important conclusion: if

1. the nuisance parameter is absent,
2. the dependence of the successive signals on their predecessors is for fixed a realized only through the values of k, and
3. the conditional probabilities $p(k^j|s^{j-1})$ defining the interdependence of the k^j do not depend on a,

then the learning is realized just as though the signals were independent, i.e., by maximizing the product of the densities (2.12).

3.2 Learning with Independent Nuisance Parameters

The expression (3.7) for the likelihood function is highly complex and therefore not easy to apply under practical circumstances.

We have considered the case when the signals are interdependent and the nuisance parameter is absent; we now turn to the case in which the parameters b^j are present and have an objectively existing but perhaps unknown probability distribution. We suppose that the successive b^j are independently distributed, and that the interdependence of the signals v^j is mediated for fixed a only via the recognition parameters k^j.

Then the state s^j does not depend on the b^j and is defined by (3.2); the distribution $p(k^j, b^j | s^{j-1})$ has the form

$$p(k^j, b^j | s^{j-1}) = p(b^j | k^j) p(k^j | s^{j-1}), \tag{3.10}$$

where $p(b^j | k^j)$ does not depend on the state s^{j-1} and does depend solely on k^j. We insert (3.10) in (3.6) and obtain:

$$p(\mathcal{L}_{j,l} | a, s^{j-1}) = \sum_{b^j} p(v^j | E(k^j, a, b^j)) p(b^j | k^j) p(k^j | s^{j-1}) p(\mathcal{L}_{j+1,l} | a, s^j).$$

$$\tag{3.11}$$

Our assumptions guarantee that the two rightmost factors in (3.11) do not depend on b^j, and they can be removed from the scope of the summation sign:

$$p(\mathcal{L}_{j,l} | a, s^{j-1}) = \left[\sum_{b^j} p(v^j | E(k^j, a, b^j)) p(b^j | k^j) \right]$$

$$\times p(k^j | s^{j-1}) p(\mathcal{L}_{j+1,l} | a, s^j). \tag{3.12}$$

The index j of the parameter b was needed to account for the influence of the jth realization of b on the state s^j. When this influence is absent, we can omit the index. According to the recursive relation (3.12) the probability density for the whole sample, and therefore the likelihood function, is given by

$$p(\mathcal{L}_{1,l} | a, s^0) = \prod_{j=1}^{l} \sum_{b} p(v^j | E(k^j, a, b))$$

$$\times p(b | k^j) \prod_{j=1}^{l} p(k^j | s^{j-1}). \tag{3.13}$$

Here the sequence of states s^{j-1} is defined by the given sequence of the k^j via (3.2).

If the product of the distributions $\prod_{j=1}^{l} p(k^j | s^{j-1})$ of the recognition parameter k is independent of a, the estimate of a itself can be obtained by maximizing the product of the sums:

$$\prod_{j=1}^{l} \sum_{b} p\big(v^j \,|\, E(k^j, a, b)\big) p(b \,|\, k^j). \qquad (3.14)$$

Thus, in the presence of the nuisance parameter, even when its successive realizations are independent, the learning problem is essentially different from the problem without it, for which the likelihood function is the product of the densities (2.12). The expression analogous to (2.12), but containing the nuisance parameters b^j in addition to the recognition parameters k^j, has the form

$$\prod_{j=1}^{l} p\big(v^j \,|\, E(k^j, a, b^j)\big). \qquad (3.14a)$$

This expression is usable for estimating the constant parameter only if each input signal v^j in the training sample is accompanied by the true values of *all* the parameters that vary from one input to another, i.e., the values of k^j and b^j. In other words the teacher must supply not only the class index k^j, but also the value of the nuisance parameter b^j.

Suppose, for instance, that we are to solve the learning problem, confining ourselves to the creation of prototype images of typescript on the basis of the observed images. Suppose, for simplicity, that the mean gray shade and contrast of the images are fixed. Even with these constraints the maximization of the product of the probabilities (3.14a) will fail to solve the problem unless the teacher provides for each observed image both the class index and the value of some centering coordinates as well; these centering coordinates locate the image with reference to the edges of the field of view, and refer to the position of the type block at the instant of contact with the paper rather than to the centroid or "edges" of the diffuse gray spot that is the observed image of the character. The parameters b^j that appear in a learning process regulated by (3.14a) are of course not nuisance parameters but observables, whose effect can be trivially excluded by inserting the measured values in the expression for the probability density

$$p\big(v_j \,|\, E(k^j, a, b^j)\big).$$

When the distribution $p(b \,|\, k)$ of the nuisance parameter is known, the parameter a is estimated by maximizing (3.14) with respect to a. If $p(b \,|\, k)$ is unknown, we must estimate its parameters jointly with a. We shall suppose that b is discrete and that it takes on only a finite set of values. Then $p(b \,|\, k)$ is defined for all k by a finite number of parameters, which are merely the conditional probabilities of the several discrete values of b. We can estimate these, along with a, by maximizing (3.14).

The problem of estimating the constant parameter jointly with the parameters of the prior distribution of b resembles the problem of self-learning, which was solved by M. I. Šlezinger [72] (see Section 1.4). In the particular case when the pair of values (k,a) determines some parameter a_k and the dependence of E on k and a is expressed solely through the parameter a_k:

$$E(k,a,b) = E'((a_k,b)),$$

the individual values of the a_k $(k = 1,2, \ldots , n)$ can be estimated separately. For this purpose the training sample must be divided into n subsamples over each of which the value of k is constant. For each k we compute the likelihood function

$$\prod_{j=1}^{l_k} \sum_b p\left(v^{jk} \,|\, E'(a_k,b)\right)p\,(b\,|\,k), \qquad (3.15)$$

where l_k is the length of the kth subsample and v^{jk} is the jth observation in the kth subsample. The problem of estimating the a_k and the parameters of the distribution $p(b|k)$ coincides in detail with the self-learning problem [72].

This last case is interesting from the viewpoint of learning application for the construction of prototypes (templates) of characters for use in reading machines. In this case we must find for each class k the set of parameters a_k that define the prototype image of the kth character.

When there is no stationary distribution $p(b|k)$ we can still obtain an estimate for a by maximizing (3.14) with respect to a and $p(b|k^j)$, where the latter may be viewed as relative frequencies of the corresponding values of b in the given sample.

3.3 Learning as the Minimization of the Conditional Risk

We now consider the learning problem as one of minimizing the mean conditional risk of a recognition error with the given training sample [34]; as we noted earlier, this formulation corresponds most closely to the requirements of practice. We need to show how the optimal procedure in this case differs from the above procedure of estimating an unknown parameter by means of the sample.

We suppose that we are given a model of the form (2.4), i.e., that we know the distribution $p(v\,|\,E(k,a,b))$. We shall also suppose that the prior distributions of the recognition parameter k and the nuisance parameter b are given to within the values of some unknown parameters. The distribution of b may depend on k. We recall that k, a, and b are in general multidimensional; we may therefore suppose that a includes among its components the parameters of the prior distributions of k and b. Thus we may suppose that the distributions $p(k\,|\,a)$ and $p(b\,|\,k,a)$ are known.

Whenever, for one reason or another, the parameters k and b are not to be thought of as random variables with known probability distributions, we should deal with the maximum value of the risk with respect to k and b rather than the mean. This represents a more complex problem, and we shall not treat it here.

We need the prior distribution $p(a)$, which we assume will embody all our *a priori* knowledge about the possible values of a. This knowledge, implicit or explicit, is commonly used in recreating distributions that depend on parameters; for instance, if we suppose that the set of the possible parameter values is given, this differs little from saying that the probability of these values is equal to zero everywhere except on the given set of values.

We also suppose that the loss matrix $w(k,d)$ is given; its elements represent the magnitude of the loss concerned with making the decision d when the true class index of the signal is k.

With these data, the learning experiment can be described as follows: With probability $p(a)$ the constant parameter takes on a value a, which is constant throughout the experiment but unknown. Then the recognition parameter k takes on the sequence of values $k^1, k^2, \ldots, k^l$ with the probabilities $p(k^1|a), p(k^2|a), \ldots, p(k^l|a)$, where a is the unknown value of the constant parameter, and the values of k are independently distributed. The parameter b takes on the values $b^1, b^2, \ldots, b^l$ with the respective probabilities $p(b^j|k^j,a)$, $j = 1, 2, \ldots, l$, and the signal v takes on the values $v^1, v^2, \ldots, v^l$ with probabilities $p(v^j|E(k^j,a,b^j))$. The values of b are not observed, however. Thus we have the observed training sample

$$\mathcal{L} = \{(v^1, k^1), (v^2, k^2), \ldots, (v^l, k^l)\}.$$

After the learning, and with the same value of the constant parameter a, we carry out a test, in which we feed the recognizer a set of signals with the same probability distributions of the k and v, but we supply only the signals v and not the recognition parameters k. The machine is to estimate the values of k, corresponding to the input signals v, by producing decisions d based on the training sample, in such a way as to minimize the risk (i.e., the mean loss). In other words, we must find an optimal decision rule $d = \hat{\mathcal{F}}(v, \mathcal{L})$ such that the risk is minimized.

For an arbitrary decision rule $d = \mathcal{F}(v)$ the Bayesian risk, i.e., the conditional mean loss $w(k,d)$, is

$$R(\mathcal{L}, \mathcal{F}) = \sum_k \sum_v w(k, \mathcal{F}(v)) p(v, k | \mathcal{L}). \qquad (3.16)$$

The conditional density $p(v,k|\mathcal{L})$ can be expressed by functions which we assume to be known, and we write it out as follows:

$$p(v,k|\mathcal{L}) = \sum_a p(a|\mathcal{L}) \sum_b p(v,k|a,b,\mathcal{L}) p(b|a,\mathcal{L}). \qquad (3.17)$$

If a is given, the training sample $\mathcal{L}$ gives no further information about k, b, and v. Therefore $p(b\,|\,a,\mathcal{L}) = p(b\,|\,a)$ and

$$p(v,k\,|\,a,b,\mathcal{L}) = p(v,k\,|\,a,b) = p(v\,|\,k,a,b)p(k\,|\,a,b)$$

$$= p(v\,|\,E(k,a,b))p(k\,|\,a,b). \tag{3.18}$$

We substitute (3.18) into (3.17), then we replace, according to Bayes' formula, $p(b\,|\,a)p(k\,|\,a,b)$ by $p(b\,|\,k,a)p(k\,|\,a)$ and introduce for brevity the notation

$$p(v\,|\,k,a) = \sum_b p(v\,|\,E(k,a,b))p(b\,|\,k,a). \tag{3.19}$$

Then

$$p(v,k\,|\,\mathcal{L}) = \sum_a p(v\,|\,k,a)p(k\,|\,a)p(a\,|\,\mathcal{L}). \tag{3.20}$$

By Bayes' formula we get

$$p(a\,|\,\mathcal{L}) = cp(\mathcal{L}\,|\,a)p(a), \tag{3.21}$$

where the coefficient c is found from the normalization

$$\sum_a cp(\mathcal{L}\,|\,a)p(a) = 1. \tag{3.22}$$

The density $p(\mathcal{L}\,|\,a)$ is given by

$$p(\mathcal{L}\,|\,a) = \prod_{j=1}^l p(v^j\,|\,k^j,a)p(k^j\,|\,a), \tag{3.23}$$

in accordance with (2.12), when the several pairs of observables in the training sample are independent. Substituting (3.23) into (3.21), and putting the result into (3.20), we obtain

$$p(v,k\,|\,\mathcal{L}) = c\sum_a p(k\,|\,a)p(v\,|\,k,a)p(a) \prod_{j=1}^l p(v^j\,|\,k^j,a)p(k^j\,|\,a), \tag{3.24}$$

where the density $p(v^j\,|\,k^j,a)$ is defined by (3.19). Using (3.24), we can define the risk (3.16) in terms of known quantities.

The optimal decision rule is defined as it was for the Bayesian problem considered in Section 1.4. If we have an antidiagonal loss matrix

$$w(k,d) = \ulcorner k \neq d \urcorner$$

where the corners $\ulcorner$ $\urcorner$ have the meaning assigned in Section 1.1, and the optimal decision rule has the form

$$\hat{\mathcal{F}}(v,\mathcal{L}) = \arg\max_k p(v,k\,|\,\mathcal{L}), \tag{3.25}$$

in which $p(v,k\,|\,\mathcal{L})$ is defined by (3.20) or, more precisely, by (3.24).

As can be seen from (3.20) and (3.25), the solution is obtained by maximizing the joint probability of v and k, convolved with the posterior distribution $p(a \mid \mathcal{L})$. This procedure differs essentially from the one applied for learning by estimating the parameter a. In fact, the discriminant function (3.20) does not even belong to the class of discriminant functions $p(v, k \mid a)$ from which we make a choice when we estimate a and substitute its value into $p(v, k \mid a)$.

The sharper the maximum of the posterior distribution $p(a \mid \mathcal{L})$, the closer the results of these two procedures. Therefore, if an increase in sample length sharpens the extremum of $p(a \mid \mathcal{L})$, so that it approaches the δ-function, the two procedures are asymptotically equivalent.

3.4 Conclusions

The general form of the likelihood function that we have obtained for a training sample shows that learning with mutually dependent signals, in the presence of nuisance parameters, represents a problem of the estimation of parameters from a composite sample.

The learning procedure with a sample in which the signals are interdependent (with constant a) may be performed by the same algorithm as with independent signals if the teacher provides the values of all the parameters that interconnect the signals. This means that in the presence of nuisance parameters the traditional statistical learning algorithms are applicable only if the teacher supplies the values of the nuisance parameter along with the value of the recognition parameter indicating the class to which the presented image belongs.

It is difficult to see how the true values of the nuisance parameter can be determined by the teacher in the case of image recognition, and therefore difficult to see how such a learning process can be implemented. In the customary procedure, when nuisance parameters are present but the teacher supplies only the value of the recognition parameter, the learning amounts to estimating a parameter from a composite sample, and in this sense is similar to the parametric self-learning procedure. The latter is much more complex than those commonly used for learning, because the likelihood function is much more complex and much less amenable to optimization. The problem of learning with nuisance parameters may be thought of as a generalization of the parametric learning and self-learning problems considered in Chapter I.

The alternative formulation, in which the parametric learning problem is seen as the minimization of the conditional risk for a given sample, leads to a procedure which differs essentially from the estimation of parameter values. It leads to a decision rule that does not belong to the class of rules that are optimal for fixed parameter values.

CHAPTER IV

On the Criteria for the Information Content of a System of Features

As we noted in Chapter II, one of the most important problems in recognition is the choice of features, or the initial description of the images to be recognized. In this chapter we shall consider some questions concerned with methods of assessing the value of a system of features. To this end, we establish a connection between the concepts of sufficient statistic, quantity of information, and the probability of a correct recognition.

4.1 On the Choice of Primary and Secondary Features

As we remarked in Section 1.1, the primary features represent the results of direct physical measurements on the images, that is, some functionals of the distribution of gray shades $v(x, y)$. We may suppose that the set of direct measurements is given to us. For images, it consists of the set of linear functionals of the distribution of gray shades, with nonnegative weight functions. The nonnegativity of the weight functions implies that if the brightness increases at a point of the image the result of the measurement cannot decrease. The following are examples of such linear functionals: the signal at the output of an optical correlator, the instantaneous value of the signal output from a television transmitting tube, etc.

For the initial measurements, or primary features, we may choose any set of measurements such that an *arbitrary* functional of the image $v(x, y)$

can be represented with sufficient accuracy by the results of these initial measurements. The simplest example of such a "complete" set is the digitization of an image by means of a very fine retina (cf. Section 1.1). If the cell diameter is several times smaller than the smallest detail of the image, then the image can be approximated well enough by its digitized representation, and an arbitrary linear functional can be represented as a linear function of its components. Therefore, we normally use the components of a digitized representation as our set of primary features.

We now ask whether we can find a more economical description of the image, by using secondary features, fewer in number or with less information capacity than the primary features, but yielding an approximately equal probability p_c of correct recognition. Clearly, it would be wrong to ask for the minimum number of secondary features for a given value of p_c; the simple and trivial answer to this requirement is: the best feature is the optimal decision function that we are looking for. It may be regarded as a single secondary feature yielding at the same time the minimum error probability.

The proper approach to the choice of the secondary features must take into account the complexity of their calculation or measurement, as well as the complexity of the decision functions into which they enter as arguments. In other words, we must take account of the complexity of the whole process—from the presented image right through to the decision—and try to minimize the total complexity for a given reliability of recognition. This amounts to saying that we want to minimize the complexity of the recognition algorithm as a whole. Which secondary features to consider, and how to choose them, remains unclear. Usually one introduces some auxiliary criterion concerning the quality of the secondary features and uses it in the selection process. However, unless we know the connection between the criterion and the error probability and the complexity of the recognition algorithm as a whole, the superiority of the system selected by means of the criterion, as against an arbitrary system, must be counted as doubtful. We do not know of any formal statement of the problem of choosing a set of secondary features that is free of this defect.

Although this is how matters stand in the general case, we may formulate some particular problems concerning the transformations of features in which difficulties of this kind do not arise—for instance, the consolidation of retinal cells by joining them up, or discarding of some part of the features, provided that the algorithm that will process them further is fixed to within parameter values. In these cases, the transformation of the features is accompanied by a monotone simplification of the recognition algorithm, since the number of features decreases, the complexity of the measurement of each remains the same, and the decision rule decreases in complexity with a decrease in the number of features. We may consolidate retinal cells or discard subsets of the set of features until the probability of correct recognition decreases from its initial value to some preset limit. Therefore we need to know how to compute the probability of correct recognition when we are given a set of features, and how to compute the changes in it when they are subjected to a transformation.

The notion of a sufficient statistic underlies all the criteria for the information content of a set of features, as described below. We shall investigate the interconnection between various criteria, in particular the conditional entropy and the error probability. The results we obtain will be useful in practical tasks related to the choice of a set of features or, more generally, in connection with the preprocessing of images. Furthermore, they have a certain cognitive value, since they call attention to the connection between some fundamental concepts of mathematical statistics, information theory, amd pattern recognition.

4.2 Sufficient Statistics

A given image may be characterized by different sets of features, i.e., by different *descriptions*. The term "description" here means the same as "signal", but it is much more convenient to speak of two different descriptions of an image than to speak of two different signals; the latter terminology is sometimes incomprehensible.

In going from a set of primary features to a set of secondary features, we are replacing the original description v by another description u. The transformed description u is a function of v, i.e., $u = u(v)$. Every function of an observation or measurement is called a *statistic*, so $u(v)$ is a statistic; we shall also refer to it as a *transformed description*.

When we obtain a simplified description u from the original description v, we perform a mapping of many different values of v into one value of u, and in fact this is what the simplification consists of. It occurs when we average some components of v, when we digitize them, or subject a description to various other transformations. If we know only the transformed descriptions u, we cannot always re-create the original v that gave rise to them.

Let us consider the conditions under which such a joining or "intermixing" of different descriptions v does not lead to a deterioration of the recognition, i.e., does not increase the risk. We begin with the Bayesian risk [cf. Section 1.4, Equation (1.12)].

If we do not confound values of v that correspond to different decisions in the recognition process, we can make the same decisions on the basis of u as we can on the basis of v. Therefore, to conserve the risk function it is necessary and sufficient that values $v^{(1)}$ and $v^{(2)}$ which generate different decisions $\mathscr{F}(v^{(1)}) \neq \mathscr{F}(v^{(2)})$ should also map into values $u(v^{(1)}) \neq u(v^{(2)})$.

Since the optimal decision depends on the loss matrix, it may happen that a given transformation of v into u will satisfy our condition for one loss matrix and not satisfy it for another. The set of optimal Bayesian decisions for an arbitrary loss matrix is produced via the posterior probabilities $p(k|v)$ or $p(k|u)$. Therefore, to find an optimal solution *for an arbitrary loss matrix* it is sufficient to distinguish those values of v for which the sets of posterior probabilities differ. The transformed description $u(v)$ will generate the same risk function as v for an arbitrary loss matrix if it confounds only those values of v for which the posterior probability distributions are identical. For such a transformation the posterior distribution is conserved: $p(k|u(v)) = p(k|v)$ for all $k = 1, 2, \ldots, n$. The transformed description is then known as a *sufficient statistic*.

There is another definition of a sufficient statistic, which can be found in most texts on mathematical statistics, e.g., [44]. It applies to the more general case in which the prior distribution of the parameter k is unknown —or even nonexistent, i.e., when the parameter k is not necessarily a random variable. Let $p(v|k)$ be the generalized probability density distribution [23] of the random variable v, i.e., let $p(v|k)$ be the probability density if v is continuous, and the probability of the individual values if v is discrete. The quantity $p(v|k)$ is a conditional generalized probability density for a given k, $k \in K$, if the parameter k is a random variable.* Let $u(v)$ be a function of v. It is called a *sufficient statistic for the parameter k* or for the family of densities $\{p(v|k): k \in K\}$ if the conditional density $p(v|u, k)$ does not depend on k.

We shall show how this definition is connected with the one given earlier, namely, we will show that a function $u(v)$ satisfying the first definition also satisfies the second.

To avoid complicating the exposition, we shall assume throughout the rest of this chapter that *the random variable v takes on discrete values*. Then the expression $p(v|k)$ denotes the probability of the discrete value v, dependent on k, i.e., the conditional probability of the value v for a given value of k. All of our results can evidently be carried over in a natural way to the case when v takes on a continuous set of values.

Let us suppose, thus, that k is a random variable and that the posterior probability distributions

$$p(k|v^1) = p(k|v^2)$$

are identical for two given values of v, say v^1 and v^2. We express the posterior probability via the probabilities $p(v|k)$:

$$p(k|v) = \frac{p(v|k)p(k)}{\sum_k p(v|k)p(k)}.$$

We shall suppose that $p(k) > 0$ for all k, since in the Bayesian problem only such distributions make sense. Then we see that the posterior

---

* If k is not a random variable, it makes no sense to speak of the conditional probability distribution $p(v|k)$. It is convenient, however, to keep the same notation for a distribution depending on k as a parameter, since it does not lead to misunderstanding.

distributions for the values v^1 and v^2 will be identical if and only if the distributions $p(v^1|k)$ and $p(v^2|k)$, as functions of k, are proportional for all values of k, i.e.,

$$p(v^1|k) = cp(v^2|k),$$

where the factor c does not depend on k. Since the $p(v|k)$ are looked on here as functions of k, we shall call them likelihood functions.

Suppose there exists a set $V_1 = \{v^j\}$ of values of v such that the distribution $p(k|v^j)$ is the same for all v^j in V_1. Then for all these values v^j the likelihood functions are proportional to one and the same function of k:

$$p(v^j|k) = \varphi(v^j) \cdot \psi(k).$$

Now if $u(v)$ is such that all the values $v^j \in V_1$ correspond to the same value of u, the density $p(u|k)$, which is given by

$$p(u|k) = \sum_{v \in V_1} p(v|k),$$

turns out to be proportional to the same function of k:

$$p(u|k) = \varphi'(u)\psi(k).$$

Then the conditional probability $p(v|u,k)$, which is given by the ratio $p(v|k)/p(u|k)$, does not depend on k for a given u.

If the whole set of the values of v is divided into subsets like V_1, such that in each of them the density splits into factors of the form $\varphi(v)$ and $\psi(k)$, and to every such subset V_u there corresponds a different value of u, then the conditional probability $p(v|u,k)$ will not depend on k for arbitrary u, and this corresponds to our definition.

We note that, together with the definitions just given, a *characteristic of a sufficient statistic* is that the likelihood functions are all proportional to a single function of k, or that for each of the subsets of values of v corresponding to a single value of u the density $p(v|k)$ splits into factors.

4.3 A Measure of Insufficiency

For the solution of practical problems, it is profitable to use strictly sufficient descriptions only in the simplest cases. For the most part, it is worthwhile to simplify the initial description at the outset by applying very simple transformations such as averaging and digitization. Only after this is done should the apparatus of mathematical statistics be brought into play for the separation of classes. To simplify a description we must make it more economical than a sufficient description. We must, however, be able to estimate the numerical distance of the new description from a sufficient one. An estimate of this kind can be generated on the basis of the following considerations. (For simplicity, we will keep to the Bayesian case.)

In going from the initial description v to the more economical description u, different values of v may map into the same point of the u-space. It is not hard to see that the posterior probabilities $p(k|v)$ are averaged under such a mapping with weights proportional to the probabilities $p(v)$ of each of the collapsed descriptions:

$$p(k|u) = \frac{\sum\limits_{v \in u} p(v)p(k|v)}{\sum\limits_{v \in u} p(v)} \tag{4.1}$$

The summation is carried out over all descriptions v mapping into the same u. Therefore

$$\sum_{v \in u} p(v) = p(u) \tag{4.2}$$

and

$$p(k|u) = \frac{1}{p(u)} \sum_{v \in u} p(v)p(k|v). \tag{4.3}$$

The more significantly the posterior distributions for the collapsed v differ among themselves, and the greater the measure of the collapsed descriptions with differing distributions, so much the further does the transformed description u fall short of sufficiency.

We can construct a numerical measure of the insufficiency of the transformed description by using the following well-known property of convex functions. Every convex function $f(x)$ satisfies the inequality

$$f\left(\sum_i \alpha_i x_i\right) \geqslant \sum_i \alpha_i f(x_i), \tag{4.4}$$

where the α_i are nonnegative numbers summing to unity, i.e., $\alpha_i \geqslant 0$, $\sum_i \alpha_i = 1$. The inequality (4.4) says that the weighted average of the values of a convex function cannot exceed the function's value for the weighted average of the arguments. If $f(x)$ is strictly convex, equality holds only when all the x_i for which $\alpha_i > 0$ are the same.

Let us apply this inequality to the quantities connected by equation (4.3). We substitute $p(v)/p(u)$ for α_i, $p(k|v)$ for x_i, and v for the summation index i. Then we get

$$f(p(k|u)) \geqslant \frac{1}{p(u)} \sum_{v \in u} p(v)f(p(k|v)),$$

or

$$p(u)f(p(k|u)) \geqslant \sum_{v \in u} p(v)f(p(k|v)).$$

Summing over all u and all k, we obtain

$$\sum_{u,k} p(u)f(p(k|u)) \geqslant \sum_{v,k} p(v)f(p(k|v)),$$

where $f(\cdot)$ is an arbitrary strictly convex function on the interval $[0,1]$. The equality will hold only when identical posterior probabilities $p(k|v)$ are averaged, i.e., when the transformed description u is sufficient for k with respect to v. Therefore the increase in the sum

$$\sum_{v,k} p(v)f(p(k|v)) \qquad (4.5)$$

when v is replaced by u measures the degree of insufficiency of the transformed description u with respect to v. We may use the difference

$$\sum_{u,k} p(u)f(p(k|u)) - \sum_{v,k} p(v)f(p(k|v)).$$

as a measure of this insufficiency.

Later we will take up the question of how to select the function $f(\cdot)$.

4.4 Generalization of the Measure of Insufficiency to the Case of Probabilistic Transformations

The case we have been looking at up to now — namely the deterministic transformation in which each v maps into only one u — is the most interesting from the point of view of image recognition. The transfer of information in the presence of noise can be looked on as a probabilistic transformation of descriptions. In this case the initial description is the information transmitted, and the transformed description is the distorted signal. Our reasonings on the measurement of the insufficiency of the transformed description can be immediately generalized to the case of probabilistic transformations.

In fact, in the general case the posterior distributions are related by the equation

$$p(k|u) = \frac{1}{p(u)} \sum_{v} p(v,u)p(k|v), \qquad (4.6)$$

where $p(v,u)$ is the joint distribution of v and u. The summation takes place over all v. In the deterministic case $p(v,u)$ is equal to $p(v)$ when v maps into u, and is zero otherwise. As before, we use the inequality (4.4) and make the substitutions $p(k|v)$ for x_i, $p(v,u)|p(u)$ for α_i, and v for the index i. Then using (4.6) we find

$$f(p(k|u)) \geqslant \frac{1}{p(u)} \sum_{v} p(v,u)f(p(k|v)).$$

Multiplying both sides by the positive quantities $p(u)$ and summing over u and k, we obtain

$$\sum_{u,k} p(u)f(p(k|u)) \geq \sum_{v,k} \sum_u p(v,u)f(p(k|v)).$$

Since

$$\sum_u p(v,u) = p(v),$$

we have as before

$$\sum_{u,k} p(u)f(p(k|u)) \geq \sum_{v,k} p(v)f(p(k|v)).$$

Thus, for probabilistic transformations also, the increment of the sum (4.5) can be used as a measure of the insufficiency of the new description with respect to the initial one.

We remark that in the function $f(\cdot)$ which appears in the expression for the measure of insufficiency we may use as arguments not only the posterior probabilities $p(k|v)$ but also other quantities by means of which we can distinguish only those values of the description that differ in their posterior distributions. These are the so-called *necessary and sufficient statistics*.

In constructing expressions like (4.5) it is of course necessary to use rather simple rules for transforming descriptions that are to serve as arguments for convex functions. For example consider the normalized probabilities

$$\rho_k(v) = \frac{p(v|k)}{\sum_k p(v|k)}.$$

Here $p(v|k)$ denotes the conditional probability of a discrete variable v. Everything that we are about to say, however, still holds true when v is continuous and $p(v|k)$ is a probability density.

When the $p(k)$ are nonzero (and this is the only case that makes sense, since otherwise we would exclude the null cases and consider the smaller number of nonzero cases), the sets of values $\{\rho_k(v): k = 1, 2, \ldots, n\}$ will correspond one-to-one with the sets of values $\{p(k|v): k = 1, 2, \ldots, n\}$. This follows immediately from Bayes' Theorem, which allows us to express the $p(v|k)$ and $p(k|v)$ in terms of one another when $p(k) > 0$.

Thus the normalized probabilities $\rho_k(v)$ form a necessary and sufficient statistic. Under a mapping of descriptions the $\rho_k(v)$ are averaged with the same weights as the posterior probabilities $p(k|v)$. This is easily seen if we note that $\rho_k(v) = p(k|v)$ when the prior probabilities $p(k)$ are all equal, $p(k) = 1/n$, and the weights do not depend on $p(k)$.

Thus, we may use the normalized probabilities as arguments for the convex function in (4.5) to obtain a measure of insufficiency. Later we shall look at another example of the choice of arguments and the construction of a measure of insufficiency.

4.5 Entropy as a Measure of Insufficiency

The following argument is a natural one when we want to choose a concrete function $f(\cdot)$. It would be useful if the expression (4.5) reduced to zero for an "ideal" description, one that led to an error-free identification of the classes. For such a description all the posterior probabilities $p(k|v)$ but one will vanish. Therefore the function $f(p)$ should also vanish for $p = 0$ and $p = 1$.

When we pass from the classification of individual objects to the classification of sets containing l such objects (for instance from the recognition of characters to the recognition of words), it is natural to require that the measure of insufficiency should be proportional to the number l of objects in a set. Since the number of classes increases exponentially as n^l, it is useful to choose a measure proportional to the logarithm of the number of classes.

As we know from information theory, the requirements we have just listed are satisfied by the convex function

$$f(p) = -p \log p.$$

For this choice of function, the expression (4.5) becomes the conditional entropy of a class for a given description v:

$$H(K|V) = -\sum_v p(v) \sum_k p(k|v) \log p(k|v). \qquad (4.7)$$

Here K symbolizes the set of classes and V the set of descriptions. The entropy $H(K|V)$ may be interpreted as a measure of the insufficiency of the description v with respect to an ideal description which infallibly identifies the classes. In information theory, the conditional entropy is interpreted as a measure of the indeterminacy of the information contained in the description v about the class it describes, or as the loss of information (dissipation) suffered when we go from the ideal description to the given one.

We conclude that the concepts of "indeterminacy" and "loss of information" can be interpreted from the point of view of mathematical statistics as measures of insufficiency.

In the general case, when an initial description v is transformed by some process into a second description u, the difference in the conditional entropies of the two descriptions,

$$H(K|U) - H(K|V) = -\sum_u p(u) \sum_k {}'p(k|u) \log p(k|u)$$
$$+ \sum_v p(v) \sum_k p(k|v) \log p(k|v),$$

will serve as a measure of the insufficiency of u relative to v. This difference may be interpreted as the loss of information about the class k that is suffered when we go from v to u.

A theorem asserting that the equality of the conditional entropies, $H(K|U) = H(K|V)$, is necessary and sufficient for u to be sufficient for v has been proved by Lindley [45].

As we pointed out earlier, when we measure the insufficiency by using (4.5) the posterior probabilities may be replaced by the normalized probabilities

$$\rho_k(v) = \frac{p(v|k)}{\sum\limits_k p(v|k)} .$$

Therefore, if we use the normalized probabilities $\rho_k(v)$ instead of the posterior probabilities $p(k|v)$ in the conditional entropy (4.7), we obtain another measure of insufficiency. It coincides numerically with the conditional entropy when the classes are equiprobable. Thus the entropy as a measure of insufficiency is completely expressible even in the important case when the prior probabilities $p(k)$ of the classes are not known and we have only the conditional probabilities $p(v|k)$ at our disposal.

4.6 On the Kullback Divergence

Kullback [42] considers a quantity characterizing the distinguishability of two hypotheses (or two classes of signals) on the basis of a given description v. The quantity is called the divergence, or distance, between the two hypotheses. In our notation, the divergence is given by

$$\text{div}_v = \sum_v [p(v|1) - p(v|2)]\log \frac{p(v|1)}{p(v|2)} .$$

When $p(v|1) \equiv p(v|2)$ and the classes are indistinguishable on the basis of v, the divergence vanishes. When the classes are separable without error, so that for any v one or other of the conditional probabilities must be zero, the divergence becomes infinite. A transformation of v into a new description u will in general change the divergence.

It is not hard to see that the divergence, represented as

$$\text{div}_v = -\sum_v p(v|1)\log \frac{p(v|2)}{p(v|1)} - \sum_v p(v|2)\log \frac{p(v|1)}{p(v|2)} ,$$

is the sum of two quantities, each capable of serving as a measure of insufficiency. Let us look at the sum

$$\sum_v p(v|1)\log \frac{p(v|2)}{p(v|1)} . \tag{4.8}$$

The ratio $p(v|2)/p(v|1)$ is a necessary and sufficient description for the two classes, and under a mapping from v to u it is averaged with weights proportional to $p(v|1)$. It appears in (4.8) as the argument of the convex function $\log x$. This function is summed with weights $p(v|1)$, which are proportional to the averaging weights. Therefore (4.8) is constructed on the same principle as the more general expression (4.5), and may serve as a measure of insufficiency. The divergence, however, has a smaller domain of applicability than the entropy, since the summand has a discontinuity whenever either $p(v|1)$ or $p(v|2)$ vanishes. As a result of this, the divergence cannot detect an insufficiency whenever one of the probabilities is zero on a set of descriptions with nonzero measure. For example, both the distributions shown in Figure 4.1 have infinite divergence, although the second distribution is clearly insufficient for the first. What we have said amounts to a proof of the following:

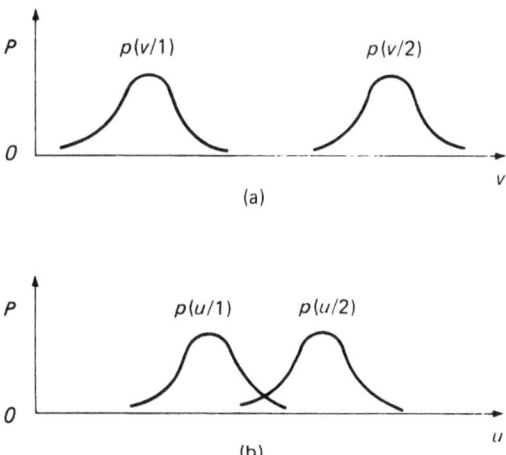

(a)

(b)

Figure 4.1 Sufficient and insufficient descriptions that are indistinguishable by Kullback's divergence.

Assertion. *When the divergences div_v and div_u are finite, the description u will be a sufficient statistic for v if and only if the two divergences are equal.*

The divergence, which was introduced by Kullback for two classes, can be generalized to an arbitrary number of classes. We take as our necessary and sufficient statistics the set of ratios of the probabilities $p(v|k)$ to one of them, say to the first:

$$\frac{p(v|k)}{p(v|1)} \qquad (k = 1, 2, \ldots, n).$$

This set can be looked on as a generalization of the likelihood ratio for n classes.

We have already noted that under a mapping of the description v into the description u the relative probabilities just introduced are averaged with weights proportional to their common denominator $p(v \mid 1)$:

$$\frac{p(u \mid k)}{p(u \mid 1)} = \frac{1}{\sum\limits_{v \in u} p(v \mid 1)} \sum\limits_{v \in u} p(v \mid 1) \frac{p(v \mid k)}{p(v \mid 1)} \qquad (k = 1, 2, \ldots, n),$$

which follows from the obvious equation

$$p(u \mid k) = \sum\limits_{v \in u} p(v \mid k).$$

Applying the inequality (4.4) with $f(\cdot) = \log(\cdot)$, we get

$$\log \frac{p(u \mid k)}{p(u \mid 1)} \geq \frac{1}{p(u \mid 1)} \sum\limits_{v \in u} p(v \mid 1) \log \frac{p(v \mid k)}{p(v \mid 1)},$$

whence, after multiplying by $p(u \mid 1)$ and summing over both u and k, we have

$$\sum\limits_{u} p(u \mid 1) \sum\limits_{k} \log \frac{p(u \mid k)}{p(u \mid 1)} \geq \sum\limits_{v} p(v \mid 1) \sum\limits_{k} \log \frac{p(v \mid k)}{p(v \mid 1)}.$$

Therefore the sum

$$\sum\limits_{v} p(v \mid 1) \sum\limits_{k} \log \frac{p(v \mid k)}{p(v \mid 1)} \tag{4.9}$$

is a measure of insufficiency.

We can construct an expression which is symmetric with respect to the classes by writing down a sum in which each term is similar to (4.9) but is specialized to each of the classes in turn, i.e.:

$$\mathrm{div}_v = \sum\limits_{j} \sum\limits_{v} p(v \mid j) \sum\limits_{k} \log \frac{p(v \mid k)}{p(v \mid j)}. \tag{4.10}$$

This is the desired generalized divergence. It coincides with Kullback's divergence for $n = 2$.

The expression (4.10) is clumsy and is useless when one of the probabilities vanishes and the others do not. The conditional entropy is a much more suitable measure of insufficiency.

4.7 Entropy and Error Probability

We have seen that for a given description the conditional entropy of a class is an important characteristic of that description. The change in the conditional entropy when the description is transformed into a new one measures the insufficiency of the new description and characterizes the loss in recognition reliability. Nevertheless, a more expedient measure of reliability is the error probability, which we have already defined and expressed in quantitative form.

The error probability is normally used to characterize a recognition system, but we may also use it to characterize the descriptions of objects to be recognized. For this purpose, we shall agree that the error probability for a set of features or a description v will be defined as the smallest error probability that can be obtained by an optimal decision rule working on the given description v. In other words, from now on, unless the contrary is stated, we shall mean by error probability the minimum probability of a false decision for a given description method. Since the error probability is only a particular value of the risk function, the entropy is left with its valuable role as a measure of the insufficiency of a description.

We now come to an interesting question: Knowing the entropy how do we estimate the error probability, and vice versa? It turns out that in general there is no functional relationship between these two quantities. Nevertheless, for a given value of the entropy the error probability can vary only between definite limits; also, for a given error probability P, the entropy lies between limits depending on P. These bounds are defined by the expression given below and derived in Section 4.9. The exact value of the entropy for a given error probability depends on the concrete form of the posterior probability distribution for all possible values of v.

The maximum entropy for a given error probability P is defined by the relationship

$$H_{max}(P) = -P\log P - (1 - P)\log(1 - P) + P\log(n - 1). \quad (4.11)$$

The corresponding graph is shown in Figure 4.2 for various values of n.

The minimum entropy for an infinite set V with a continuous measure is defined by the piecewise linear relationship

$$H_{min}(P) = \log m + m(m + 1)\left(\log \frac{m + 1}{m}\right)\left(P - \frac{m - 1}{m}\right), \quad (4.12)$$

where the integer m is such that

$$\frac{m - 1}{m} \leqslant P < \frac{m}{m + 1}. \quad (4.13)$$

In the general case, when the set V is arbitrary, the minimum entropy $\min H$ for a given P may fail to attain the bound $H_{min}(P)$. However, for arbitrary V and $p(v)$ we can find a form for the posterior distribution such that

$$H(K|V) \leqslant h_{min}(P),$$

where $h_{min}(P)$ is the minimum value of the specific entropy (see definition on p. 82), for fixed v and under the condition that P represents the error

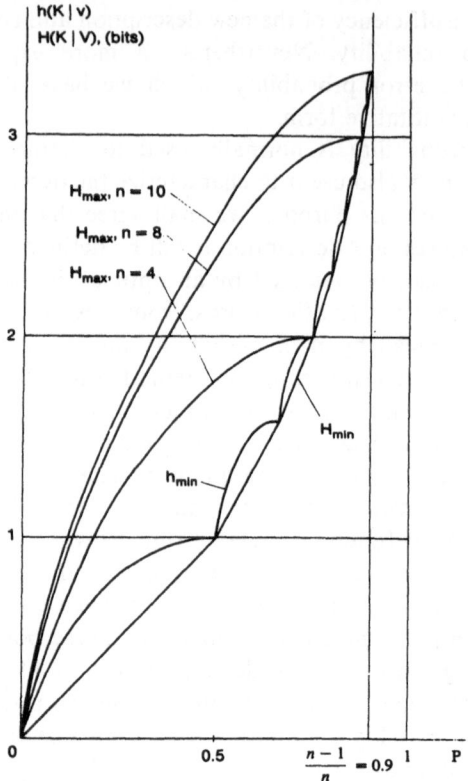

Figure 4.2 Relationship between the minimum error probability P and the conditional entropy $H(K|V)$ of a class for a given description.

probability of the optimal decision for the given v. The value of $h_{min}(P)$ (cf. Figure 4.2) is defined by

$$h_{min}(P) = -m(1 - P)\log(1 - P)$$

$$- (1 - m(1 - P))\log(1 - m(1 - P)), \qquad (4.14)$$

where the integer m has the same meaning as in (4.13). (We note in passing that the largest value of the specific entropy is defined by (4.11), as it is also for the mean entropy.) We can now say that the following relationship holds in the general case:

$$H_{min}(P) \leqslant H(K|V) \leqslant H_{max}(P), \qquad (4.15)$$

where $H_{min}(P)$ and $H_{max}(P)$ are defined by (4.12) and (4.11). A proof of (4.11) [but not of (4.12) nor (4.14)] which differs from the one given here will be found in a book by Feinstein [64].

4.8 The Information Content of the Optimal Decision

The recognition process consists in going (exactly or approximately) from an initial description to an optimal decision, which can also be thought of as an ultimately simplified description indicating the class having the maximum probability of containing the given signal. An optimal decision is not in general a sufficient description, since several different descriptions with different posterior probabilities may correspond to one decision. The insufficiency of the decision, or the loss of information in going from the initial description to the decision, obviously depends on the insufficiency of the initial description with respect to the hypothetical ideal description, which generates an error-free decision as to the class to which the signal belongs. In other words, the incremental entropy generated on passing from the description to the decision, $\Delta H = H(K|D) - H(K|V)$, depends on the entropy for the given description $H(K|V)$. For example, if the entropy for the initial description $H(K|V)$ is zero, so is the entropy for the optimal decision.

In the general case we consider the dependence of the entropy for the decision $H(K|D)$ on the entropy for the description $H(K|V)$. We note first that since the decision is a function of the description $d = \mathcal{F}(v)$, the inequality

$$H(K|D) \geqslant H(K|V)$$

is always true. The equality holds only when the decision is a sufficient description, that is, when for all v corresponding to one decision all the posterior distributions coincide.

The excess of the entropy for the decision, $H(K|D)$, over the entropy for the description, $H(K|V)$, depends on the concrete form of the posterior distribution $p(k|v)$. The upper bound of the decision entropy can be found by using (4.15). Since the decision can be thought of as a description, and (4.15) is applicable to an arbitrary description, we have

$$H(K|D) \leqslant H_{\max}(P_{\max}), \tag{4.16}$$

where $P_{\max}$ is the maximum error probability achievable with the given entropy $H(K|V)$ of the description.

For a given $H(K|V)$ we find $P_{\max}$ by using (4.12) and

$$H_{\min}(P_{\max}) = H(K|V). \tag{4.17}$$

The inequality (4.16), together with (4.17), yields an upper bound for the entropy for a decision. We shall show in Section 4.9 (Theorem 5) that there exists a posterior distribution for which this bound is attained, so that (4.16) gives an exact upper bound for the entropy for the optimal decision when the entropy for the description is prescribed.

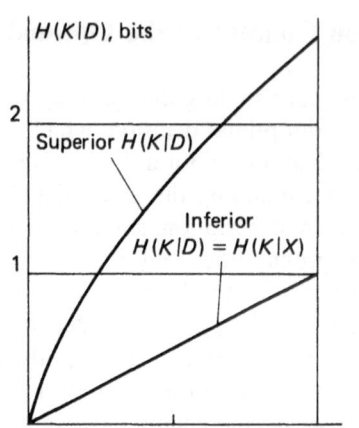

Figure 4.3   Relationship between the conditional entropy $H(K|V)$ for a description and the conditional entropy $H(K|D)$ for the optimal decision.

Since by (4.12) the function $H_{min}(P_{max})$ is piecewise linear, (4.17) is easily solved for P_{max}. Thus in the most interesting case when $H(K|V) < 1$ bit, when the error probability does not exceed $\frac{1}{2}$, the equation (4.12) (after we put $m = 1$) takes on the form

$$H_{min}(P) = 2P.$$

Putting this into (4.17) we find

$$P_{max} = H(K|V)/2,$$

whence

$$H(K|V) \leqslant H(K|D) \leqslant H_{max}\left(\frac{H(K|V)}{2} \right). \tag{4.18}$$

The corresponding graph is shown in Figure 4.3 for the case $n = 10$. This relationship allows us to estimate the loss of information on passing from a given description to an optimal decision.

In our opinion, these arguments allow us to comprehend and interpret the processes of pattern recognition from the point of view of mathematical statistics and information theory.

4.9 Theorems on the Relation between the Conditional Entropy and the Error Probability

In studying the relationship between the mean conditional entropy $H(K|V)$ and the mean error probability, it is worth while to begin by looking at the relationship between the specific conditional entropy and the specific error probability. The *specific conditional entropy of a class* for a given individual description v is defined as

$$h(K|v) = - \sum_{k=1}^{n} p(k|v)\log p(k|v),$$

where the $p(k|v)$ are the posterior probabilities of the classes for a given v.

The *specific error probability* $p_M(v)$ is defined as the minimum value of the conditional error probability $p_e(v)$ under a decision optimal for the given v. As we know (cf. p. 27),

$$p_M(v) = 1 - \max_k p(k|v).$$

Since the probabilities $p(k|v)$ sum to unity, $\max_k p(k|v)$ cannot be less than $1/n$, where n is the number of classes. It follows that

$$p_M(v) \leqslant 1 - \frac{1}{n}.$$

To prove the following theorems we shall need the property of convex functions that we listed earlier: the weighted mean of the values of a convex function does not exceed the value of the function at the weighted mean of the arguments, i.e.,

$$f\left(\sum_k a_k x_k\right) \geqslant \sum_k a_k f(x_k), \tag{4.19}$$

where $f(\cdot)$ is an arbitrary convex function on the interval $[a,b]$, the x_k are arbitrary numbers in the same interval, and the a_k are nonnegative weights which sum to unity, i.e., $\sum_k a_k = 1$, $a_k \geqslant 0$. The equality holds when all the x_k are equal to their mean value. This is easily seen, after direct substitution. We can formulate the foregoing briefly as follows: if

$$\sum_k a_k x_k = \text{const},$$

then

$$\sup \sum_k a_k f(x_k) = f\left(\sum_k a_k x_k\right). \tag{4.20}$$

Theorem 1.   *The exact upper bound $h_{\max}(P)$ of the specific conditional entropy $h(K|V)$ for a given specific error probability $p_M(P)$ is attained when all the posterior probabilities, with perhaps the exception of one, are equal to $P/(n-1)$. The bound is*

$$h_{\max}(P) = -P\log P - (1-P)\log(1-P) + P\log(n-1).$$

PROOF.   When we prescribe the error probability we at the same time prescribe the sum of $n-1$ of the posterior probabilities $p(k|v)$. Without loss of generality, we may suppose that the probability $p(1|v)$ is maximal; then

$$p(1|v) = 1 - P.$$

We rewrite the expression for the specific entropy in the form

$$h(K|v) = -(1 - P)\log(1 - P) - \sum_{k=2}^{n} p(k|v)\log p(k|v). \qquad (4.21)$$

The sum appearing in (4.21) is, to within a constant multiplier, equal to the mean value of the convex function $f(x) = -x\log x$; all the weights a_k are equal, i.e., $a_k = 1/(n-1)$, and the arguments are $x_k = p(k|v)$. The mean of the arguments has the value

$$\frac{1}{n-1} \sum_{k=2}^{n} p(k|v) = \frac{P}{n-1},$$

and therefore, by (4.20),

$$\sup\left(-\frac{1}{n-1} \sum_{k=2}^{n} p(k|v)\log p(k|v)\right) = -\frac{P}{n-1} \log \frac{P}{n-1}.$$

Comparing this with (4.21), we find that the exact upper bound of the specific entropy is defined by the equation

$$\sup h(K|v) = h_{\max}(P)$$

$$= -(1 - P)\log(1 - P) - P\log \frac{P}{n-1}$$

$$= -P\log P - (1 - P)\log(1 - P) + P\log(n - 1). \quad \square$$

Theorem 2. *The exact lower bound $h_{\min}(P)$ of the specific conditional entropy $h(K|v)$ for a given specific error probability $p_M(v)$ is attained when all the posterior probabilities, with the possible exception of one, are either zero or equal to $1 - P$. The exact lower bound is given by*

$$h_{\min}(P) = -m(1 - P)\log(1 - P)$$

$$- (1 - m(1 - P))\log(1 - m(1 - P)),$$

where the integer m is defined by the inequalities

$$\frac{m-1}{m} \leqslant P < \frac{m}{m+1}.$$

PROOF. As in the preceding case, when we prescribe the error probability we also prescribe

$$\max_{k} p(k|v) = p(1|v) = 1 - P.$$

Therefore, for all $p(k|v)$ we have the inequality

$$0 \leqslant p(k|v) \leqslant 1 - P.$$

The idea of the proof consists in the following. If we move apart two values of a pair of arguments $p(k|v)$ and $p(l|v)$ while holding their sum constant, we thereby decrease the mean value of the convex function of these arguments, i.e., we decrease the entropy. Further movement is impossible when all values of the $p(k|v)$, with the possible exception of one, lie on the boundaries of the interval of possible values.

In fact, let us suppose that some two values of $p(k|v)$ are different from zero and $1 - P$; let these be the pair $p(2|v)$ and $p(3|v)$. Then we separate them, i.e., replace them by $p^*(2|v)$ and $p^*(3|v)$, which are chosen to be closer to zero and $1 - P$, in such a way that

$$p^*(2|v) < p(2|v) < p^*(3|v);$$

$$p^*(2|v) < p(3|v) < p^*(3|v). \tag{4.22}$$

This alteration can always be done while conserving the sum

$$p^*(2|v) + p^*(3|v) = p(2|v) + p(3|v) \tag{4.23}$$

and therefore not violating the condition

$$\sum_{k=2}^{n} p(k|v) = P.$$

The values of $p(2|v)$ and $p(3|v)$, lying between $p^*(2|v)$ and $p^*(3|v)$, can be represented as weighted means of the latter:

$$p(2|v) = \alpha p^*(2|v) + (1 - \alpha)p^*(3|v),$$

$$p(3|v) = \beta_p^*(2|v) + (1 - \beta)p^*(3|v).$$

Putting these into (4.23), and remembering that $p^*(3|v) - p^*(2|v) \neq 0$, we find that

$$\alpha + \beta = 1. \tag{4.24}$$

Using (4.19) and noting that the arguments $p^*(2|v)$ and $p^*(3|v)$ are not equal to their mean, we obtain the inequalities

$$f(p(2|v)) \leqslant \alpha f(p^*(2|v)) + (1 - \alpha)f(p^*(3|v)),$$

$$f(p(3|v)) < \beta f(p^*(2|v)) + (1 - \beta)f(p^*(3|v)).$$

Now using (4.24), we get the inequality

$$f(p(2|v)) + f(p(3|v)) > f(p^*(2|v)) + f(p^*(3|v)).$$

Setting $f(P) = -P \log P$, we reach the conclusion that on separation of the pairs of values of $p(k|v)$ the corresponding terms in the entropy expression (4.21) decrease, and with them the entropy $h(K|v)$ itself.

No further decrease is possible if all the $p(k|v)$ are equal to zero or $1 - P$, since for the given error probability P the $p(k|v)$ must lie in the interval $[0, 1 - P]$. No decrease is possible either when only one of the $p(k|v)$ fails to lie on the boundaries of the interval, since it cannot be changed without altering the given error probability.

To find the value $h_{min}(P)$ of the exact lower bound of the entropy we take the reciprocal of the maximum value of $p(k|v) = 1 - P$. The integer portion m of the resulting ratio determines the number of the $p(k|v)$ that are to be set equal to $1 - P$. One of the $p(k|v)$ is to be set equal to $1 - m(1 - P)$, and the rest are to be set equal to zero. Then

$$\inf h(K|v) = h_{\min}(P) = -m(1 - P)\log(1 - P)$$

$$- (1 - m(1 - P))\log(1 - m(1 - P)),$$

where the integer m is defined by the inequalities $m \leqslant 1/(1 - P) < m + 1$ or, equivalently,

$$\frac{m - 1}{m} \leqslant P < \frac{m}{m + 1} . \quad \Box$$

The graph of $h_{\min}(P)$ is shown in Figure 4.2.

Theorem 3.   *The exact upper bound of the mean conditional entropy $H(K|V)$ for a given mean error probability P is attained when all the specific error probabilities are equal to P. This bound is defined by the same function $h_{max}(P)$ that was found for the specific entropy.*

PROOF.   The mean conditional entropy is equal to the mean of the values of the specific entropies taken over all possible descriptions v:

$$H(K|V) = \sum_v p(v)h(K|v) = - \sum_v p(v) \sum_k p(k|v)\log p(k|v).$$

By Theorem 1,

$$\sup h(K|v) = h_{\max}(p_m(v)),$$

where $p_M(v)$ is the specific error probability, and therefore

$$\sup H(K|V) = \sup \sum_v p(v)h_{\max}(p_M(v)),$$

where the function $h_{\max}(\cdot)$ is convex. Accordingly, taking (4.20) into account, we find

$$\sup \sum_v p(v)h_{\max}(p_M(v)) = h_{\max}\left(\sum_v p(v)p_M(v)\right).$$

But the argument of $h_{\max}(\cdot)$ on the right-hand side of this equation is precisely the mean error probability:

$$\sum_v p(v)p_M(v) = P.$$

Therefore

$$\sup H(K|V) = H_{\max}(P) = h_{\max}(P),$$

or

$$H_{\max}(P) = -P \log P - (1 - P)\log(1 - P) + P \log(n - 1). \quad \Box$$

Theorem 4.   *The lower bound of the mean conditional entropy $H(K|V)$ for a given mean error probability P lies on the open polygon that joins the* *neighboring singular points of the curve $h_{\min}(P)$. The bound is attained when all the specific error probabilities lie on the boundary of the interval $[(m-1)/m, \, m/(m+1)]$ that includes the value of P. This is possible for arbitrary P if the unconditional measure given on the set of descriptions V is continuous.*

PROOF.   By Theorem 2

$$\inf h(K|v) = h_{\min}(p_M(v)),$$

and therefore

$$H(K|V) = \sum_v p(v)h(K|v) \geqslant \sum_v p(v)h_{\min}(p_M(v)).$$

The function $h_{\min}(\cdot)$ is not convex. We construct the open polygon that we have considered earlier:

$$L(P) = \log m + m(m+1)\left(\log \frac{m+1}{m}\right)\left(P - \frac{m-1}{m}\right),$$

where the integer m satisfies the inequalities

$$\frac{m-1}{m} < P < \frac{m}{m+1}.$$

Since this polygon nowhere lies above the curve $h_{\min}(P)$,

$$H(K|V) \geqslant \sum_v p(v)L(p_M(v)). \tag{4.25}$$

But the polygon $L(P)$ is concave, i.e., the function $-L(P)$ is convex. Therefore the assertion (4.20) is applicable if we replace the upper bound by the lower bound. Then, under the condition $\sum_v p(v)p_M(v) = P$, we have

$$\inf \sum p(v)L(p_M(v)) = L(P)$$

and

$$H(K|V) \geqslant L(P).$$

Let us now look at the conditions under which $H(K|V) = L(P)$, and choose the integer m satisfying the inequalities

$$\frac{m-1}{m} < P < \frac{m}{m+1};$$

then we can find an $a \geqslant 0$ such that

$$a\frac{m-1}{m} + (1-a)\frac{m}{m+1} = P. \tag{4.26}$$

If we can find a subset of measure a in V, we write for all v in this subset

$$p_M(v) = \frac{m-1}{m},$$

and for the remaining v we write

$$p_M(v) = \frac{m}{m+1}.$$

According to (4.26) the equality

$$\sum_v p(v)p_M(v) = P,$$

will be satisfied. For each v we choose the posterior probabilities such that the specific entropy is minimal:

$$h(K|v) = h_{min}(p_M(v));$$

and then

$$H(K|V) = ah_{min}\left(\frac{m-1}{m}\right) + (1-a)h_{min}\left(\frac{m}{m+1}\right).$$

But at the points $(m-1)/m$ and $m/(m+1)$ the functions $h_{min}(P)$ and $L(P)$ coincide, and therefore

$$H(K|V) = aL\left(\frac{m-1}{m}\right) + (1-a)L\left(\frac{m}{m+1}\right).$$

Because $L(P)$ is linear on the interval $[(m-1)/m, m/(m+1)]$ we have

$$aL\left(\frac{m-1}{m}\right) + (1-a)L\left(\frac{m}{m+1}\right) = L\left(a\frac{m-1}{m} + (1-a)\frac{m}{m+1}\right)$$

$$= L(P).$$

Thus if there exists a subset of V having the measure a, the mean conditional entropy $H(K|V)$ can attain its lower bound $L(P)$. But such a subset always exists if the unconditional measure given on V is continuous.   □

Theorem 5. *Given the mean conditional entropy $H(K|V)$ of a class, for a description v, the upper bound of the entropy $H(K|D)$ for an optimal decision is given by $H_{max}(P_{max})$, where P_{max} is defined by the equation $L(P_{max}) = H(K|V)$. This bound is exact for $H(K|D)$ if the unconditional measure on the set V of descriptions is continuous.*

PROOF.   For a given description entropy $H(K|V)$ the error probability cannot exceed P_{max} as defined by the equation $L(P_{max}) = H(K|V)$. Here $L(P)$ is the open polygon that marks out the minimum value of the entropy $H(K|V)$ for given P. In fact, if the error probability were greater than P_{max}, then by Theorem 4 the value of $H(K|V)$ would be less than its lower bound, which is impossible.

If the error probability is equal to P_{max}, Theorem 3 says that for an arbitrary description the entropy cannot exceed $H_{max}(P_{max})$, which is therefore an upper bound for $H(K|D)$.

We now show that this bound is attained, by finding a posterior distribution $p(k|v)$ for which $H(K|V)$ has a prescribed value $H(K|V) = H$ and $H(K|D) = H_{max}(P_{max})$.

We choose an integer m satisfying the inequalities $\log m \leqslant H < \log(m+1)$, where H is the given value of the description entropy $H(K|V)$; then we can find a nonnegative a such that

$$H = a\log m + (1-a)\log(m+1). \tag{4.27}$$

We consider a subset V_1 of descriptions for which the optimal decision has the value 1, i.e., $\mathscr{F}(v) = 1$ if $v \in V_1$. We divide this subset into two subsets V_{11} and

Table 4.1

Descriptions and sums of probabilities for two groups		Posterior Probabilities of the classes					Specific error probabilities $p_M(v)$	Specific entropies $h(K\|v)$
		$p(1\|v)$	$p(2\|v)$	$p(3\|v)$	$p(4\|v)$	$p(5\|v)$		
$a = 1 - H$ $= 1 - 2P$	v^1	1	0	0	0	0	0	0
	v^2	1	0	0	0	0	0	0
$1 - a = H$ $= 2P$	v^3	1/2	1/2	0	0	0	1/2	1
	v^4	1/2	0	1/2	0	0	1/2	1
	v^5	1/2	0	0	1/2	0	1/2	1
	v^6	1/2	0	0	0	1/2	1/2	1
Means		$1 - P$	$P/4$	$P/4$	$P/4$	$P/4$	P	$2P = H$

V_{12} such that the conditional measure of V_{11} with respect to V_1 is equal to a, i.e.,

$$p(V_{11})/p(V_1) = a.$$

For all v in V_{11} we choose the posterior distribution $p(k\|v)$ so that m of the values, including $p(1\|v)$, are equal to $1/m$ and the rest vanish.

For all v in V_{12} we set $m + 1$ of the probabilities $p(k\|v)$, including $p(1\|v)$, equal to $1/(m + 1)$ and set the remainder equal to zero. We stipulate that all the possible distributions of the zeros into $n - 1$ places, except the first place, are equiprobable. The first place will always be assigned the probability $p(1\|v) = 1/(m + 1)$, which is different from zero. An example of such a distribution for five classes and a value of H not exceeding one binary unit is given in Table 4.1. In this case $m = 1$.

For this posterior distribution the specific entropy h_1 for $v \in V_{11}$ is given by $h_1 = \log m$, and for $v \in V_{12}$ we have $h_2 = \log(m + 1)$. If we construct distributions of this kind for all the subsets V_k corresponding to the other decisions, we find for the mean conditional entropy

$$H(K\|V) = ah_1 + (1 - a)h_2$$
$$= a \log m + (1 - a)\log(m + 1).$$

By Equation (4.27) this is equal to the given value of H. The error probability for $v \in V_{11}$ is $P_1 = (m - 1)/m$, and for $v \in V_{12}$ it is $P_2 = m/(m + 1)$. We average these with the weights a and $1 - a$, to find the mean error probability

$$P = a\,\frac{m - 1}{m} + (1 - a)\,\frac{m}{m + 1}\ .$$

We recall that the quantities $(m - 1)/m$ and $m/(m + 1)$ are the abscissas of neighboring vertices of the polygon $L(P)$ (cf. Theorem 4). Therefore the point with the coordinates

$$P = a\,\frac{m - 1}{m} + (1 - a)\,\frac{m}{m + 1}\ ,$$
$$H = a \log m + (1 - a)\log(m + 1)$$

lies on the polygon $L(P)$, and the value of P corresponds to the maximum error probability for the given H,

$$P = P_{\max}.$$

Next we find the entropy for the optimal decision. The posterior probability $p(k\,|\,1)$ of the classes for a given decision $d = 1$ can be computed by averaging the $p(k\,|\,v)$ with weights proportional to $p(v)$. Also [by (4.27)]

$$p(1\,|\,1) = a\,\frac{1}{m} + (1 - a)\,\frac{1}{m + 1} = 1 - P_{\max}.$$

The remaining probabilities $p(k\,|\,1)$ $(k = 2, 3, \ldots, n)$ are equal among themselves because of the equiprobable distribution of the zero and nonzero values of the $p(k\,|\,v)$ at all places except the first. Therefore $p(k\,|\,1) = P_{\max}/(n - 1)$ $(k = 2, 3, \ldots, n)$ and, for the decision $d = 1$, the specific entropy $h(k\,|\,1) = H_{\max}(P_{\max})$ (cf. Theorem 1).

Since the distributions for all the subsets V_k corresponding to other decisions are constructed in the same manner, the specific entropies corresponding to the other decisions have the same value, and therefore the mean conditional entropy of the optimal decision is

$$H(K\,|\,D) = H_{\max}(P_{\max}).$$

Thus for a given description entropy $H(K\,|\,V)$ the entropy for the optimal decision lies between the bounds

$$H(K\,|\,V) \leqslant H(K\,|\,D) \leqslant H_{\max}(P_{\max}),$$

where $L(P_{\max}) = H(K\,|\,V)$. The graph of the relationship between the exact upper bound $\sup H(K\,|\,D) = H_{\max}(P_{\max})$ and $H(K\,|\,V)$ is shown in Figure 4.3.   □

4.10 Conclusions

The mean value of an arbitrary convex function of the posterior probabilities of the recognition parameter k, when the signal v is given, characterizes the statistical sufficiency of the signal considered as a statistic for the estimation of k. It increases as the distance of the statistic from sufficiency increases, and may therefore be taken as a measure of insufficiency. The measure of insufficiency is determined by the distributions $p(v\,|\,k)$ and $p(k)$ and therefore is a characteristic of the signal which is specific for a given concrete task. The conditional entropy and the Kullback divergence are particular instances of the measure of insufficiency.

The minimum error probability, defined as the minimum Bayesian risk for an antidiagonal loss matrix, is another important characteristic of a concrete recognition problem (but not of the method of solution). The theorems proved in this chapter allow us to establish bounds between which the conditional entropy must lie for a given minimal error probability. The Bayesian decision (like every other decision) generally gives us incomplete information about the recognition parameter. This means that the conditional entropy $H(K\,|\,D)$ for a given Bayesian decision usually exceeds the conditional entropy $H(K\,|\,V)$ for the given signal.

These results are useful in choosing a set of features for describing the images to be recognized.

CHAPTER V

The Method of Admissible Transformations

In practical recognition problems we choose decision rules that correspond with our prior information about the classes or abstract images to be recognized. In most cases class membership is an invariant of certain given transformations of images. It seems intuitively right that two images which differ only by a translation or rotation through not too large an angle should belong to the same class; therefore the decision rule should also be an invariant of the corresponding transformations.

We proceed to consider the formal statement and solution methods for the recognition problem, with this property of the image classes in mind.

5.1 Sets That Are Closed under Transformations

One way to sharpen and formalize the notion of the invariance of a decision rule under given transformations lies in the use of familiar mathematical methods for describing the affine transformations of points in the infinite plane. We shall see whether these methods are suitable for describing the set of images that would be assigned to a single class in accordance with the intuitive notions we have just put forward.

We shall attempt to define the recognition classes as sets that are closed under certain transformations. To do this, we must meet two requirements: First, we must give a formal definition of the transformation of an image defined in a finite region, i.e., in a bounded field of view rather than in the infinite plane. Second, we must define the set of transformations (which may be a group) in such a way that the transformed images shall not be spoiled. This means that under a translation and change of scale no essential portion of the image shall lie outside the field of view, and under a rotation no image shall be turned through an inadmissibly large angle with respect to the original "upright" image. If the latter rule is not obeyed, a "Ш" may become an "E" via a rotation through 90°, and a "9" may become a "6" via a rotation through 180°.

The first requirement will be met if we extend every image lying in the field of view by a homogeneous white background or by periodically repeating images. This latter variant is equivalent to the introduction of a toroidal retina [48]. The transformation in both cases is to be taken as the corresponding transformation of the infinite plane.

This process is acceptable at least for the recognition of characters, or more generally, of images that are placed against a white background, provided the second condition is met. It is however difficult to meet the second condition since transformations of the plane that meet this requirement for one image may fail it for another. For example, the acceptability of a given translation for a given image depends on how far the essential portions of the image lie from the nearest edge of the field of view. The acceptability of a rotation through a given angle depends on how far the given image has already been rotated away from the upright version. In general, the acceptability of any transformation of the plane, for a given image, depends on the values of the parameters characterizing the position of the image with respect to some fixed image rigidly attached to the field of view.

If we assume that an arbitrary transformation of the plane is applicable to an arbitrary image in a given class, then we may apply it to a transformed image, and to a twice transformed image, etc. The result will be an image for which the location parameters lie far from the values of those characterizing the original image. They may have passed beyond the acceptable limits. What we have said amounts to a proof that there exists no subset of the transformations of the plane under which the class of images satisfying the second condition is closed. This path to the formal definition of the properties of image classes that interest us is blocked, and we must look for another.

5.2 Admissible Transformations and the Formalization of the Notion of "Similarity"

In most practical applications the images to be recognized are given in a field of view of finite size. The classes of images are such that a given class contains only those images for which the parameter values characterizing their size and their location with respect to the boundaries of the field of view lie within definite limits. As we have just explained, the image classes satisfying this demand cannot be sets that are closed under some fixed subset of the affine transformations of the plane.

The constraints on the set of admissible parameter values can be stated by means of the following formal scheme. Let there be given for each class k an image that will serve as a preimage or ancestor of all the images in the given class. Its digitized representation on a given retina with N cells will be called the archetype* and will be denoted by the N-dimensional vector $e^{(k)}$. Its possible values belong to the set V of images v. Suppose we are also given a set of *admissible transformations* $\mathfrak{T}_b$, parametrized by the nuisance parameter b, and applicable only to the archetype and not at all to the observed images. The result of applying $\mathfrak{T}_b$ to the archetype $e^{(k)}$ is a *transformed prototype*

$$E(k,b) = \mathfrak{T}_b\, e^{(k)}$$

whose values also belong to V. The transformation parameter b may be multidimensional. We are given the set B_k of admissible values of b, which in general depend on k. This defines the set of admissible transformations.

This set may contain affine transformations of the plane (their application requires that the archetype be extended by a homogeneous background), or topological transformations of a very general nature, and others not representable as transformations of the plane. The latter include changes in the contrast of the images, darkening of the background, changes in the distribution of blackness across the character strokes (changes in the stroke width), and other such changes. By proper choice of the set B_k of admissible transformations we can guarantee that the transformed prototypes are not spoiled, i.e., that no essential portion of the image lies outside the field of view, that the angle of rotation of the transformed image, relative to the original, is not too large, that the stroke width lies within acceptable limits, etc.

The set of values assumed by the prototype $E(k,b)$ for fixed k and for all possible b [that is, the domain of values of the $E(k,b)$] will be called the *domain of prototypes* of the kth class.

The observed images, or more exactly their digitized representations v on the same retina on which the prototypes are set, do not necessarily belong to any domain of prototypes. In our scheme they are realizations of an N-dimensional random variable with a known probability distribution $p(v|E(k,b))$, depending on the transformed prototype $E(k,b)$ as a multidimensional parameter, which is either the mean or the mode of this distribution.

It is easy to see that this formal scheme allows us to define sets of transformations meeting the requirements listed in Section 5.1. It also allows us to solve the recognition problem for a known distribution $p(v|E)$ and a known functional dependence of the transformed $E(k,b)$ on the parameters k and b. In the process of deciding on the value of the recognition parameter k, b appears as a nuisance parameter. Therefore the distribution $p(v|E(k,b))$ is a special case of the distribution (2.4),

---

* This concept was used in the example on p. 47.

corresponding to the parametric model of the image-generating process introduced in Chapter II.

It corresponds to the assumption that the value of the parameter a is given in advance or has been defined during the learning process. To solve the recognition problem we now have in mind we may apply the method of maximum likelihood, just as in the general case (cf. Chapter II). The density $p(v \mid E(k,b))$ for an observed image v is regarded as a function of the parameters k and b. This is the *likelihood function*. In arriving at a decision regarding the value of the parameter k, we must maximize the likelihood function with respect to k and b, and choose for the decision d the value of k for which the maximum is attained:

$$d = \arg\max_{k} \max_{b \in B_k} p(v \mid E(k,b)) \tag{5.1}$$

(the notation $\arg\max$ was introduced in Section 1.1).

The decision rule (5.1) has a peculiarity that in many cases simplifies the calculations needed for the decision. The decision d remains the same if we replace the likelihood function by an arbitrary function of the parameters which depends in a monotone increasing way on $p(v \mid E(k,b))$. In other words, if $g(v, E)$ is an arbitrary function of v and E, satisfying the equation

$$p(v \mid E) = f(g(v, E)), \tag{5.2}$$

where $f(\cdot)$ is a monotone increasing function, the rule (5.1) can be replaced by

$$d = \arg\max_{k} \max_{b \in B_k} g(v, E(k,b)). \tag{5.3}$$

The value of any function $g(v, E)$ satisfying (5.2) may be interpreted as a measure of the similarity between the prototype E and the image v. Then the decision rule (5.3) may be interpreted as the search for those values d and $\hat{b}$ of the parameters k and b that maximize the similarity between the observed image v and the transformed prototype $E(k,b)$. The value E of the transformed prototype for which the maximum is attained is called the *prototype of maximum similarity* for v:

$$\hat{E} = E(d, \hat{b}),$$

where d is defined by the rule (5.3) and

$$\hat{b} = \arg\max_{b \in B_k} \max_{k} g(v, E(k,b)).$$

The quantity $\max_{b \in B_k} g(v, E(k,b))$ in (5.3) may be interpreted as a discriminant function. Then, as usual,

$$d = \arg\max_{k} \tilde{f}_k(v), \tag{5.3'}$$

where

$$\tilde{f}_k(v) = \max_{b \in B_k} g(v, E(k, b)). \tag{5.3''}$$

Accordingly, the discriminant function in this case is defined as the maximum of the similarity function with respect to the nuisance parameter.

The condition (5.2) is a formal definition of similarity. It is clear that if p is a monotone function of g, then g is also a monotone function of p. Therefore the definition of similarity can also be written in the form

$$g(v, E) = f(p(v \mid E)),$$

i.e., any monotone increasing function of the likelihood is a similarity function.

If $f(\cdot)$ in (5.2) is a monotone decreasing function, $g(v, E)$ characterizes the difference between v and E rather than the similarity. In this case we should seek the minimum rather than the maximum, and then we have

$$d = \arg\min_k \min_{b \in B_k} g(v, E(k, b)). \tag{5.4}$$

It is clear that if $g(v, E)$ is a monotone decreasing function of the likelihood $p(v \mid E(k, b))$, then $-g(v, E)$ is a monotone increasing function. These two cases are so trivially distinguished that it is worthwhile to apply the name "similarity" also to monotone decreasing functions of the likelihood. Thus, for instance, if $v, E \in R^N$, and the distribution $p(v, E)$ is normal with unit covariance matrix and mean E, the likelihood function depends monotonely on the Euclidean distance between the points v and E. In this case, the distance can be used as a measure of similarity.

We can now slightly extend the definition of similarity: We shall say that any function $g(v, E)$ satisfying (5.2) with $f(\cdot)$ monotone is a similarity function.

A similarity function is in general not symmetric, i.e.,

$$g(v, E) \neq g(E, v).$$

For example, if the signal and prototype are binary vectors, and the noise is described by the unequal probabilities ψ_0 and ψ_1 of distortion of the zero and unit components of the prototype, the likelihood function is asymmetric (this example was discussed in more detail in Section 2.3). If the two probabilities ψ_0 and ψ_1 are equal, the likelihood function is symmetric, and the similarity is measured by the Hamming distance, i.e., the number of binary components of v that disagree in value with the corresponding binary components of E.

For an additive noise the model (2.4) has the form

$$p(v \mid E(k, b)) = p_{\text{noise}}(v - E(k, b)). \tag{5.5}$$

The similarity function is symmetric if the noise density $p_{noise}(r)$ is constant with respect to the sign of r. This is true, for example, for the normal distribution $p_{noise}(r)$.

We may put forward the proposition that whenever, in solving the recognition problem on the basis of arguments other than those given above, a notion of nearness of a signal to some prototype is introduced, the criteria of nearness will represent a more or less successful intuitive approximation of the above described formal notion of similarity. Our formalism may be seen as the basis of the concept of nearness, or similarity, using the method of maximum likelihood.

We may sum up the *method of admissible transformations* in the following way: We assume that the set of images v belonging to a single class is described by a known probability distribution $p(v|E)$, depending on a multidimensional parameter E, known as a *prototype*. The value of E belongs to the image space and is either the mean value or the mode of the distribution $p(v|E)$. For a given image class it is the result of applying some one of the *admissible transformations* $\mathfrak{T}_b$, $b \in B_k$, to the archetype $e^{(k)}$:

$$E = E(k,b) = \mathfrak{T}_b e^{(k)}, \qquad b \in B_k.$$

The decision concerning the value of the recognition parameter k is made by the maximum-likelihood method. Of course, the likelihood function $p(v|E(k,b))$ may be replaced by any monotone function of it, $g(v, E(k,b))$, which is called the similarity function, or merely the *similarity*. The decision d is found as the value of k corresponding to the absolute maximum of the similarity:

$$d = \arg\max_k \max_{b \in B_k} g(v, E(k,b)).$$

5.3 Peculiarities of the Method of Admissible Transformations

It follows from what we have just said, that the method of admissible transformations is founded on the conventional method of maximum likelihood, and needs no other foundation. Those who are concerned with applications, however, may find some value in a discussion of certain peculiarities of the method that put it ahead of other recognition methods.

Let us look first at some of its methodological aspects. The decision rules (5.3) or (5.4) allow a simultaneous estimate of the recognition parameter k and the transformation parameter b. Thus, for every observed image v we can find the prototype $\hat{E}$ of maximum similarity, and at the same time compute the value $\hat{b}$ of the parameter b, which tells us how the observed image differs from the archetype $e^{(k)}$.

With the concepts that we have so far developed, we can now formulate the intuitively perceived property of the classes that we spoke of at the beginning of the chapter. *A single class consists of those images for which the maximum similarity prototypes are admissible transforms of one and the same archetype.* In other words, the value $\hat{b}$ of the nuisance parameter in the maximum similarity prototype must belong to the set B_k of admissible values.

The decision rules (5.3) and (5.4) meet the requirement of invariance under admissible transformations. In fact, for constant k and an admissible change in the value of b, the decision on the class membership of images v generated by the new distribution $p(v \mid E(k,b))$ remains with high probability as it was.

Next let us look at the aspects connected with applications. Almost all recognition tasks meet two obstacles: the great variety of images, and the presence of random disturbances. Many of the methods described in the literature deal, at best, with one or other of these two but not both. A peculiarity of the method of admissible transformations is that it deals with both. The variety of images is taken into account by a description of the set of prototypes, in the form of the function $E(k, b)$. The noise resistance of the method is due to the fact that we do not demand exact coincidence of the image with one of the prototypes. We need only find a prototype that exhibits maximum similarity with the observed image.

In the approach that we are now discussing, the statistical aspects are removed to the background, since they influence only the selection of the criteria for similarity of the image and the prototype, or the choice of a metric in the image space. It is not difficult to see that some inexactness in our assignment of the probabilistic nature of the noise will have an insignificant effect on the probability of correct recognition. This will certainly be true if the differences between images arising from the noise are less significant than the differences due to variations in the parameters. This does not mean, of course, that we may entirely neglect the noise. On the contrary, taking account of the noise by applying criteria based on statistical methods appears as one of the most important peculiarities of our method.

We have reduced the recognition problem to the search for the maximum of some function that expresses the similarity between image and prototype. The maximization is carried out over the parameters on which the prototype depends. This task presents enormous computational difficulties, even when the number of parameters is comparatively small. In the following sections we shall consider the concrete problem of recognizing typewritten characters; for these the number of parameters in the prototype is not too large, and therefore the solution can be obtained by relatively simple methods which permit the use of simple technical implementations in a character reader (cf. Chapter IX). Chapters VII and VIII are devoted to the use of dynamic programming in the search for maximum similarity. This allows us to solve very complex recognition problems involving a large number of nuisance parameters.

5.4 Recognition by the Correlation Method

The following method [32] is a special case of the method of admissible transformations. It can be applied for the recognition of signals which may differ in their physical nature but are described by the single mathematical model introduced below. To gain maximum concreteness, however, we shall consider only the application of the method to the recognition of optical images. The description of the model will itself suggest the possibilities for generalization and the way to achieve it.

As before, we shall assume that the image to be recognized is described by an N-dimensional vector v with components v_i, which in their ensemble form a digitized representation of the image on a retina with N cells. In the specific case that we have in mind, however, and in contrast to the example given on p. 47 we shall assume that the components v_i represent the mean *brightness* and not the blackness of the corresponding cells. This assumption allows us to assume that they may assume arbitrary positive values, while the blackness remains in the interval $[0, 1]$. Thus the image space V is the positive quadrant of the N-dimensional Euclidean space R^N.

The brightness of an optical image usually depends on the illumination of the corresponding physical object, for instance a picture consisting of an unevenly distributed layer of color on paper. The average brightness of the ith cell of the retina is equal to the product of the illumination, taken to be constant over the whole set of cells, and the mean coefficient of reflectivity of the cell. Scattered light may appear, and this leads to a uniform increase in the brightness of all the cells. We define the ith component $e_i^{(k)}$ of the archetype of the kth class to be the brightness of the corresponding cell of some ideal image under unit illumination. Then under arbitrary illumination the brightness of the ith cell will be

$$E_i(k, \alpha, \beta) = \alpha e_i^{(k)} + \beta \qquad (i = 1, 2, \ldots, N), \qquad (5.6)$$

where $e_i^{(k)}$ and $E(k, \alpha, \beta)$ are the components of the archetype and the transformed prototype, α is the illumination, and β the intensity of the scattered light. The ratio α/β clearly measures the contrast of the image, and β is its uniform increment of brightness. Thus, in the case of recognition of optical images, we must accept as admissible transformations the multiplication of the components of the archetype by a positive constant and the addition to all components of another positive constant. We shall call these *optical transformations*. If there are other admissible transformations than the optical, say $\mathfrak{T}_\zeta$, depending on a set of parameters ζ, Equation (5.6) becomes

$$E_i(k, \alpha, \beta, \zeta) = \alpha e_i(k, \zeta) + \beta \qquad (i = 1, 2, \ldots, N), \qquad (5.7)$$

or, in vector form,

$$E(k, \alpha, \beta, \zeta) = \alpha e(k, \zeta) + \beta I, \qquad (5.8)$$

where I is a vector with all components equal to unity and the vector $e(k,\zeta)$ is a partially transformed prototype, i.e., the result of applying $\mathfrak{T}_\zeta$ to the archetype $e^{(k)}$. For example, ζ may include the parameters of the translation of the archetype within the field of view, of the change of scale in the axes of x and y, of the rotation, etc. Thus the set of nuisance parameters denoted by b in our general model (5.1) now consists of the set ζ and two more parameters α and β.

We shall suppose that the observed images are described by the model (2.2) (cf. p. 45), which for optical transformations takes the form

$$v = \alpha e(k,\zeta) + \beta I + r. \tag{5.9}$$

Thus we assume the noise to be additive. We shall also suppose that the probability density $p_{\text{noise}}(r)$ of the noise r is a monotone decreasing function $f(\cdot)$ of the sum of the squares of its components:

$$p_{\text{noise}}(r) = f(r^2), \tag{5.10}$$

where $r^2 = \sum_{i=1}^{N} r_i^2$, and the r_i are the components of the noise vector. Our assumption is valid, for instance, for the spherically symmetrical normal distribution. As we explained earlier (Section 2.2, pp. 45–49), such assumptions concerning the noise should not essentially narrow the domain of practical application of the results obtained by their adoption, since a method that works well for the spherical-normal assumption will work well enough for an arbitrary noise with independent components and sufficiently small variance.

In accordance with (5.5) and (5.10) the likelihood function has the form

$$p_{\text{noise}}(v - E(k,\alpha,\beta,\zeta)) = f((v - E(k,\alpha,\beta,\zeta))^2), \tag{5.11}$$

i.e., under our assumptions the likelihood is a monotone decreasing function of the Euclidean distance between the points v and $E(k,\alpha,\beta,\zeta)$ in the N-dimensional space R^N of the observed images.

In keeping with the general scheme of the method of admissible transformations, we introduce the similarity as equal to this distance:

$$g(v,E) = [v - E(k,\alpha,B,\zeta)]^2. \tag{5.12}$$

Since the function $f(\cdot)$ in the expression (5.11) for the likelihood is monotone decreasing, we apply the decision rule (5.4):

$$d = \arg\min_{k} \min_{\alpha,\beta,\zeta} [v - E(k,\alpha,\beta,\zeta)]^2.$$

To minimize the quadratic distance (5.12) over all the parameters, we may always begin by finding the minimum with respect to α and β and then with respect to the remaining parameters k and ζ. Let us consider the minimization with respect to α and β.

Substituting (5.8) in (5.12), we find that the function to be minimized is quadratic in α and β. Since the domain of admissible values of these is convex ($\alpha > 0$ and $\beta > 0$), the function has a unique minimum. If in the first approximation we neglect the constraints, the minimum can be found by equating to zero the partial derivatives with respect to α and β, as was done in [32].

The same result can be achieved more rapidly with the aid of a geometric representation. For a fixed vector $e(k,\zeta)$ and varying parameters α and β, the transformed image E as defined by (5.8) remains in a two-dimensional subspace (a plane) spanned by the vectors $e(k,\zeta)$ and I. The shortest distance D from the point v to this plane is easily expressed in terms of the length of the vector v and its projection v_p on that plane (cf. Figure 5.1):

$$D^2 = v^2 - v_p^2.$$

The projection v_p is expressible in terms of projections of v on two orthogonal unit vectors lying in the plane. We choose the two vectors to be: the normalized vector I_0, collinear with I,

$$I_0 = \frac{1}{\sqrt{N}} I, \tag{5.13}$$

and the normalized component of the vector $e(k,\zeta)$ orthogonal to I,

$$c(k,\zeta) = \frac{e(k,\zeta) - [e(k,\zeta), I_0] I_0}{\|e(k,\zeta) - [e(k,\zeta), I_0] I_0\|} . \tag{5.14}$$

(The square brackets denote the scalar product.) Then the distance we want is given by

$$D^2 = v^2 - [v, I_0]^2 - [v, c(k,\zeta)]^2. \tag{5.15}$$

This expression gives us the minimum distance with respect to the optical parameters α and β. We must now find the minimum of the expression D^2 with respect to the remaining parameters k and ζ.

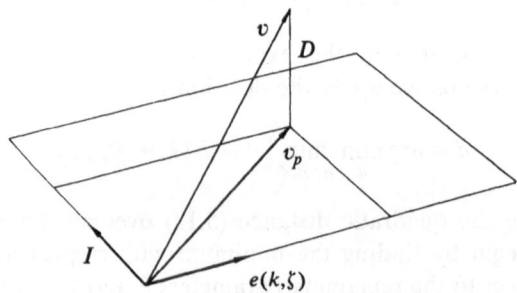

Figure 5.1 Computation of the shortest distance from the image to the hyperplane of prototypes.

We see by (5.15) that the basis of the plane was so chosen that only the term $[v, c(k, \zeta)]^2$ depends on k and ζ, and the minimum value of D^2 corresponds to the maximum value of this term. Therefore, to find the minimum distance it suffices to maximize the absolute value of the scalar product $[v, c(k, \zeta)]$, which may be interpreted as the value of the similarity maximized with respect to α and β. We denote its value by $g_{cor}(k, \zeta)$ and write it out in coordinate form:

$$g_{cor}(k, \zeta) = \sum_{i=1}^{N} v_i c_i(k, \zeta). \tag{5.16}$$

Here the $c_i(k, \zeta)$ are the components of the vector $c(k, \zeta)$.

Since v_i is the brightness of the ith retinal cell, $g_{cor}(k, \zeta)$ may be interpreted as the light flux from the image v through a mask or optical template on which the image is projected, while the transmission coefficient of the ith cell of the template is equal to $c_i(k, \zeta)$. We therefore call the vector $c(k, \zeta)$ the *orthonormal template* for the prototype $e(k, \zeta)$.

By (5.14)

$$c_i(k, \zeta) = \frac{e_i(k, \zeta) - (1/N) \sum_{i=1}^{N} e_i(k, \zeta)}{\sqrt{\sum_{i=1}^{N} e_i^2(k, \zeta) - (1/N) \left(\sum_{i=1}^{N} e_i(k, \zeta) \right)^2}}. \tag{5.17}$$

Substituting (5.17) in (5.16) we obtain

$$g_{cor}(k, \zeta) = \frac{\sum_{i=1}^{N} v_i e_i(k, \zeta) - (1/N) \sum_{i=1}^{N} v_i \left(\sum_{i=1}^{N} e_i(k, \zeta) \right)}{\sqrt{\sum_{i=1}^{N} e_i^2(k, \zeta) - (1/N) \left(\sum_{i=1}^{N} e_i(k, \zeta) \right)^2}}. \tag{5.18}$$

This expression represents the sample correlation coefficient of the set of quantities v_i and $e_i(k, \zeta)$, with one exception — that the denominator does not contain as a factor the square root of the sampling variance of the v_i. It is therefore quite natural to call $g_{cor}(k, \zeta)$ the *correlation coefficient* of the image v with the prototype $e(k, \zeta)$, unnormalized with respect to v.

As we have just shown, this correlation coefficient is the scalar product of the vector v and the orthonormal template $c(k, \zeta)$. Therefore the decision rule for the correlation method has the form

$$d = \arg\max_{k} \max_{\zeta} \left| [v, c(k, \zeta)] \right|, \tag{5.19}$$

where $c(k, \zeta)$ is the orthonormal mask of the kth class, depending on the parameter ζ of a nonoptical admissible transformation.

We must note especially that the decision rule (5.19) uses a piecewise linear discriminant function

$$\tilde{f}_k(v) = \max_{\zeta} \left| [v, c(k, \zeta)] \right|$$

and not a linear function. For this reason it may be possible to separate sets of images that cannot be even approximately called convex. As we showed at the outset of Chapter II, such sets are characteristic of all practical image recognition problems.

We shall consider the important special task of recognizing typewritten characters from a given type font. The dimensions and form of the characters are constant. We shall suppose also that any significant tilting of the characters is excluded. Therefore the admissible transformations consist of translations of the prototypes in the horizontal and vertical directions, and optical transformations. In fact, the contrast of typewritten characters depends strongly on the quality of the ribbon, the force of the stroke, and many other factors. The mean brightness or the mean blackness change with these factors, and depend also on the quality and cleanness of the paper.

With these assumptions, we must include in the set of parameters ζ two parameters ξ and η characterizing the translations of the image along the x- and y-axes, respectively. We adopt as the archetypes an idealized image of each character. This is an image corresponding precisely to the typeface on the typewriter, taking account of the thickness and elasticity of the ribbon, which influence the line width. The transforms of the archetype $e(k, \zeta)$ for fixed α and β will be obtained via all possible progressive translations of the archetype in the vertical and horizontal directions within the limits of the bounded field of view.

For the recognition of a character whose image lies in the field of view we must compute the correlation coefficient of the image with every prototype and for all possible translations of the prototypes. It suffices to find the scalar product of the vector v with the orthonormal template $c(k, \zeta)$ for all values of k and for all admissible values of the translation parameter ζ. The maximum values of the scalar product with respect to translations measure the similarity (of the image to be recognized) with each of the archetypes. The largest value shows which of the archetypes the image most resembles. The index of this archetype is the output that we desire as the result of the recognition process.

This algorithm solves the problem of the search for the maximum similarity under the assumption that there are no constraints on the optical parameters α and β. The constraints may be taken into account in the following way: It is not difficult to express the maximum-likelihood estimates of α and β in terms of the values of the scalar product in (5.15). If both these estimates are nonnegative, the value of (5.15) is a solution of the problem in the bounded case. If at least one is negative, however, we must replace the shortest distance D to the plane by the shortest distance to the boundary of the set of admissible values of α and β. When the constraints have the form $\alpha > 0$ and $\beta > 0$, the distance to the boundary is fairly easily expressed in terms of the estimates of α and β, and the value of D^2. For a negative estimate of α (or of β) the correction to D^2 is proportional to the square of the absolute value of the estimate.

It is not hard to see that a negative estimate for α may be obtained when because of noise the presented image is nearer to the negative image of the archetype than to the positive (the negative image is one in which black and white are exchanged). Usually the appearance of such a noise is most improbable. Equally improbable is the appearance of a negative estimate of β having a large absolute value. Therefore the constraints on α and β are usually not taken into account, and this omission does not lead to any significant worsening of the results of the recognition process. For the same reason the maximum of the absolute value of the correlation coefficient with respect to k and ζ is attained with very high probability for a positive value of the coefficient, and the absolute value symbols may be omitted in (5.19).

A more significant concern is presented by the constraints on α and β when the components v_i and E_i refer to values of the blackness rather than the brightness. The values of the blackness lie by definition in the interval $[0, 1]$, and therefore the admissible values of α and β must satisfy not only the inequalities $\alpha > 0$ and $\beta > 0$ but also constraints of the form

$$0 \leqslant \alpha e_i(k, \zeta) + \beta \leqslant 1.$$

Moreover, in this case we cannot assume that the noise is normally distributed, since the v_i are bounded. The recognition problem with these constraints has been solved by L. A. Svjatogor [61].

The correlation method can be generalized to the case in which the domain of prototypes is an m-dimensional linear subspace and $m > 2$ [70]. Suppose that the images, as before, have a spherical normal distribution $p(v \mid E)$ with respect to the prototype E, and that E can be represented as

$$E = \sum_{j=1}^{m} \alpha_j e(j, k, b) + \mu(k, b), \tag{5.20}$$

where $\{e(j, k, b): j = 1, 2, \ldots, m\}$ are vectors that are linearly independent for arbitrary fixed k and b, and $\mu(k, b)$ is a vector depending on k and b which, in particular, may vanish identically, as in the particular case examined above. In keeping with our assumption on $p(v \mid E)$, the Euclidean distance between v and E is a measure of similarity. We are to find the minimum of this distance with respect to the parameters $\{\alpha_j\}$, and then with respect to k and b.

We introduce an orthonormal basis $\{c(j, k, b): j = 1, 2, \ldots, m\}$ into our space. Equating to zero the gradient of the distance with respect to the

$\{\alpha_j\}$, or using the geometric model introduced earlier, we find that the shortest distance from v to the subspace, for fixed k and b, is given by

$$D^2 = (v - \mu(k,b))^2 - \sum_{j=1}^{m} [v - \mu(k,b), c(j,k,b)]^2. \qquad (5.21)$$

To obtain the maximum-likelihood estimate d of the parameter k, we must minimize D^2 with respect to k and b. In the particular case when $\mu(k,b) \equiv 0$, it is sufficient to find the maximum with respect to k and b of the sum on the right-hand side of (5.21):

$$d = \arg\max_{k} \max_{b} \sum_{j=1}^{m} [v, c(j,k,b)]^2. \qquad (5.22)$$

Let us now suppose that the distribution $p(v|E)$ is normal and that the parameters $\{\alpha_j\}$ are also normally distributed random variables.* Then, as is easily seen, the distribution of the images v for fixed k and b will be normal. Our m-dimensional subspace (5.20) is the m-dimensional regression plane for this distribution. If the variance of each of the α_j increases without limit, the distribution of the images v spreads out over the infinite m-dimensional plane, and the inverse of the covariance matrix becomes degenerate. In this case we obtain the model (5.20) with unbounded α_j. We thus arrive at a conclusion which is valuable from the methodological point of view, that the model on which the correlation method is based is simply the *limiting case of the normal distribution* which arises when the variance increases unboundedly in several directions.

This generalized correlation method can be applied to the recognition of complex images, in which the various components are subjected to different independent optical transformations. Such a model can be applied, for example, to the recognition of multicolored images, that is, images of the same object observed in light of varying wavelengths.

5.5 Experimental Results

The effectiveness of the correlation method has been tested by experiments on the recognition of typescript. The first experiments were done by simulating the recognition process on a computer. equipped with a general-purpose photoelectric image converter [21]. The converter uses a flying-spot scanner, which is guided by the computer. Under computer control the bright spot on the face of a cathode ray tube is located at a point with coordinates calculated by the computer program. The spot is projected on the corresponding point of the image on paper (or on a photographic film). The light reflected from the paper (or transmitted

---

*This case was considered in the dissertation of G. L. Gimel'farb (Kiev, Institute of Cybernetics of the Ukrainian Academy of Sciences, 1968).

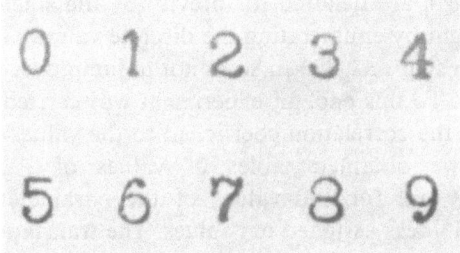

Figure 5.2   The images of the digits used as prototypes

through the film) falls on a photomultiplier and is transformed into a four-bit binary code, which is then fed to the computer. Thus the computer has access to any of 256×256 points of the image and gets a reading on the blackness of a small neighborhood of that point. Sixteen gray shades can be distinguished. By using a suitable program one can choose very different orders of inspection of the image, including those dependent on the observed gray shades. There is no need to keep the data on the gray shades in the computer memory, since the access to each image point occurs rapidly (in about 200 microseconds) and we may think of the image as part of the read-only memory of the computer. The data needed for the calculation are obtained directly from the image, and this essentially extends the possibilities for experiment as compared with devices that demand a preliminary storage of all the data describing the image.

The apparatus provides an auxiliary control CRT for visual supervision of the movement of the scanning spot over the image. By a special program, this control tube permits displaying graphic information of various types: one can inspect strongly magnified input images, display stored prototype images from memory, etc.

The experiments on the recognition of typed digits [24] were carried out on the "Kiev" computer and the image converter which we have just described. The characters were written on a "Moskva" typewriter. The archetypes were clearly printed images of the digits, as shown in Figure 5.2. These images were digitized by an 8×6-cell retina and stored in the computer memory. Each component could have any one of 16 values. Orthonormal templates were constructed for all ten classes ($k = 0, 1, 2, \ldots, 9$). The decision rule (5.19) was implemented by a suitable program.

Table 5.1 shows the results of recognizing these prototype images. The values of the correlation coefficients are shown in relative units: the figures in the ith row are the results of recognizing the image of the ith class and are equal to

$$\max_{\zeta} g_{\text{cor}}^{(j)}(k, \zeta) / \max_{\zeta} g_{\text{cor}}^{(j)}(i, \zeta) \qquad (k = 0, 1, 2, \ldots, 9).$$

To recognize an image by the rule (5.19) we seek the maximum of the correlation coefficients with respect to the parameters ξ and η. (The pair of parameters ζ and η are denoted for brevity by the single symbol ζ.) This maximum is sought by enumerating the discrete values of ξ and η. The size of the translation step was chosen so as not to jump over the neighborhood of the maximum. To this end, an experiment was carried out to determine the sensitivity of the correlation coefficient to the values of ξ and η. Using the computer, we obtained tables of values of $g_{cor}(k,\zeta)$ for every $k = 0, 1, 2, \ldots, 9$ and for 100 values of the parameter ζ. Each of the parameters ξ and η was assigned ten values. The translation step was taken as half of the distance λ between centers of the retinal cells ($\lambda \simeq 0.24$ mm). We then constructed graphs of the sections of each table, by row and column, with interpolated intermediate values of $g_{cor}(k, \zeta)$. The contours of equal value are shown for the characters $0, 1, 8$ ($k = 0, 1, 8$) in Figures 5.3, 5.4, and 5.5 respectively. The coordinate axes are labeled with the values of the translation parameters, and the unit is the value of λ.

A square is drawn in each figure, inscribed in the contour representing 80% of the maximum value; this contour is drawn with a dashed line in the

Table 5.1

	0	1	2	3	4	5	6	7	8	9
0	1.00	0.56	0.53	0.67	0.44	0.64	0.78	0.39	0.61	0.78
1	0.42	1.00	0.23	0.39	0.74	0.39	0.39	0.42	0.35	0.29
2	0.43	0.32	1.00	0.57	0.34	0.39	0.32	0.39	0.66	0.45
3	0.68	0.50	0.58	1.00	0.42	0.74	0.68	0.37	0.74	0.42
4	0.33	0.80	0.30	0.38	1.00	0.38	0.50	0.40	0.33	0.40
5	0.60	0.39	0.39	0.66	0.32	1.00	0.66	0.32	0.50	0.39
6	0.66	0.47	0.34	0.59	0.47	0.61	1.00	0.32	0.61	0.47
7	0.31	0.48	0.38	0.33	0.45	0.26	0.33	1.00	0.19	0.45
8	0.56	0.54	0.70	0.67	0.35	0.49	0.60	0.23	1.00	0.47
9	0.65	0.37	0.44	0.42	0.49	0.42	0.42	0.49	0.49	1.00

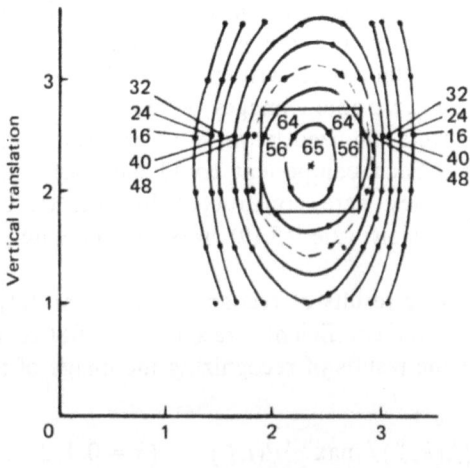

Figure 5.3 Autocorrelation function of the character "0".

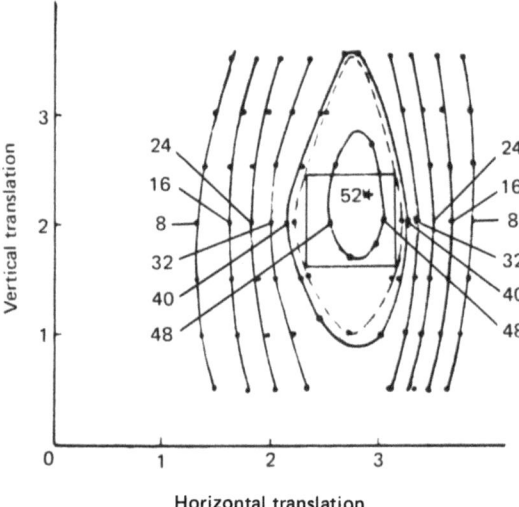

Figure 5.4   Autocorrelation function of the character "1".

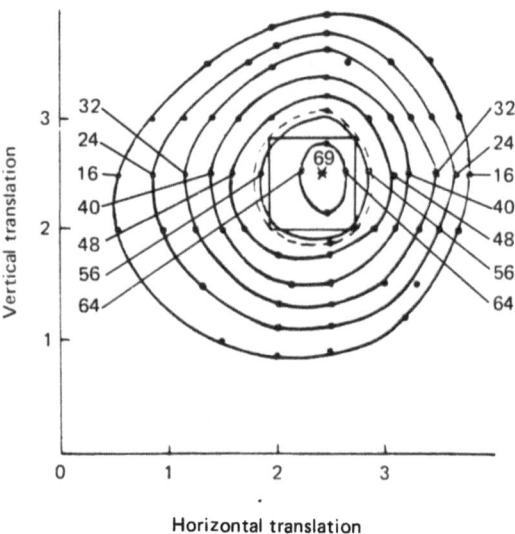

Figure 5.5   Autocorrelation function of the character "8".

figure. The 80% level was chosen because the experiments showed that the maximum of the correlation coefficient for an alien prototype very rarely exceeded 80% of the maximum of the correlation of the proper prototype. It is clear that with a translation step exceeding the length of the side of the square an erroneous recognition is possible. It will be seen from the figures that the side of the smallest square measures less than 0.83λ.

It must be noted that we studied the autocorrelation function of well-printed characters. The autocorrelation functions of characters subjected to damage may be quite different, and therefore the work done so far could only establish an upper bound for the translation step. In the subsequent experiments the step was set at 0.5λ, i.e., 0.12 mm. As is shown by a statistical study given below, a high recognition reliability was achieved with this value.

To get an estimate of the noise resistance of the algorithm a series of experiments on the recognition of digits was carried out with artificially damaged images. Three types of defect were studied: artificially broken lines (Figure 5.6); artificial fouling (Figure 5.7); and very great natural damage (Figure 5.8).

In Table 5.2 we display the results of the recognition of the three images marked out by squares in Figures 5.6–5.8. For each of the characters ten values of the maximum of the correlation coefficient $g_{cor}(k,\zeta)$ with respect to ζ were developed, corresponding to the ten values of k from 0 through 9.

The correct decisions reached in these experiments testify to the fact that the method of maximum similarity with the prototypes is sensitive even to small differences among the archetypes. Therefore it is possible to recognize severely damaged images if the appearance of noise in any part of the image decreases the similarity with the competing prototypes uniformly and the undamaged portion of the image has a greater similarity to its own prototype than to an alien. However, this property of the

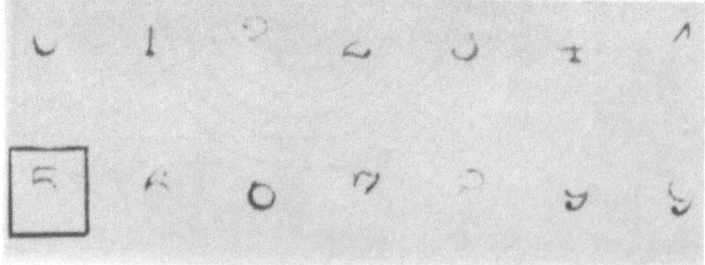

Figure 5.6   Artificial line breaks.

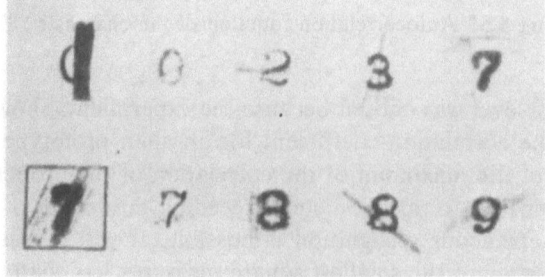

Figure 5.7   Artificial fouling.

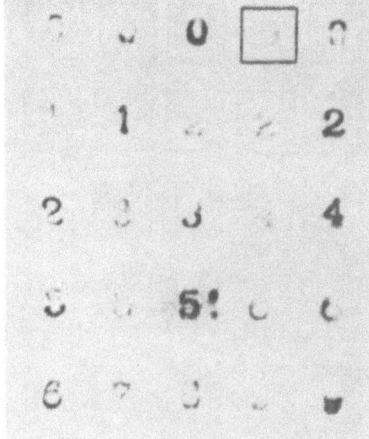

Figure 5.8   Natural damage.

Table 5.2

Prototypes	5	7	0
0	274	317	223
1	283	305	168
2	142	252	163
3	288	333	173
4	293	438	118
5	337	264	172
6	290	300	202
7	289	481	171
8	252	269	206
9	197	417	191

method is not always helpful, since it may generate errors due to insignificant differences between the archetype used to generate the images and the archetype on which the template is based. Thus, for example, on some typewriters there are planned differences between the characters standing for "zero" and for the letter "O", which are distinguished by the radii of curvature of the arcs. If the ensemble of templates contains at most one of these two, say the template for zero and none for "O", the image of the character "O" will not necessarily be assigned to the character "zero", contrary to one's expectations. A random defect might cause assignment of it to the class "C", or the process might decide to reject the image.

Some statistical studies were carried out on the results of recognizing typewritten digits, using the same program that implemented the algorithm (5.19). Five kinds of paper were used: newsprint, sized white, unsized white, yellow, and green. Four copies of the character sequence (an original and three carbon copies) were printed on each kind of paper. These were typed in random order. In all, 35,000 characters were typed. Naturally, the recognition of 35,000 characters would consume a great deal of computer time (for one image with 100 displacements, the machine

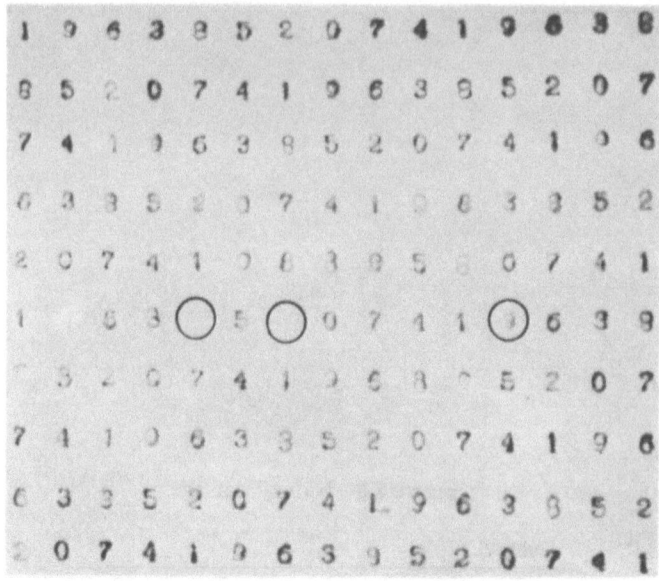

Figure 5.9   Specimen page as used in the experiments.

required about 2.5 minutes, at a speed of 7000 operations per second). To economize on computer time, the experiment was carried out as follows: As a result of experience gained during our work with the algorithm, it was possible to judge the quality of the image by eye, and to select quite confidently those printed images that would be correctly recognized. After a careful inspection of all 35,000 images, a few hundred were chosen for which proper recognition could not be guaranteed. These images were fed to the machine and recognized by the program that implemented (5.19).

Figure 5.9 shows part of a page from one of the four typewritten copies as used in this experiment. All the characters in the figure were correctly recognized.

Among the results of the experiment there were two wrong decisions and three rejections. The rejections occurred when none of the ten correlation coefficients exceeded the preassigned threshold. In the three cases observed, the images were very faint, so that a significant portion of the strokes of the characters vanished under the 16-level quantization procedure.

The errors and rejections were distributed among the original (copy 1) and the three carbon copies (2, 3, 4) as follows:

Copy No.	Errors	Rejections
1	—	—
2	1	—
3	1	1
4	1	—

If we assume that the several hundred chosen characters included all the cases in which recognition was difficult, and that there would have been no errors in recognizing the remaining characters, we may make a guideline estimate of the error probability and set it at 10^{-4}.

While weighing the relatively good experimental results in the recognition of the originals and typewritten copies, we must keep in mind the fact that the brightness was quantized into 16 levels (usually there are only two levels) and that the translation parameters were quantized in the unusually small steps of 0.12 mm, which is half the width of the thinnest stroke in any of the images. It is also important to note that only 10 character classes were recognized, and the prototypes for these are widely different.

A further trial showed that the magnitude of the translation step has an essential effect on the recognition error probability.

Special methods for constructing the templates must be used if good results are to be obtained when the step is comparable to the stroke width. As the number of recognition classes grows it becomes very difficult to achieve small error probabilities, especially for similar characters such as the Russian "Ш" and "Щ", or "3" and "Э". We shall discuss a method for solving this problem in Chapter VI.

Later on, L. S. Belobragina and V. K. Eliseev [7] made a careful statistical analysis of the results obtained by the use of the algorithm (5.19) for the recognition of typewritten characters. They found an upper confidence limit of 6×10^{-5} for recognition of the originals and 6×10^{-3} for the copies with a fiducial probability of 0.9. Their basic assumption was that the difference Δg_{cor} of the correlation coefficient between the image's own prototype and an alien prototype is normally distributed.

This hypothesis was tested for agreement with experimental data for a given significance level, i.e., with a bounded Type-I error probability [44]. They determined the mean value $\overline{\Delta g_{cor}} = \mu$ and the sampling variance σ^2 of the difference in question. The quantity μ / σ was used to compute a point estimate and upper confidence limit for the error probability. If Δg_{cor} is in fact normally distributed, this yields a more exact estimate of the error probability with a small sample than can be obtained by a simple count of the number of errors in the sample. However, the upper confidence limit for the recognition error probability does not depend on the significance level adopted for testing the hypothesis of normality, but rather on the power of the goodness-of-fit test, i.e., on the probability of a Type-II error, whose value was not stated in [7]. For small samples ($l = 10$), which were used by the authors, the probability of a Type-II error is quite high. Their findings should therefore be treated with some caution.

5.6 Potential Applications of the Correlation Method

It follows from the theory of the correlation method that it applies to any case in which the set of images in each of the recognition classes is described by a spherically symmetrical normal distribution for which the mean value (the prototype) varies within some linear subspace of the signal space. We may also consider a somewhat more general case in which the mean value belongs to one of a small finite number of linear subspaces. (We recall that in the language of admissible transformations a variation of the mean within a linear subspace is called an *optical transformation*, and a passage from one linear subspace to another is a *nonoptical* transformation.)

The number of subspaces should be small, because the likelihood function must be maximized over all possible values of the nonoptical transformation parameter by an exhaustive search, whereas the maximum over the optical parameters is computed by formula, i.e., analytically. If the number of nonoptical parameters is large, serious difficulties arise in the search for the extremum of a function of many variables.

For example, the correlation method is in principle applicable to the recognition of hand printed characters. These can be adequately represented by means of transformations such as translation, shear, change of scale, change of stroke width, etc. However, the practical solution of the problem, under the assumption that the images may have significant defects, cannot be achieved by the very simple methods used for the recognition of typescript. This is because the maximum of the correlation function cannot be found by simple enumeration of the parameter values. In the case of two parameters (translations) some hundreds of values must be explored; for six parameters the number is in the millions. It is difficult to solve this problem either on a general-purpose computer or on a specialized machine.

We may consider the correlation method as being applicable to the recognition problem when the number of archetypes is no more than a hundred, and the number of trial values of the nonoptical parameters in each act of recognition is no more that a few tens of thousands.

This does not mean, however, that the correlation method has less potential than other methods that are described in the recognition literature. When it is possible to find the maximum of the correlation coefficient over all the parameter values, the correlation method has a much higher noise resistance than any other method. If the computational difficulties prevent a precise estimate of the maximum, and rough estimates of some parameters must be made, the correlation method still has about as good a potential as any other.

To verify this, E. F. Kušner experimented with the recognition of handwritten "printed" characters by the correlation method [43]. If the characters are written carefully enough, without significant defects, blots, or fouling, it is possible to effect a kind of normalization of their images. We draw a parallelogram around the character and segment its interior into a fixed number of rhomboids forming a skewed grid. In the case of a larger character the parallelogram is also larger and, since the number of cells is fixed, it is divided into coarser cells. This digitization of the character is repeated several times, with different translations of the grid within small limits and different inclinations of the "vertical" axes. The correlation coefficients are computed for each variant of the digitization and for all prototypes, and the largest is recorded.

The search for the extremal black points is made by inspecting the horizontal and vertical strips of cells while these are moved in steps from the boundary of the field of view to the image. To avoid errors arising from isolated spots of dirt near the outline of the character, the search is carried on after the first black point is discovered. If a clear space is found beyond it, the next black point is also recorded. In this case two different parallelograms are constructed and the whole process of multiple digitization is done twice.

The experiments were carried out with the aid of a computer and a general-purpose image converter controlled by it. The experimenter prepared two or three different prototypes for some characters, in view of possible variations in their outlines.

The characters used in the experiment were handwritten versions of printed letters and digits, written at the rate of about 50 per person by 20 different persons, under no constraints (Figure 5.10). Out of the total of 750 characters, only seven were wrongly recognized.

The error probability for the most difficult characters was evaluated more carefully by the method we have already described [7], on the hypothesis that the difference Δg_{cor} between the correlation coefficients of the image with its own prototype and with alien prototypes is normally distributed (cf. Section 5.5). The results are given in Table 5.3. The ratio of the mean difference $\Delta g_{\text{cor}} = \mu$ to the root-mean-square deviation was of the order of 2.5 for most characters. Assuming the distributions are normal, we find the confidence interval for the value p_c of a correct recognition as 0.95–1.00. For some pairs of characters that are very much alike, the ratio was 1.6 and the corresponding confidence interval was 0.92–0.98 (with a fiducial probability $p_f = 0.95$).

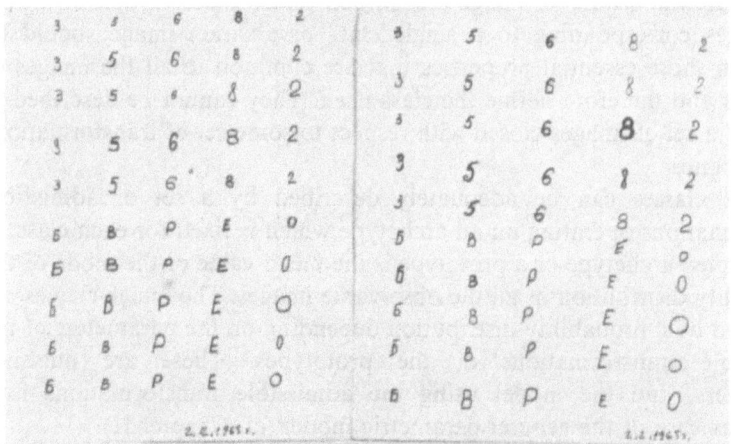

Figure 5.10 Images of the handwritten characters used in the experiments.

Table 5.3

	Class				
	"2"	"3"	"5"	"6"	"8"
Number of experiments	60	60	60	60	60
Number of errors	0	0	3	0	3
Confidence interval[a] for μ/σ	2.13–3.28	1.61–2.59	1.37–2.20	1.80–2.86	1.41–2.28
Confidence interval[a] for μ	320–400	170–230	100–140	200–250	120–160
Confidence interval[a] for σ^2	13000–27000	6000–14000	3000–7000	6000–14000	4000–9000
Confidence interval[a] for p_c	0.983–0.9995	0.946–0.995	0.915–0.986	0.964–0.998	0.921–0.989

[a] The fiducial probability is 0.95 for all confidence intervals.

These results support our assertion that by the use of various methods of normalization of the images, which may be interpreted as independent rough estimates of the parameters, the correlation method gives the same probability of correct recognition as other methods do. To take advantage of the benefits of the correlation method or the more general method of admissible transformations, one must make use of effective methods for finding the maximum similarity over the parameter space. We will consider these methods in Chapter VII.

5.7 Conclusions

It is highly important for image recognition that the description of the set of images corresponding to a single class or abstract image should be based on those essential properties that are common to all the images of the class and therefore define the class itself. They cannot be described in terms of a set of images closed with respect to some set of transformations of the plane.

Image classes can be adequately described by a set of admissible transformations operating on an archetype which is fixed for each class. A transformed archetype or a prototype is the mean value or the mode of the probability distribution of all the observable images. The image classes are described by a probability distribution depending on the parameters of the admissible transformations of the prototypes. These are nuisance parameters, and the model using the admissible transformations is a particular case of the general parametric model (cf. Chapter II).

The corresponding decision rule consists of finding the maximum-likelihood estimate of the recognition parameter k, obtained by maximizing the likelihood function over all the values of the parameters on which the transformed prototype depends. Thus the recognition problem is reduced to an optimization problem.

The values of the likelihood function, which depend on the observed image and the prototype, may be interpreted as quantitative measures of the similarity between the image and the prototype. The similarity can be defined generally as an arbitrary quantity which depends monotonically on the likelihood function. This means that we may look on the method of admissible transformations as the basis for recognition algorithms founded on a search for the prototype having maximum similarity to the observed image.

The correlation method is a particular case of the method of admissible transformations, applicable when the set of admissible values of the transformed prototype of each class is a linear subspace or the union of linear subspaces. It has been shown [32] that in this case the maximum-likelihood method leads to a decision rule with piecewise linear discriminant functions. As applied to the recognition of typewritten numbers this rule has the form

$$d = \arg\max_k \max_\zeta \left[v, c(k,\zeta) \right],$$

where the square brackers denote the scalar product and the vector $c(k,\zeta)$ is the precalculated template for the kth class, whose displacement relative to the edge of the field of view is characterized by the parameter ζ.

The peculiarities that distinguish the correlation method from others that use the scalar product for the computation of discriminant functions are as follows: (1) the scalar product is maximized over the nuisance parameters, in particular, over the translations; (2) the components of the template are chosen so that they sum to zero and the sum of their squares is unity.

Experiments on recognition by a computer equipped with a photo-electric image converter have shown that symbols from a fixed font are correctly recognized, even when there are significant defects in their images. The error probability is of the order of 10^{-4}.

The application of the correlation method to the recognition of image classes that admit a wider class of admissible transformations—e.g., handwritten characters—is hindered by the difficulty of finding the maximum of the similarity over the nuisance parameters when there are many of these. If we first normalize the images, however, which amounts to making a rough estimate of the parameters, the correlation method gives about as good a probability of correct recognition as the other known methods, i.e., about 95%. This reliability is not good enough for practical tasks. To obtain a higher reliability index in those cases where there are many nuisance parameters and the maximum similarity cannot be found by a simple search, more effective methods of optimization must be found. A recognition method based on the use of dynamic programming is given in Chapters VII and VIII.

Even when the number of nuisance parameters is relatively small, however, difficulties due to an imprecise determination of the maximum similarity may arise from the quantization of the parameter values used in the search. The effect of these errors on the recognition reliability may be minimized by proper choice of the components of the templates. This gives rise to the important and widely applicable task of optimizing a piecewise linear decision rule of bounded complexity, which in its formulation is close to the nonparametric learning problem. The next chapter is devoted to it.

CHAPTER VI

Optimization of the Parameters of a Piecewise Linear Decision Rule

This chapter is devoted to the solution of the problem formulated in Section 2.7—the optimal choice of the parameters of a piecewise linear decision rule with a bounded number of linear functions. We recall that a decision rule of the form

$$d = \arg\max_{k} \tilde{f}_k(v)$$

is said to be piecewise linear if the discriminant functions $\tilde{f}_k(v)$ are. This means that, depending on the value of v, the value of $\tilde{f}_k(v)$ coincides with the value of one of the given linear forms in the components v_i. The number of these forms is finite. For instance, the function

$$f(v) = \max_{\zeta} \left(c_0(\zeta) + \sum_{i=1}^{N} v_i c_i(\zeta) \right)$$

is piecewise linear.

Such functions can serve as adequate approximations to the optimal discriminant functions in many cases of practical importance. The optimization method described below should therefore be widely applicable. The practical need for applying it arose in the designing of a character reader, because of the difficulty of finding an exact solution for the problem of seeking the maximum of the similarity over the translation parameters in the decision rule (5.19), since these parameters take on an infinite set of values. Templates that are suitable for finding a precise maximum of the similarity over the translation parameters of the template are unsuitable when the precise solution is to be replaced by an approximation based on a search over discrete values of these parameters. This difficulty was noted and analyzed by R. A. Našljunas and P. P. Jašinskas [52]. It was partially overcome in [71]. We shall consider a more general problem, consisting of the search for an optimal collection of templates, containing a given finite number of them, while the nuisance parameters take on an infinite number of values. In a particular case, the nuisance parameter may be the translation parameter of the images, and the translation parameter of the template may assume only a predetermined finite number of values.

The idea on which the theoretical solution to this problem is based is due to M. I. Šlesinger. His papers [73, 74] on this problem do not exhaust his contribution, and he should be understood to be a co-author of this chapter.

6.1 The Adequacy of a Piecewise Linear Rule and Formulation of the Optimization Problem

In Section 5.2 we obtained the decision rule (5.3), which follows from the maximum-likelihood method and from some very general assumptions about the probability distribution of the images v that are to be recognized. It is not hard to see that (5.3) will be piecewise linear if the similarity $g(v, E)$ is a linear function of v and the nuisance parameter b takes on only a finite number of values.

This happens, for instance, when each class is defined by a set of normal distributions with a constant covariance matrix—i.e., a matrix not depending on k and b—and with mean values lying in several linear subspaces of small dimensionality. This case was studied in Section 5.4. A particular instance is provided by classes, each characterized simply by a few normal distributions with the same covariance matrix. In this case, the subspaces have dimension zero.

There is another important case in which a piecewise linear function provides an exact solution for the maximum-likelihood problem, namely when each component v_i can assume only two values, and the v_i are all independent random variables for fixed values of k and b. The statistical independence of the v_i is the only constraint imposed on the distrlbutions $p(v \mid E(k, b))$ in this case. The linear property follows from the independence for binary v_i, since because of the independence the logarithm of the likelihood function is a sum of terms each depending on only one of the components v_i. But an arbitrary function of a binary variable is representable in linear form:

$$f(v_i) = f(1)v_i + f(0)(1 - v_i).$$

Therefore the logarithm of the likelihood function, as the sum of N linear functions, is itself linear in v. The coefficients of the v_i depend on k and b, and if there are only a finite number of values of b, the discriminant function according to (5.3″) is piecewise linear.

There are problems in which these conditions are only approximately satisfied—for instance, the recognition of classes each defined by many normal distributions with *arbitrary* covariance matrices, or recognition of classes defined by a model of the form $p(v|E(k,b))$ when an infinite set of values of the nuisance parameter b can be approximated by a finite set of discrete values. Then a piecewise linear decision rule, which is relatively easy to compute or to implement technically, can serve as a satisfactory approximation of the optimal decision rule. For any concrete task one must select from among all piecewise linear decision rules the one that is in some definite sense the best.

We shall consider rules analogous to (5.19), expressible in the form

$$d = \arg\max_k \max_\zeta \left(c_0(k,\zeta) + \sum_{i=1}^{N} v_i c_i(k,\zeta) \right). \tag{6.1}$$

The introduction of the free term $c_0(k,\zeta)$ broadens the class to a certain extent, as compared to (5.19), where the free term was set equal to zero because in Section 5.4 we were considering a problem in which the multiplication of all the image components by a positive constant was an admissible transformation. In the general case this is not so, and we must work with the more general expression (6.1).

In order to preserve the compact notation for linear forms as scalar products, we shall look on $c_0(k,\zeta)$ as a component of an $(N+1)$-dimensional vector $c(k,\zeta)$, so that the index i in the expression $c_i(k,\zeta)$ takes on the values $0, 1, \ldots, N$ and the extra component v_0 of the $(N+1)$-dimensional vector v is permanently set equal to 1. Then the decision rule (6.1) is

$$d = \arg\max_k \max_\zeta [v, c(k,\zeta)], \tag{6.2}$$

where $[v, c(k,\zeta)] = \sum_{i=0}^{N} v_i c_i(k,\zeta)$. According to the arguments set forth in Section 5.3, we may, as before, call the vectors $c(k,\zeta)$ templates, and the scalar product $[v, c(k,\zeta)]$ may be called the similarity of the image v and the template $c(k,\zeta)$.

In the general case we may impose some constraints on the values of the components of the templates. For instance, if we take ζ to be a translation parameter of the templates over an integral number of rows and columns of the retina, the decision rule can be simplified, since in this case there is no need to store in memory the vectors $c(k,\zeta)$ for all values of ζ. Knowing $c(k,\zeta)$ for some initial value of ζ, we can find it for any other arbitrary value. To realize this simplification, we must solve the problem of the optimal choice of the templates $c(k,\zeta)$ subject to a constraint requiring the templates for different values of ζ to differ only by a translation.

In Chapter V, we searched for a decision rule without constraints, and we used the method of maximum likelihood, assuming that this method makes the probability of a wrong recognition close to its minimum value. However, when choosing the optimum rule from a given class, say linear or piecewise linear rules, it is hardly possible to use maximum likelihood. Rather, it is more profitable to go directly to the criterion of minimum error probability for the choice of the optimal decision rule, since this criterion is of great practical importance. When the computation of the error probability is difficult, we may compute an upper bound for it and use this as a criterion of optimality. In particular, if the probability distribution of the parameters k and b is either unknown or nonexistent, we can use for the upper bound the maximum with respect to k and b of the error probabilities for fixed k and b. This criterion is in any case stronger than one based on the mean error probability. A known value of the upper bound carries a guarantee that it will not be exceeded by the error probability for any values of k and b. Moreover, as will be seen later, it is easier to optimize a decision rule under a minimax criterion than by Bayesian methods. We therefore adopt the minimax criterion and arrive at the following formulation of the problem.

We are given a model of the set of images to be recognized, represented in the form

$$p(v|E(k,b)). \tag{6.3}$$

The recognition parameter k takes on a finite number of values $k = 1, 2, \ldots, n$. The set B_k of values of the nuisance parameter b is given for every k and may be infinite.

We are given a class of piecewise linear decision rules in the form (6.2), i.e.,

$$d = \arg\max_k \max_\zeta \left[v, c(k,\zeta) \right],$$

where the parameter k takes on the same set of n values as in (6.3). The parameter ζ takes on a finite, not too large, set of values $\zeta = 1, 2, \ldots, m$, making it possible to find a maximum with respect to ζ by exhaustive enumeration. The collection C of templates is subject to the restriction that it be chosen from the set of admissible collections.

We must find a collection $\hat{C}$ satisfying the constraints and such that the error probability for images with the distribution $p(v|E(k,b))$, maximized over b and k, shall be the smallest achievable by selection of $\hat{C}$:

$$\hat{C} = \arg\min_C \max_k \max_b \mathbf{P}_{k,b}(d_C \neq k), \tag{6.4}$$

with d_C a decision depending on the collection C in accordance with (6.2).

This task may be looked on as a generalization of the problem formulated in Section 1.3 (p. 20), that of nonparametric learning, which consists in the search for the optimal separating hyperplane [10, 41]. For, suppose that $p(v|E(k,b))$ is a normal distribution with mean $E(k,b)$ and unit covariance matrix. Let there be two classes, and let the values of

$E(k,b)$ coincide with the signals from the training sample, so that the value of k is supplied by the teacher, and the value of b is simply the ordinal number of the particular signal realization in the kth subsample. Suppose that for each class there is only one mask $c(k)$, i.e., that the parameter ζ has a single unique value, and the decision rule (6.2) defines the unique separating hyperplane

$$[v,(c(1) - c(2))] = 0.$$

For fixed k and b the error probability is equal to the probability that the signal v will appear on the wrong side of the separating hyperplane, corresponding to an alien class. If the covariance matrices are the same for all values of k and b, the error probability depends monotonely on the Euclidean distance from the point $E(k,b)$ to the hyperplane. Therefore the templates that minimize the error probability define a hyperplane that is optimal in the sense of maximizing the shortest distance from the sample points.

Our current problem is an essential generalization of the problem of finding the optimal hyperplane: (1) we consider a more general class of distributions $p(v \mid E(k,b))$; (2) the number of classses may be greater than two; (3) there may be more than one template for a given class, i.e., the decision rule is not necessarily linear, and may be piecewise linear.

6.2 The Linear Decision Rule as a Special Case

Let us first look at the properties of our chosen criterion of optimality for the simplest special case. Suppose that for each class we provide only one template $c(k)$ and that no restrictions are placed on its components. Then the decision rule is

$$d_C = \arg\max_k \left[v, c(k) \right], \tag{6.5}$$

i.e., it is linear. The indexing of d_C reminds us that the decision depends on the choice of the collection C of templates $c(k)$ as a parameter. We compute the criterion of optimality, which we denote by $\mathfrak{R}(C)$,

$$\mathfrak{R}(C) = \max_k \max_b \mathbf{P}_{k,b}(d_C \neq k), \tag{6.6}$$

where $\mathbf{P}_{k,b}(d_C \neq k)$ is the probability of a wrong decision $d_C \neq k$ for an image with the distribution $p(v \mid E(k,b))$. According to the rule (6.5) there will be a wrong decision $d_C \neq k$ whenever the inequality

$$[v,c(k)] < \max_{k' \neq k} [v,c(k')] \tag{6.7}$$

holds, that is, one of the inequalities

$$[v,c(k)] < [v,c(k')] \tag{6.8}$$

holds, with k' taking on $n - 1$ values different from k. Let us denote by $p^*(k,b,k',C)$ the probability that (6.8) will be satisfied:

$$p^*(k,b,k',C) = \mathbf{P}_{k,b}([v,c(k)] - [v,c(k')] < 0). \qquad (6.9)$$

The event (6.7) is the sum of the events (6.8). Therefore the probability $\mathbf{P}_{k,b}(d_C \neq k)$, which is equal to the probability of the event (6.7), is related to the probability $p^*(k,b,b',C)$ of the event (6.8) by the following inequalities:

$$\max_{k'} p^*(k,b,k',C) \leqslant \mathbf{P}_{k,b}(d_C \neq k) \leqslant \sum_{k' \neq k} p^*(k,b,k',C). \qquad (6.10)$$

Unfortunately, it is not easy to compute the quantity $\mathbf{P}_{k,b}(d_C \neq k)$. We must be satisfied with an upper bound for it. In our later calculations it is inconvenient to use the sum on the right-hand side of (6.10) for this upper bound. We therefore adopt a rougher estimate

$$\mathbf{P}_{k,b}(d_C \neq k) \leqslant (n - 1) \max_{k'} p^*(k,b,k',C), \qquad (6.11)$$

where n is the number of recognition classes.

In order to calculate the probability $p^*(k,b,b',C)$ we return to (6.9) and consider the random variable Δg, the difference in similarities between v and its "proper" template* on the one hand, and v and an "alien" template on the other hand:

$$\Delta g = [v,c(k)] - [v,c(k')] = [v,c(k) - c(k')]. \qquad (6.12)$$

When $p(v|E(k,b))$ is a normal distribution, the variable Δg will be also normally distributed for fixed values of the parameters, and will have mean value

$$\mathbf{M}_{k,b}\Delta g = \mu(k,b,k',C)$$

and variance

$$\mathbf{D}_{k,b}\Delta g = \sigma^2(k,b,k',C).$$

The normalized variable $\Delta g^* = (\Delta g - \mu)/\sigma$ has the standard normal distribution.[†] Therefore

$$p^*(k,b,k',C) = \mathbf{P}_{k,b}(\Delta g < 0) = \mathbf{P}_{k,b}(\Delta g^* < -\mu/\sigma)$$

$$= \Phi(-\mu/\sigma),$$

---

* We shall call the template having the same class index k as the considered images v with the distribution $p(v|E(k,b))$ the *proper template*. All other templates will be referred to as alien templates.

† The parameters on which μ and σ depend are omitted here to avoid a clumsy notation.

i.e.,

$$p^*(k,b,k',C) = \Phi(-\mu/\sigma), \tag{6.13}$$

where $\Phi(\cdot)$ is the standard normal distribution function

$$\Phi(x) = \frac{1}{\sqrt{2\pi}} \int_{-\infty}^{x} e^{-x^2/2} dx.$$

Substituting (6.13) into (6.11), and putting the result into (6.6), we find

$$\mathfrak{R}(C) \leqslant (n-1) \max_{k} \max_{b} \max_{k'} \Phi\left(-\frac{\mu(k,b,k',C)}{\sigma(k,b,k',C)}\right). \tag{6.14}$$

Since the function $\Phi(\cdot)$ is monotone, the maximum of $\Phi(-\mu/\sigma)$ in (6.14) can be found by finding the minimum value of μ/σ. We adopt the notation

$$\mathbf{EPA}(k,b,k',C) = \frac{\mu(k,b,k',C)}{\sigma(k,b,k',C)} . \tag{6.15}$$

where the abbreviation **EPA** stands for "the *error probability argument*". By (6.13), the **EPA** defines the value of the specific error probability $p^*(k,b,k',C)$.

If the distribution $p(v|E(k,b))$ has the mean value $M_{k,b}v = E(k,b)$ and the covariance matrix **K**, then the numerator μ and the denominator σ in the ratio **EPA** for a given ensemble of masks $C = \{c(k)\}$ are computed as follows:

$$\mu(k,b,k',C) = \sum_{i=0} E_i(k,b)(c_i(k) - c_i(k')), \tag{6.16}$$

$$\sigma^2(k,b,k',C) = \sum_{i=1}^{N} \sum_{j=1}^{N} (c_i(k) - c_i(k'))(c_j(k) - c_j(k'))\mathbf{K}_{ij}. \tag{6.17}$$

Here the $E_i(k,b)$ are the components of the mean value vector, i.e., of the prototype $E(k,b)$, with $E_0(k,b) \equiv 1$. In the general case the covariance matrix **K** depends on k and b.

We may use the quantity **EPA** in estimating the error probability even when the distribution is not normal. Chebyshev's inequality for a random variable with an arbitrary distribution and variance **D**, says that the probability of deviating by more than ϵ from the mean value does not exceed $\mathbf{D}/\epsilon^2$. In our case this gives an estimate of the error probability as $\sigma^2/\mu^2 = 1/\mathbf{EPA}^2$. If the distribution is close to the normal, this estimate is rougher than $\Phi(-\mu/\sigma)$. However, distributions exist for which Chebyshev's estimate is attained. Therefore in the most general case there is no better estimate. It is important to stress the fact that for an arbitrary distribution of the quantity Δg the error probability can be bounded above by a monotone decreasing function of the **EPA**. The **EPA** is therefore a general-purpose criterion for estimating the quality of a linear decision rule. To compute the value of the **EPA** for the ensemble of templates C, even for an arbitrary distribution $p(v|k,b)$ we need only know the mean value $M_{k,b}v = E$ and the covariance matrix $\mathbf{K}$ of the distribution, and substitute these in (6.16) and (6.17) respectively.

In addition to the normal distribution, it is important to study distributions with independent components. Then Δg, in accordance with (6.12), represents the sum of a large number of independent terms. The central limit theorem says that the distribution of the sum of a number of independent random variables tends to normality with an increase in the number of terms whose variance differs from the maximum variance (of the terms in question) by no more than a fixed constant.

When the sum (6.12) satisfies these fairly standard conditions, Δg has a distribution close to the normal, and an estimate of the error probability can therefore be found for an arbitrary distribution with independent components in the same way as for the normal distribution, i.e., by use of the **EPA**.

The numerator μ of the **EPA** is computed by (6.16) in this case also. The variance σ^2 is computed as a weighted sum of the variances of the components,

$$\sigma^2 = \sum_{i=1}^{N} (c_i(k) - c_i(k'))^2 \mathbf{D}_{k,b}v_i, \qquad (6.18)$$

because the components are independent. Here $\mathbf{D}_{k,b}v_i$ is the variance of the ith component of the image v with the distribution $p(v|E(k,b))$. We remark that the $\mathbf{D}_{k,b}v_i$ depend on k and b. The zero component ($i = 0$) in (6.18) is of course absent, since its variance is zero.

Let us summarize the foregoing calculations. An upper bound for the probability that an image of the kth class, with the distribution $p(v|E(k,b))$, will be wrongly assigned to the class k' by a recognizer using the decision rule (6.5) and the system $C = \{c(k)\}$ of templates, depends monotonely on the **EPA**:

$$\mathbf{EPA}(k,b,k',C) = \frac{\mu(k,b,k',C)}{\sigma(k,b,k',C)}.$$

Here the quantity $\mu(k,b,k',C)$ characterizes the conditional mean value of the difference in the similarities of v and the kth and k'th templates in the collection C, and is defined by (6.16). The quantity $\sigma(k,b,k',C)$ is the standard deviation of this difference; it is given by (6.17) for a normal distribution and by (6.18) for a distribution with independent components.

The quality of the collection of templates C is characterized by the minimum value of the **EPA**:

$$\mathbf{EPA}^*(C) = \min_k \min_b \min_{k'} \mathbf{EPA}(k,b,k',C). \qquad (6.19)$$

6.3 The Optimization Problem and Its Solution

We shall study the properties of $\textbf{EPA}^*(C)$ as a function of the collection C of templates $c(k)$ and show that it is strictly quasiconvex in the region where it is positive. We begin with a *definition*: Let some two values x_1 and x_2 of the argument of the function $f(x)$ be such that

$$f(x_1) < f(x_2). \qquad (6.20)$$

If for all x_1 and x_2 in a region X that satisfy (6.20), and for all convex combinations

$$x = \alpha x_1 + (1 - \alpha)x_2,$$

where $0 < \alpha < 1$, the inequality

$$f(x) \geqslant f(x_1)$$

holds, then $f(x)$ is said to be *quasiconvex upward* in the region X. If the strict relationship

$$f(x) > f(x_1)$$

holds, $f(x)$ is said to be *strictly quasiconvex*.

It is not hard to see that the foregoing definition of a quasiconvex function coincides with the customary one, i.e.: a function is said to be quasiconvex if for arbitrary ϑ the set of values of x for which $f(x) \geqslant \vartheta$ is convex. The concept of quasiconvexity that we need for our own purposes is, however, more difficult to express in terms of the latter definition.

Every function that is quasiconvex upward has a unique maximum. If it is strictly quasiconvex, the maximum can be found by the gradient method of optimization. Therefore the quasiconvexity of $\textbf{EPA}^*(C)$ is highly important for the solution of our problem. The quasiconvexity of $\textbf{EPA}^*(C)$, as first proved by M. I. Šlezinger, follows, as explained below, from the quasiconvexity of $\textbf{EPA}(k, b, k', C)$ with respect to C.

The variable $\textbf{EPA}$ is a fraction, whose numerator μ is a linear function of C, by (6.16), and whose denominator σ contains under the radical a positive definite quadratic form, by either (6.17) or (6.18), that is, as a function of C it is convex downward. Given only these facts about the numerator and denominator, nothing can be said about the convexity of $\textbf{EPA}$, as a function of C, over the whole range of values of C. Nevertheless, it can be shown that $\textbf{EPA}$ is quasiconvex where it is positive.

In fact, it is not hard to see that the quotient $f(x) = \varphi(x)/\psi(x)$, obtained by dividing a positive upward-convex function $\varphi(x)$ by a positive downward convex function $\psi(x)$, is quasiconvex upward. Let us prove that this is so. Let x_1 and x_2 satisfy (6.20), and let x satisfy (6.21). By the definitions of upward- and downward-convex functions,

$$\varphi(x) \geqslant \alpha\varphi(x_1) + (1 - \alpha)\varphi(x_2),$$

$$\psi(x) \leqslant \alpha\psi(x_1) + (1 - \alpha)\psi(x_2).$$

Since *both sides of each* of these inequalities are positive, we may divide the first by the second:

$$\frac{\varphi(x)}{\psi(x)} > \frac{\alpha\varphi(x_1) + (1 - \alpha)\varphi(x_2)}{\alpha\psi(x_1) + (1 - \alpha)\psi(x_2)} \cdot \tag{6.22}$$

Now, using (6.20) we may write

$$\frac{\varphi(x_1)}{\psi(x_1)} < \frac{\varphi(x_2)}{\psi(x_2)} \,,$$

or, since $\psi(x_2)$ is positive,

$$\varphi(x_2) > \frac{\varphi(x_1)}{\psi(x_1)} \psi(x_2). \tag{6.23}$$

Substituting the right-hand side of (6.23) in (6.22), we have

$$\frac{\varphi(x)}{\psi(x)} > \frac{\alpha\varphi(x_1) + (1 - \alpha)\varphi(x_1)\psi(x_2)/\psi(x_1)}{\alpha\psi(x_1) + (1 - \alpha)\psi(x_2)} \cdot$$

By simple transformations we find that the right-hand side of the above inequality is equal to $\varphi(x_1)/\psi(x_1)$. Then we have

$$\frac{\varphi(x)}{\psi(x)} > \frac{\varphi(x_1)}{\psi(x_1)} \,,$$

which, in view of the fact that x_1 and x_2 were chosen arbitrarily, shows that $f(x) = \varphi(x)/\psi(x)$ is strictly quasiconvex upward.

The function **EPA**(k, b, k', C) is the ratio of $\mu(k, b, k', C)$ to $\sigma(k, b, k', C)$, satisfying all the above requirements except for the positivity of μ. This property must be separately specified, i.e., **EPA** is quasiconvex if $\mu > 0$. We shall now show that the function **EPA***(C) is also strictly quasiconvex. We consider the function $F(x) = \min_s f_s(x)$, where the parameter s assumes a finite number of values, and all the $f_s(x)$ are strictly quasiconvex. Let x_1 and x_2 satisfy the condition $F(x_1) < F(x_2)$, and let x satisfy (6.21). Then by the strict quasiconvexity of the $f_s(x)$ we have for all s

$$f_s(x) > \min_{i=1,2} f_s(x_i).$$

We minimize both sides of this inequality with respect to s:

$$\min_s f_s(x) > \min_s \min_{i=1,2} f_s(x_i) \tag{6.23'}$$

and interchange the places of $\min_s$ and $\min_{i=1,2}$ on the right-hand side of (6.23'). Remembering the definition of $F(x)$, we have

$$F(x) > \min_{i=1,2} F(x_i) = F(x_1),$$

which is what we were to prove.

To find the maximum of a quasiconvex function we may use any method that allows us to go from points with smaller values of the function to points with larger values. For differentiable functions we may use the gradient method. But by (6.19) the function **EPA***(C) is nondifferentiable at those points where the minimum is attained for more than one of the functions within the scope of the "min" symbol. N. Z. Šor has developed a generalized gradient method [75] to find the maximum of a nondifferentiable convex function. A vector $\mathcal{G}$ in the n-dimensional space R^n is said to be the generalized gradient of the convex function $F(x)$ at the point $x^* \in R^n$ if the inequality

$$[\mathcal{G}, x - x^*] \geqslant F(x) - F(x^*)$$

holds for all x.

We note that in $(n + 1)$-dimensional space the hyperplane

$$y = [\mathcal{G}, x - x^*] + F(x^*)$$

is a generalized tangent to the surface $y = F(x)$ at the point $x = x^*$ (Figure 6.1).

The gradient of $F(x)$ coincides with the generalized gradient at each point where it exists, i.e., where $F(x)$ is differentiable. At the singular points, where the gradient is discontinuous, the generalized gradient is multiply defined, as for instance at the point x^* in Figure 6.1, and a displacement along it does not necessarily correspond to an increase in the function.

Nevertheless, Šor proved [75] that an iterated motion along the generalized gradient, with a corresponding control of the step length, converges to the maximum. Suppose the function to be maximized has the

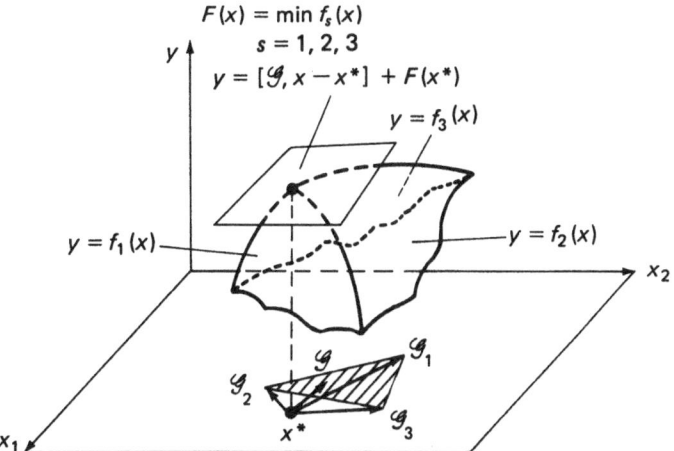

Figure 6.1   Generalized tangent and generalized gradient $\mathcal{G}$ for a function $F(x)$ at the point x^*.

form

$$F(x) = \min_s f_s(x), \tag{6.24}$$

where the $f_s(x)$ are convex. If the minimum with respect to the discrete parameter s is attained at the point x^* for one value of s only, the gradient of $F(x)$ at that point is

$$\mathcal{G}(x^*) = \operatorname{grad} f_\theta(x^*), \tag{6.25}$$

where

$$\theta = \arg\min_s f_s(x^*). \tag{6.26}$$

The gradient of the function (6.24) does not exist at x^* if the minimum is attained there for more than one value of s:

$$f_\theta(x^*) = \min_s f_s(x^*); \qquad \theta = s_1, s_2, \ldots, s_m, \quad m \geqslant 2.$$

At such a point we must use the generalized gradient. It can be found by computing the gradient of any one of the functions $f_\theta(x)$ that agrees with the minimum at x^*, i.e., it can be found as before, by (6.25). For, $f_\theta(x)$ is convex, and therefore

$$\left[\mathcal{G}(x^*), x - x^*\right] \geqslant f_\theta(x) - f_\theta(x^*). \tag{6.27}$$

But at the point x^* (6.26) implies that $f_\theta(x^*) = F(x^*)$. Moreover, (6.24) implies that for all x we have the inequality $f_\theta(x) \geqslant F(x)$. It therefore follows from (6.27) that

$$\left[\mathcal{G}(x^*), x - x^*\right] \geqslant F(x) - F(x^*),$$

i.e., a vector $\mathcal{G}(x^*)$ satisfying (6.25) and (6.26) is by definition a generalized gradient.

The function **EPA***(C)$ is not convex. However, we may obviously suppose that a continuous function which is strictly quasiconvex (in the sense of the first definition, p. 125)—as the function **EPA***(C)$ is—may be represented in the form $F(\varphi(C))$, where $\varphi(C)$ is convex and $F(\cdot)$ is monotone. In this case the maximization of **EPA***(C)$ may be replaced by the maximization of $\varphi(C)$, and for this we need the generalized gradient of $\varphi(C)$. But the gradients computed in accordance with (6.25), for functions that are monotonely related, are obviously collinear. This is at the root of the fact that the maximization of **EPA***(C)$ can be accomplished by motion along the generalized gradient computed via (6.25). The role of $f_s(X)$ is played by **EPA**(k, b, k', C), and the role of s by the set of parameters (k, b, k').

To construct the optimization algorithm for **EPA***(C)$ we now need only a method for choosing an initial approximation. Since the quasiconvexity of **EPA***(C)$ has been proved only for positive values, we may begin the optimization by means of the generalized gradient only for that collection $C^{(\text{in})}$ for which $\textbf{EPA}^*(C^{(\text{in})}) > 0$, i.e., $\textbf{EPA}(k,b,k',C^{(\text{in})}) > 0$ for all admissible parameter values.

To find such a $C^{(\text{in})}$ we use the same algorithm, but now the function to be maximized is the minimum of the numerator in $\textbf{EPA}$:

$$\mu^*(C) = \min_{k,b,k'} \mu(k,b,k',C).$$

This function is convex for all its values. Since the denominator in $\textbf{EPA}$ is always positive, a positive value of $\mu^*(C)$ guarantees a positive value of $\textbf{EPA}^*(C)$, and can be used to start the optimization process. Thus the initial value $C^{(\text{in})}$ with which the optimization of $\textbf{EPA}^*(C)$ is begun, is to be found as the result of an iterative procedure. The initial approximation for this procedure (let us call it the *null approximation* $C^{(0)}$) may be arbitrary, but to cut down the length of the iteration it is worth while to choose $C^{(0)}$ near to the desired optimal collection.

One obvious way to choose the null approximation of the kth template consists in taking the mean value with respect to b for the $E(k,b)$ in the distribution $p(v \mid E(k,b))$, for fixed k:

$$c^{(0)}(k) = \frac{1}{|B_k^*|} \sum_{b \in B_k^*} E(k,b),$$

where $|B_k^*|$ is the number of values of the parameter b in a finite subset $B_k^* \subset B_k$ approximating B_k. The collection $C^{(0)}$ consists of the n templates $c^{(0)}(k)$, $k = 1, 2, \ldots, n$.

The outline of the iterative algorithm for the solution of (6.4) is as follows: Each iteration in turn begins with the current approximation of the collection C of templates $c(k)$, and for the various values of k, b, and k' computes the values of $\textbf{EPA}(k,b,k',C)$ and finds the value of

$$\min_{k'} \min_{k} \min_{b} \textbf{EPA}(k,b,k',C)$$

by exhaustive enumeration of the parameter values. The parameters k and k' take on all of the values $k, k' = 1, 2, \ldots, n$ for which $k \neq k'$; b runs over the finite subset B_k^* of B_k. The number of these values, defined by the digitization quantum, must be determined experimentally. The value of $\min_{b \in B_k} \textbf{EPA}(k,b,k',C)$ can only decrease as the quantum decreases; when the digitization steps are small enough, no further decrease is observed.

To help the exposition we introduce a vector s whose components are the parameters k, k', and b. After we have found the minimum of $\textbf{EPA}$ for all values of s, we record its value θ for which the minimum was attained (and if there are several such values, we choose any one of them). Then for this value θ we compute the gradient of $\textbf{EPA}$ with respect to C, and the current approximation of C is changed by an amount proportional to the gradient. With this the iteration is ended and the next one begins. The number of iterations is determined experimentally by observation of the rate of change of the variable **EPA*(C)**.

To summarize, we may state an algorithm for optimizing the collection of templates C, with the following structure:

Begin: Calcùlate the null approximation $C^{(0)}$. Set the current collection $C = C^{(0)}$ and the number of completed iterations = 0.

Iteration: Set the initial values of k, b, k'. Set **EPA*** = $+\infty$.

Enumeration: Compute **EPA** for the current values of the parameters. If **EPA** < **EPA***, set **EPA*** = **EPA** and replace the components of θ by the current values of the parameters. Change the values of the parameters. If the list of parameter values is not exhausted, go to "Enumeration."

End Enumeration.

If the value obtained for **EPA*** is less than zero (or some fixed positive number) go to "Without Denominator," else if **EPA*** is greater than another predetermined threshold go to "Output," else compute the gradient of **EPA** for the value of θ developed in "Enumeration." Go to "Step."

Without Denominator: Compute the gradient of the numerator μ for the value of θ developed in "Enumeration."

Step: Compute the length of the iteration step depending on the current value of the iteration index. Multiply by the gradient and add the resulting vector to the vector C. Increment the iteration index by 1. If the number of iterations does not exceed the predetermined limit, go to "Iteration."

End Iteration.

Output: Print the value of **EPA*** and list the components of all the templates. Stop.

End Algorithm.

6.4 Solution of the Optimization Problem for a Piecewise Linear Rule

The problem that we have solved in Sections 6.2 and 6.3, namely that of optimizing the choice of parameters in a linear decision rule, may be interpreted as the problem of approximating, by a *single* template, the set of prototypes $E(k, b)$ corresponding to a single value of k and all possible values of the nuisance parameter b. When the convex hulls of these sets of prototypes do not intersect for different values of k, the approximation of each set by a single template can yield a high probability of correct recognition. If, however, the convex hulls do intersect, considerably better results can be obtained by providing several templates for each class. In

this case the decision rule must be piecewise linear and must have the form
(6.2), i.e.,

$$d_C = \arg\max_k \max_\zeta \left[v, c(k, \zeta) \right].$$

As before, the set C of templates $c(k, \zeta)$ must be chosen to minimize an
upper bound for the error probability. For this purpose, we estimate the
probability $\mathbf{P}_{k,b}(d_C \neq k)$ that an image with the distribution $p(v \mid E(k, b))$
will be wrongly recognized by the decision rule (6.2). An error occurs
whenever

$$\max_\zeta \left[v, c(k, \zeta) \right] < \max_{k' \neq k} \max_{\zeta'} \left[v, c(k', \zeta') \right]. \tag{6.28}$$

This event, in contrast to (6.7) which we considered in the case of a linear
decision rule, is the product of several events, namely

$$\left[v, c(k, \zeta) \right] < \max_{k' \neq k} \max_{\zeta'} \left[v, c(k', \zeta') \right], \tag{6.29}$$

for all values of $\zeta = 1, 2, \ldots, m_k$. Therefore the probability of any one of
the events (6.29) is an upper bound for the probability of the event (6.28)
in which we are in fact interested. However, it is easy to see that
minimizing the probability of (6.29) for fixed ζ is not useful. In fact, if we
merely fix ζ and go ahead with (6.29) as we did earlier with the inequality
(6.8), the task reduces in reality to the finding of a single optimal template
for each class. Instead, we want to use several templates, in order to
approximate the set of prototypes $E(k, b)$ for all $b \in B_k$ more exactly than
we can by using a single template.

To accord with the method of admissible transformations, *every* value of
the nuisance parameter b should have its own template. However, as we
noted in Section 6.1, we are pursuing the goal of obtaining a satisfactory
recognition reliability by the use of a comparatively small number of
templates. To achieve this goal, we must divide the set of prototypes
$\{ E(b, k) : b \in B_k \}$ into subsets of "neighboring" prototypes in such a way
that the convex hulls of every subset of the kth class do not intersect any
of the hulls of subsets belonging to other classes. We assign a single
template to each subset.

It is not easy to make such a subdivision by an optimization process. We
shall therefore assume that the partition of the sets of prototypes into
subsets and the attachment of one of the optimized templates $c(k, \zeta)$ to
each subset is done on the basis of various intuitive considerations, as for
instance merely by dividing the range of each of the components of the
parameter b into equal intervals. The templates may be assigned by use of
the function

$$\zeta = Z(b) \tag{6.30}$$

which maps each value of b into some of the discrete values of the
parameter ζ. A very simple example is provided by the case in which b has

only one component, the thickness of the strokes in a character. We divide the interval $[b^{(1)}, b^{(2)}]$ of values of the stroke width into m subintervals of length $b = (b^{(2)} - b^{(1)})/m$, and we assign to each subinterval a single template $c(k, \zeta)$. This assignment corresponds to the function

$$Z(b) = \text{Ent}\left\{ \frac{b - b^{(1)}}{\Delta b} \right\}, \tag{6.31}$$

where $\text{Ent}\{\cdot\}$ is the integer part of a number.

An assignment based on heuristic arguments may of course be unsuccessful. The result will be an unsatisfactory outcome of the optimization process, i.e., a high estimate of the error probability. Then we must try other methods of assignment, or increase the number of templates for some or all of the classes.

Using the assignment function (6.30), we can estimate for each value of the pair of parameters k and b the probability of a wrong decision taken via maximum similarity of the image to the template *assigned* to the given value of b. For an arbitrary template assignment this probability, by our earlier line of reasoning, provides an upper bound for the probability of an erroneous decision made by the rule (6.2). Therefore, as an estimate of the probability of the event (6.28), which is what interests us, we may take the probability of the inequality (6.29) for the value of ζ corresponding to (6.30). This probability can in turn be estimated, as for (6.11), by using the variable $p^*(k, b, k', \zeta', C)$ computed by formulae similar to (6.9), (6.13), (6.15), and (6.17), namely:

$$p^*(k, b, k', \zeta', C) = \mathbf{P}_{k, b}\big([v, c(k, Z(b))] - [v, c(k', \zeta')] < 0\big)$$

$$= \Phi(-\mathbf{EPA}(k, b, k', \zeta', C)),$$

where the collection of templates C is given by $C = \{c(k, \zeta) : \zeta = 1, 2, \ldots, m_k; k = 1, 2, \ldots, n\}$.

We may use as the optimization criterion the quantity

$$\mathbf{EPA}^*(C) = \min_{k, b} \min_{k', \zeta'} \mathbf{EPA}(k, b, k', \zeta', C), \tag{6.32}$$

computed by formulae analogous to (6.16)–(6.18). The maximization of (6.32) over the collection C is similar to the optimization derived in Sections 6.2 and 6.3 for a linear decision rule with the number of classes equal to the number of templates, i.e., equal to $\sum_{k=1}^{n} m_k$. The difference consists only in the fact that now $\mathbf{EPA}$ is not computed for all pairs of templates; namely it is not computed when both templates in the pair correspond to the same value of k. This difference does not affect the strict quasiconvexity of $\mathbf{EPA}^*(C)$, and therefore the optimization can be carried out by the algorithm described at the end of Section 6.3. The changes in the algorithm amount to this: that now $\mathbf{EPA}(k, b, k', \zeta', C)$ depends on four parameters rather than three, and we must find the minimum by enumeration of the values of all these four parameters.

In the foregoing example, several templates were assigned to each class, one for each interval of the values of the line width. By the same process we can introduce different templates for different subsets of the values of other components of the nuisance parameter b. As we remarked in Chapter V, b may be thought of as the parameter of the set of admissible transformations of a prototype. Among these there may be some simple ones such that we can predict the corresponding variations of the templates before doing the optimizing. The translation of a prototype over an integral number of rows and columns of the retina is a transformation of this kind. We shall call it an *integer translation*.

Let us consider the case in which b has three components, t, x, and y, expressing respectively the stroke width (thickness) and the translations in the horizontal and vertical directions. We partition the set of admissible prototypes $E(k,t,x,y)$ into subsets such that one can be obtained from another by an integer translation of all of its members. It is easy to picture these subsets by setting up a correspondence between the prototype $E(k,t,x,y)$ and the point in the field of view with the coordinates (x,y). Then one subset includes all the prototypes for which the points (x,y) fall in a single retinal cell. Let this be the cell $\Omega_{\xi,\eta}$ lying in the column with index ξ and the row with index η. The subset of prototypes $E(k,t,x,y)$ such that

$$(x, y) \in \Omega_{\xi, \eta}, \tag{6.33}$$

is assigned the template $\tilde{c}(k,\tau,\xi,\eta)$, where the value of the parameter τ is defined by an assignment function $T(t)$ similar to (6.31). The values of ξ and η are also defined by assignment functions which we may assume are defined by (6.33). Then we have

$$\tau = \mathrm{T}(t), \qquad \xi = \Xi(x), \qquad \eta = \mathrm{H}(y). \tag{6.34}$$

It can probably be proved that the templates $\tilde{c}(k,\tau,\xi,\eta)$ for different values of ξ and η differ only by an integer translation. If we accept this assumption, we can represent the templates $\tilde{c}(k,\tau,\xi,\eta)$ in the form

$$\tilde{c}(k,\tau,\xi,\eta) = \mathfrak{T}_{\xi,\eta}\, c(k,\tau), \tag{6.35}$$

where $\mathfrak{T}_{\xi,\eta}$ is an integer translation by ξ columns and η rows, and $c(k,\tau)$ is an original template corresponding to some fixed values of ξ and η, say zero, i.e.,

$$c(k,\tau) = \tilde{c}(k,\tau,0,0).$$

Then the decision rule becomes

$$d = \arg\max_{k}\ \max_{\tau}\ \max_{\xi,\eta} \left[v, \mathfrak{T}_{\xi,\eta}\, c(k,\tau) \right]. \tag{6.36}$$

The introduction of the transformation $\mathfrak{T}_{\xi,\eta}$ simplifies the decision rule, since we no longer need to keep in recognizer memory all the $c(k,\tau,\xi,\eta)$

corresponding to the different values of ξ and η. Instead, they can be obtained from a single template $c(k, \tau)$ by applying the simple transformation $\mathfrak{T}_{\xi, \eta}$.

We now ask how the optimization of $\mathbf{EPA}^*(C)$ for a collection of templates is changed by the introduction of the transformation $\mathfrak{T}_{\xi, \eta}$. This case may be also regarded as the case with several templates per class; in fact, we may assume that we are optimizing the collection $\tilde{C}$ of templates $\tilde{c}(k, \tau, \xi, \eta)$, in which there are as many templates for each class as there are values of the parameter triplet (τ, ξ, η). However, a constraint has been imposed on these templates, namely that those corresponding to different values of ξ and η are connected by (6.35).

The integer translation $\mathfrak{T}_{\xi, \eta}$ can be written as a linear transformation. Therefore the equations (6.35) define a linear subspace in the space of the values of the collection $\tilde{C}$ of templates $\tilde{c}(k, \tau, \xi, \eta)$. Then the search for the maximum value of $\mathbf{EPA}^*(\tilde{C})$ should be carried out over the subspace (6.35). A linear subspace is always convex, and therefore $\mathbf{EPA}^*(\tilde{C})$, which is quasiconvex in the space of values of $\tilde{C}$, is also quasiconvex in the subspace (6.35). It follows that the optimization algorithm defined at the end of Section 6.3 is applicable here with one change, namely that the gradient of EPA with respect to the collection C of templates $c(k, \zeta)$ must now be taken to be the projection of the gradient of $\mathbf{EPA}$ with respect to the extended collection $\tilde{C}$ of templates $\tilde{c}(k, \tau, \xi, \eta)$ on the subspace (6.35). Thus because of the special simplicity of the integer translations, we may replace the search over the collection $\tilde{C}$ of templates $\tilde{c}(k, \tau, \xi, \eta)$ by a search over the smaller collection C of templates $c(k, \tau)$.

Certain not very stringent arguments can be brought forth in support of the idea that under certain conditions we should not optimize over the whole range of the admissible values of the translation parameters x and y for the prototype $E(k, t, x, y)$ but should restrict ourselves to values corresponding to a fixed subset (6.33). This means that we consider only those prototypes that are translated within the limits of a single retina cell. In this case the number of computed values of $\mathbf{EPA}$ is somewhat reduced and the optimization problem becomes

$$\hat{C} = \arg\max_{C} \min_{k, t} \min_{x, y \in \Omega_\infty} \min_{k', \tau'} \min_{\xi' \eta'} \mathbf{EPA}(k, t, x, y, k', \tau', \xi', \eta', C).$$

In the computation of $\mathbf{EPA}$ the parameters τ, ξ, and η of the "proper" kth template are defined by the assignment function (6.34), with $\xi = 0$ and $\eta = 0$, since $x, y \in \Omega_{0, 0}$. The parameters k', τ', ξ', and η' of the alien template take on all possible values.

Just as in the optimization of the linear decision rule [cf. (6.14)], the estimate of the error probability has the form

$$\mathcal{R}(C) \leqslant m\Phi(-\widetilde{\mathbf{EPA}}(C)), \tag{6.37}$$

where

$$\widetilde{\mathbf{EPA}}(C) = \min_{k, t} \min_{x, y} \min_{k', \tau'} \min_{\xi', \eta'} \mathbf{EPA}(k, t, x, y, k', \tau', \xi', \eta', C),$$

and $m = \max_k \sum_{k' \neq k} m_{k'}$; $m_{k'}$ is the number of different templates $\tilde{c}$ for the class k', including those that differ only by integer translations.

The estimate (6.37) is generally greatly inflated, since for the most part only a few of the great number of alien templates are close to the proper template in the sense that the value of **EPA** for them is close to the minimum. A more practical (but unproven) estimate can be obtained by setting $m = 2$ or $m = 3$ in (6.37).

The problem of optimizing a piecewise linear decision rule under constraints like (6.35) arises as a practical problem in the design of character readers. We will look at its solution in the next section.

6.5 An Application to the Recognition of Alphanumeric Characters by a Character Reader

The algorithm that we have defined for optimizing the parameters of a piecewise linear decision rule has been used in the development of a character reader (cf. Chapter IX). In this application the solution consisted of several independent stages:

1. the elaboration of an adequate parametric model of the set of images to be recognized, allowing the calculation of the parameters of the probability distribution $p(v \mid E(k, b))$;
2. writing a computer program to implement the optimizing algorithm;
3. organizing the computing process, in which the task of optimization over a large number of classes was broken down into subtasks of lesser dimensionality; and
4. verifying the results by experiment.

All these stages are described in this section, which is largely devoted to a description of the model of the set of images. This model, which is essential to the application, also serves as a concrete example of the parametric model developed in its general form in Chapter II. We therefore describe it in some detail.

We remarked in Section 2.2 that the parametric model must represent a process that generates sets of images identical to the classes of observables that we intend to recognize. The images modeled must be sampled and quantized in the same way as the images to which we shall apply the decision rule that is to be optimized.

The model is shown in Figure 6.2.

The block labelled "Archetype" stores in memory the skeletons of the symbols in the given alphabet. The *skeleton* is a standardized outline of the corresponding typeface on the typewriter (Figure 6.3). For each character we record the parameters of the straight line segments and arcs of circles that make up the skeleton.

The "Admissible Transformations" block realizes the translations of the archetypes by horizontal and vertical displacements x and y respectively. This block also fleshes out the skeleton with a black band whose width (i.e., the width of the lines in the image) is defined by the value of the

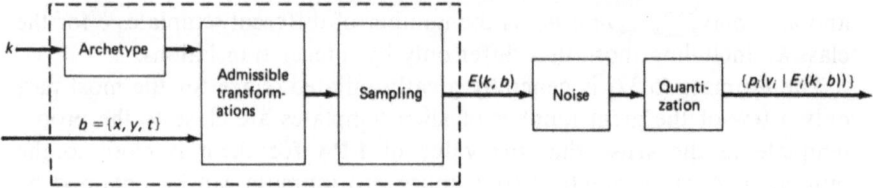

Figure 6.2   Schematic model of the process generating the images of typewritten characters to be recognized.

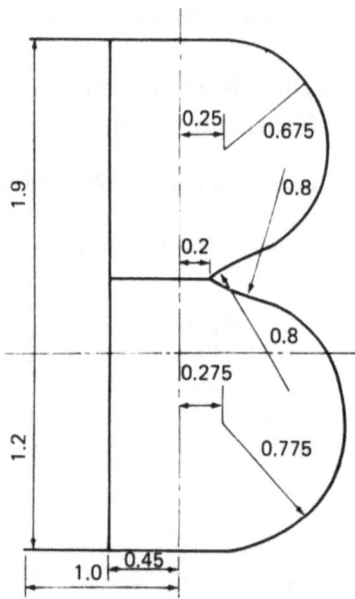

Figure 6.3   Lengths of segments, centers, and radii of curvature of the arcs, in the skeleton of the character "B".

parameter t (Figure 6.4). The parameters x, y, and t should be interpreted as the components of the three-dimensional nuisance parameter b, and we shall denote the triplet by the single symbol b.

The "Sampling" block projects the prototype images—the result of the admissible transformations—on the retina, a grid made up of cells, and determines the blackness of each cell, which is proportional to the area of the blackened portion of the cell, i.e., the portion covered by the black field of the prototype image.

The "Noise" block simulates the signals at the outputs of the light-sensing elements that measure the flux reflected from each of the cells. The signals are supposed to be normally distributed with a given variance which is the same for all cells, and mean value equal to the blackness of the corresponding cell.

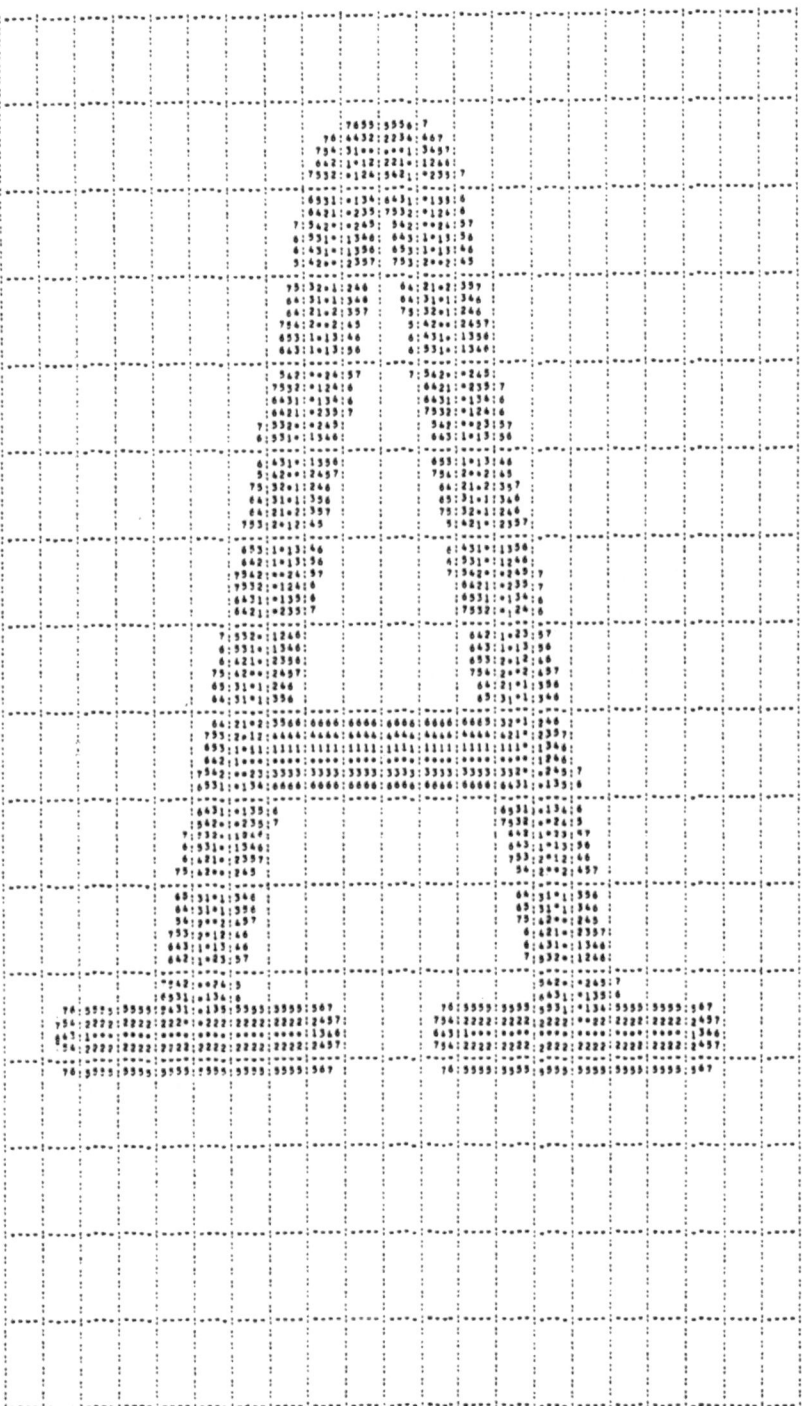

Figure 6.4 Transformed prototype, point lattice, and retina.

```
6 6 6 6 6 6 6 6 6 6 6 6 6 5 3
I 5 2 I 3 6 ✕ 6 I I I I 2 6 6 6 6
        6 ✕ 6                          6 ✕ 6
      I 6 ✕ 6                          6 ✕ 6
      I 6 ✕ 6                          6 ✕ 6
      I 6 ✕ 6        I I 2 6 6 6 6
      I 6 ✕ 6 6 6 6 6 6 6 6 5 3
      I 6 ✕ 4
      I 6 ✕ 6
        6 ✕ 4
6 6 6 6 6 6 6 6 6 6 6 6
I 5 2                 I 4 3
```

Figure 6.5 Example of the set of probabilities $p_i(k,b)$ for concrete values of the parameters.

The "Quantization" block simulates the quantization process that is implemented in the developed character reader. The noise-distorted value of the blackness is compared with a threshold which is a function of the blacknesses of several neighboring cells. The result of the comparison is a binary variable v_i, equal to 0 or 1. For each cell, and for given values of k and b, the probability that $v_i = 1$ is computed. It is assumed that the random variables v_i are independent for fixed k and and b. Then the ensemble of probabilities $\{p_i(k,b): i = 1,2,\ldots,N\}$ defines the probability distribution

$$p(v\,|\,E(k,b)) = \prod_{i=1}^{N} (v_i p_i(k,b) + (1 - v_i)(1 - p_i(k,b))).$$

This is the output of the model. The distribution $p(v\,|\,E(k,b))$ is used in the optimization of the parameters of the decision rule applied by the reader. If necessary, it can be used to generate images by means of a random number generator.

An example of the set of probabilities $p_i(k,b)$ is shown in Figure 6.5. The values of the probabilities, coded on a nonuniform scale, are placed in the corresponding retina cell locations. The codes are shown in Table 6.1.

Table 6.1

Probability values $p_i(k,b)$	Symbol used in Figure 6.5
$p = 0.01$	Blank
$0.01 < p \leqslant 0.03$	.
$0.03 < p \leqslant 0.1$	1
$0.1 < p \leqslant 0.3$	2
$0.3 < p \leqslant 0.7$	3
$0.7 < p \leqslant 0.9$	4
$0.9 < p \leqslant 0.97$	5
$0.97 < p < 0.99$	6
$p = 0.99$	✱

Images with different stroke widths were segmented into cells by a computational device that simplified the calculations significantly. A point lattice was constructed with a mesh much finer than that of the retina; this was used to estimate the magnitude of the black area in each cell by a count of the number of points falling in the blackened portion of the cell. For each point of the lattice, the shortest distance to the skeleton of the prototype was determined and recorded. When the prototype was displaced relative to the retina, so was the lattice; therefore this distance did not change. For a given stroke width those points of the lattice for which the distance did not exceed half the width were counted as black. This device obviated many repeated and tedious computations of the distance.

An example of the point lattice is shown in Figure 6.4, together with the distances of the points from the skeletons of the character "A". The values are rounded and expressed in relative units. The retina cells are also shown in the figure.

This model was implemented by a program for the BESM-6 computer. The original alphabet contained 53 characters: numerical digits, Russian capital letters, and arithmetic and other symbols used on the "Optima" typewriter. The retina consisted of 15×20 cells of dimension 0.31×0.135 mm^2.

The optimization program was constructed according to the most general scheme described in Section 6.4. The decision rule embodied in the reader has the form (6.36), in which ξ and η are taken as the parameters of integer translations. For most of the classes the parameter τ takes on only a single value, i.e., for these only a single template is provided. For the symbols that are more difficult to distinguish, as for instance, "Ш" and "Щ" two templates per class are provided (two values of τ), and for "3" and "Э" as many as four. The total number of templates came to 72, including a blank template.

The structure of the program agrees with the algorithm given in Section 6.3. Since the retina contains $15 \times 20 = 300$ cells, every template has 301 components [including the free term $c_0(k, \tau)$; cf. (6.1)]. The total number of components of all templates, i.e., the number of variables over which the optimization is carried out, comes to $72 \times 301 = 21672$. With such a number of variables, the optimization cannot be carried out, even on a computer of the BESM-6 class. It was necessary to divide the alphabet into groups of similar characters and construct optimal templates for each group. Examples are: 8, 3, Н, В, Я, or ь, Б, В, Н.

Using a magnetic drum and a packed information representation in memory (several quantities per memory word), we succeeded in writing a program that would construct 14 templates for 8 classes. When the same class appeared in several groups, its template was constructed for one group and adopted with no change for the other groups. For example, after the templates for the group 8, 3, Н, В, Я wėre constructed, we proceeded to construct the templates for ь, Б В, Н. Those for B and и (two per class) were merely lifted from the first group and transferred without change. However, they were used in the computation of **EPA** for all possible pairs of classes in the second group, and so influenced the optimization of the templates for ь and Б. Since there were some character groups that did not intersect at all, it was necessary to solve an additional normalization problem after all the templates were constructed—i.e., to set the values of $c_0(k, \tau)$ so that the quantity **EPA***(C) for the complete collection of 72 templates was maximized. This task is similar to the maximization of **EPA***(C) that we have already studied, and consists of finding a max min over all 72 variables $c_0(k, \tau)$.

The program was written in FORTRAN for the BESM-6. Some subprograms were written in the assembly language MADLEN, to speed up the work. All the subprograms were stored in a magnetic tape library, and were called into the operational memory as needed. As a whole, the program contained about 800 executable statements. A single iteration required 15 to 20 seconds, depending on the mode of computation and the number of templates being optimized. The construction of a group of 14 templates consumed about four hours. The output of the program consisted of 72 templates for 53 classes, including the class for the blank character, with the value **EPA***$(C) = 3.2$.

Table 6.2 displays a more detailed characterization of the collection of templates, in the form of the values of

$$\widetilde{\mathbf{EPA}}(k, k', \hat{C}) = \min_{b, \tau'} \min_{\xi', \eta'} \mathbf{EPA}(k, b, k', \tau', \xi', \eta', \hat{C}),$$

for certain pairs of classes k and k'. This represents an upper bound for the probability that an image of the kth class will be wrongly assigned to the class k', given the worst-case values of b, τ', ξ', and η'. It is clear from Table 6.2 that there are comparatively few classes for which $\widetilde{\mathbf{EPA}}(k, k', C)$ does not exceed 4.0.

Table 6.2

	В₁	В₂	Я₁	Я₂	Н₁	Н₂	ь₁	ь₂	Б₁	Б₂	И₁	И₂
В₁			—	—	6.1	6.4	3.9	4.8	3.7	4.0	—	—
В₂			—	—	5.6	6.1	6.9	4.5	4.0	4.0	—	—
Я₁	8.6	—			5.3	6.3	—	—	—	—	7.7	8.7
Я₂	7.6	9.4			5.0	5.2	—	—	—	—	8.4	7.2
Н₁	5.4	6.3	4.7	6.0			—	—	6.9	5.0	3.7	4.7
Н₂	5.1	6.1	4.2	4.5			—	—	7.7	5.7	4.9	4.2
ь₁	3.5	5.1	—	—	—	8.8			3.9	5.1	—	—
ь₂	3.7	4.4	—	—	—	—			5.3	5.6	—	—
Б₁	4.4	3.2	—	—	9.0	7.7	4.1	5.3			—	—
Б₂	5.1	3.5	—	—	8.8	9.1	5.9	5.1			—	—
И₁	—	—	—	—	6.0	7.8	—	—	—	—		
И₂	—	—	—	—	9.3	8.6	—	—	—	—		

Figure 6.6 Templates constructed for the characters "P", "Г", "E". The numbers represent rounded values of the positive (white) components; the letters E, д, T, ч, П, represent negative (black) components, from −1 to −5, respectively. The components of the background are omitted, for better visual comprehension.

Figure 6.6 displays representations of some templates generated by the program. The components are represented by symbols corresponding to rounded values as described in the caption of the figure. For practical use of the templates in the reader, a special subroutine was written to convert the values of the components into resistances that would embody the components in the machine. They were rounded off to standard resistance values, and the values of **EPA***(C) were tested after the rounding; a supplementary correction of the components was made whenever as a result of the rounding the value of **EPA***(C) was significantly decreased.

The effectiveness of the templates, measured by the error probability, was tested experimentally in two steps. In the first step, the recognition process was modeled on the BESM-6 computer. For this purpose typewritten documents were produced, containing 72 images for each symbol of the alphabet, with varying stroke widths and differing degrees of

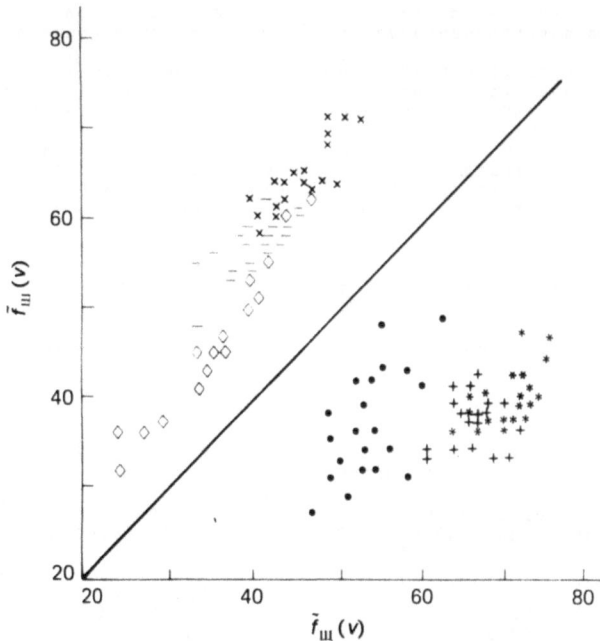

Figure 6.7 Two-dimensional similarity diagram for the characters "Ш" and "Щ"; ◊ and · represent images with thin lines; × and ∗ those with lines of medium thickness; - and + those with thick lines.

The two-dimensional diagram is descriptive, and permits us to see how the similarity is affected by random defects together with such factors as stroke width, contrast, etc. It can be used to obtain a sampling estimate of **EPA**, compare it with the values of **EPA** computed during the construction of the templates and, more importantly, make informal corrections to the decision rule to provide a minimum error probability for the real images rather than the model images. In this way, the error probability for some classes was significantly lowered by changes in the values of $c_0(k, \tau)$. The construction of a large number of such diagrams enabled us to detect a number of previously unknown pairs of classes difficult for recognition, and permitted us to analyse and to remove the causes of errors [12].

In the second step of the verification, the templates were realized by circuits in the reader, and were tested by multiple readings of a large mass of documents, containing more than 100,000 symbols. This trial showed that with medium quality print, attainable on ordinary typing paper, with ordinary ribbons (medium inking), the upper confidence limit for the error probability at the 95% fiducial probability was 2.7×10^{-4} for the whole alphabet, and 2.4×10^{-5} for numerical characters [16]. The results of these experiments are described in more detail in Section 9.5.

contrast; in all, there were 3744 images. These documents were fed to the scanning unit of the reader, and the digitized images were punched on tape and sent to the computer. A special computer program emulated exactly the decision rule embodied in the reader. The computer tallied the number of errors and rejections and printed out all the information needed for analysis of the cause of the errors.

Another special program constructed the so-called two-dimensional diagrams of the similarity. In such a diagram, for each image used in the experiment a point is plotted with coordinates equal to the values of the two discriminant functions

$$\tilde{f}_k(v) = \max_\tau \max_{\xi, \eta} \left[v, \mathcal{T}_{\xi, \eta} c(k, \tau) \right], \qquad k = k^1, k^2.$$

Each function is equal to the maximum similarity of the given image v for all templates of the kth class and for all admissible translations. For the images of a given class, the maximum similarity was determined with respect to the proper templates of the class and the templates of an alien class. A specimen diagram is displayed in Figure 6.7 for the classes Ш and Ш.

6.6 Conclusions

The method that we have described for optimizing piecewise linear decision rules allows us to solve the important applied problem of designing the recognizer for a character reader. It can be widely applied to the solution of various problems of learning and recognition. It is applicable when the available information on the sets of images (or more generally, signals) to be recognized allows us to count on achieving a satisfactory probability of correct recognition by the use of a piecewise linear decision rule containing a limited number of linear components. This occurs when the signals corresponding to the different classes can be divided into subsets such that the convex hulls of subsets belonging to different classes do not intersect. If the probability distributions of the signals can be approximated satisfactorily by the normal distribution depending on a nuisance parameter b, or by a distribution with independent components likewise depending on the parameter b, the success of the method depends on the size of the set B_k consisting of the values assumed by the nuisance parameter for each class k.

It would appear that the optimization process can be improved and simplified by introducing for each class a criterion of Neyman–Pearson type, with the given class as hypothesis and all other classes as alternatives. The criteria should be chosen so that for a given k and all $b \in B_k$ the probability of a Type-I error does not exceed a predetermined significance level α, and the probability of a Type-II error, maximized over all the other classes, should be minimal. Every such criterion for the kth class may be piecewise linear, i.e., may have the form

$$f_k(v) = \ulcorner \max_\tau \max_{\xi, \eta} \left[v, \mathcal{T}_{\xi, \eta} c(k, \tau) \right] > \vartheta \urcorner,$$

where $\mathcal{T}_{\xi, \eta}$ is an integer translation. The decision rule will have the form

$$d = \left(\sum_k k f_k(v) \right) \ulcorner \sum_k f_k(v) = 1 \urcorner,$$

i.e., $d = k$ if $f_k(v) = 1$ and $f_{k'}(v) = 0$ for all $k' \neq k$. If $f_k(v) = 1$ for more than one value of k, the decision will be to reject, i.e., to conclude that the image v is not legible. Such a decision corresponds to the value $d = 0$. The collection C of templates $c(k, \tau)$ should be chosen so as to minimize the maximum value of the probability of rejection, evaluated over all values of k and b.

This formulation of the problem permits us to choose the parameters of the criteria, and in particular the components of the templates for a given class, independently of the criteria for other classes; and this essentially simplifies the solution of the optimization problem. Moreover, it guarantees that the error probability for an arbitrary class does not exceed the predetermined significance level. The success of the optimization influences only the probability of rejection. The solution of the optimization problem can be obtained by the method described above. We may expect that the solution of this problem will yield good results in its applications.

CHAPTER VII

The Reference-Sequence Method

In Chapter V we studied a general approach to the recognition problem, based on the construction of a model of the image-generating process. Such a model yields a parametrized set of reference images, or prototypes. The observed images arise by superposition of random noise onto the prototypes. The criterion of similarity between the observed image and the prototype is the corresponding likelihood, treated as a function of the parameters of the prototype. Recognition consists in determining those values of the parameters that maximize the similarity between the prototype and the observed image.

The maximization of a function of many variables is very difficult in the general case. In Chapter V we described the correlation method for recognition; this is successful in the relatively simple case when the prototype is characterized by four nuisance parameters only. If there are many nuisance parameters, we cannot find the maximum similarity by an enumeration of all parameter values. There exists, however, a rather broad class of recognition problems for which certain assumptions about the properties of the images allow us to apply the methods of dynamic programming in the search for this maximum. These assumptions deal with the structure of the prototypes and with the characteristics of the noise.

The task of recognizing a complex image by means of dynamic programming was first formulated in connection with the separation of the noisy images of typewritten lines into different symbols [35]. A similar method for the recognition of speech signals was independently developed in 1967 by T. K. Vincjuk. Later a few papers of other authors on speech recognition by dynamic-programming methods appeared. The technique was applied to image recognition by the author [38–40, 84] and by a few others: W. Görke [80], V. M. Šarypanov and M. I. Šlezinger [68] and A. Martelli and U. Montanari [85]. There are more recent papers by T. Huang and K. S. Fu [81] on stochastic grammars, in which a similar though essentially different approach is described.

7.1 Formal Statement of the Structural-Description Problem

The recognition parameter k in an image-processing problem is not necessarily a simple class index. It may be necessary, in some cases, to find a structural description of an image, i.e., to indicate how it was assembled from a collection of predefined parts, and how these parts are distributed in the image. This problem has been studied by Kirsch [82], Narasimhan [50, 51], Romanov [59], and others.

As explained in Section 1.1, the term "structural description" has a special meaning different from that of the general term "description" used throughout Chapter IV. We shall consider here, in Chapter VII, only the structural descriptions, though the term "structural" may be omitted for brevity. In most of the published papers the structural description has been seen as the result of syntactical analysis of the images, which are composed by definite rules like the phrases in a formal grammar. However, a description resulting from syntactical analysis can be obtained only for ideal images composed in strict accord with the given syntactical rules. Real images are distorted by random noise and therefore cannot be subject to syntactical analysis. We are greatly interested in a formal statement of the problem of describing real images and in methods for its solution.

As before, we shall think of an observed image as the result of the distortion by noise of some prototype depending on certain parameters; that is, we shall begin with the model of an image class described by (2.4). We shall suppose that the prototypes are complex images composed of given elementary images according to definite rules, and that the random noise is described by some known probability distribution.

We look on the problem of describing the image as a search for those elementary images and that sequence of rules for which the composite prototype has maximum similarity to the observed image. The rules for composing a prototype from elementary images, and those images themselves, must conform to those syntactical rules and elementary concepts in terms of which the desired structural description is to be expressed.

Thus, instead of one single recognition parameter we shall consider a whole collection of parameters characterizing the different parts of the prototype and their mutual collocations. We had just such a situation in mind at the end of Chapter II when we proposed to consider the recognition parameter as multidimensional in the general case.

We may pose several different recognition problems for a single class of images. Depending on the concrete problem, we may regard the same parameters as the recognition or the nuisance parameters. In the maximum-likelihood method there is no distinction; the maximum must be sought over all values of both the recognition and the nuisance parameters. Therefore in this chapter we shall not make the distinction. We shall suppose that in the general case the recognition parameters are functions of a collection of parameters that completely describes the elementary images from which the prototypes are made up according to the given rules.

When the prototypes depend on many parameters we shall mean by recognition the verification of certain conditions superposed on the parameter estimates (as opposed to the problem of structural description, as just now formulated). These conditions must be satisfied if the given image is a member of a definite class.

As an example of such a problem with many recognition parameters we may cite the recognition of sequences of letters, which we treat in Chapter VIII. In this task for each unsegmented typewritten line we must define the class (the name) of each of the characters and in some cases even their joint collocations.

7.2 Formal Syntactical Rules For Constructing Composite Images

The synthesis of composite images from elementary images is founded on formal rules governing the composition of the elements. These rules are a species of formal grammar, and they impose definite restrictions on the images constructed in accordance with them and on the descriptions that can be obtained via the process of structural analysis. Therefore, the formal language for description of images is related to the structure of the images in the class under consideration.

In the theory of formal languages [19] a *grammar* is a collection of rules of a definite form, by which we construct sequences (phrases) from a given alphabet $\mathfrak{B} = \{ \beta_i : i = 1, 2, \ldots, n_T \}$ of *terminal symbols*. There is also an auxiliary alphabet of n_{NT} nonterminal symbols:

$$\mathfrak{S} = \{ \sigma_k : k = 0, 1, 2, \ldots, (n_{NT} - 1) \}.$$

The rules take the form of substitutions. Each rule permits substitution of a short chain of adjacent terminal and nonterminal symbols in place of some other such chain. The sequence of substitutions must begin with a substitution applied to an initial symbol σ_0.

The simplest grammars are the *finite-state* ones, in which the substitution rules are customarily of the form

$$\sigma_k \rightarrow \beta_i \sigma_l, \tag{7.1}$$

where σ_k and σ_l are nonterminal symbols and β_i is a terminal symbol. The arrow symbol between σ_k and $\sigma_i\beta_l$ denotes the substitution of the string $\sigma_i\beta_l$ in place of σ_k. For instance, the sequence of substitutions

$$\sigma_0 \rightarrow \beta_1\sigma_1; \quad \sigma_1 \rightarrow \beta_2\sigma_2; \quad \sigma_2 \rightarrow \beta_3\sigma_3,$$

applied to the given initial nonterminal σ_0 and to the successive substitution results, yields the sequence of successively transformed strings

$$\sigma_0; \quad \beta_1\sigma_1; \quad \beta_1\beta_2\sigma_2; \quad \beta_1\beta_2\beta_3\sigma_3.$$

Every rule of the form (7.1) states which of the terminal symbols β_i may be written at the right end of a given string of terminal symbols followed by a nonterminal σ_k. Furthermore, it indicates that the continuation of the string to the right of β_i should be of type σ_l. In other words, the rule (7.1) deciphers the first step of the admitted extension of the string being constructed, if this extension is of type σ_k, and also shows that the next step (following the first) in the extension should be a continuation of type σ_l.

To represent a two-dimensional image as a sequence, we must consider the *process* of composing an image from elementary images or *elements*. The elements, which must be pictured one after the other in a definite order to obtain a composite image, form a sequence corresponding to that image. We may imagine that we have prepared in advance a set of thin transparent cards, of a standard size and shape, each bearing some elementary image $e(b)$. The variable b may take on the values $\beta_1, \beta_2, \ldots$, i.e., in place of b we may substitute some terminal symbol. To each terminal symbol β_i of the given alphabet there will now correspond a definite elementary image $e(\beta_i)$, where b is a parameter characterizing this image and β_i is its value. The rules of the grammar say which card we should choose to place on the stack of images already chosen, in such a way that the edges of the cards coincide. The result of stacking all the chosen cards is a composite image E, composed according to the given rules.

We shall suppose, as before, that E and $e(b)$ are represented by N-dimensional vectors whose components express the gray shade of retina cells. We construct E from the elementary images by an operation on the components which corresponds to the superposition of elementary images:

$$E = \mathop{J}_{j=1}^{m} e(b_j), \tag{7.2}$$

where j is the index of the steps in the construction of E. The operation J may be the ordinary addition of the components, or their disjunction if they are binary, or any other suitable operation. Each of the variables b_j, $j = 1, 2, \ldots, m$, in (7.2) assumes one of the values β_i belonging to the alphabet $\mathfrak{B}$ of terminal symbols.

The various images E may be composed by constructing different sequences $b_1, b_2, \ldots, b_m$ in accordance with the rules of the given grammar.

Let us now look at a graphical method for writing the rules for forming a sequence, which will be more suitable than (7.1) in our future work. We note first that the grammar may specify more than one sequence resulting from the initial nonterminal symbol σ_0, and then there will be more than one substitution corresponding to some given nonterminal σ_k. The substitutions in this case will be written briefly in the form

$$\sigma_k \to \beta_{i_1}\sigma_{l_1} \mid \beta_{i_2}\sigma_{l_2} \mid \ldots \mid \beta_{i_p}\sigma_{l_p}. \tag{7.3}$$

We shall enumerate all the substitutions containing the same symbol σ_k on the left-hand side, using a parameter u which assumes integer values. We call it the *control* parameter. When constructing a composite image its value is chosen arbitrarily for each step. The choice of one sequence of control values as against another defines the selection of one concrete image made up according to the given rules.

By using the control variable, a substitution of the type of (7.3) can be written in functional form:

$$b_{j+1} = b(s_j, u_{j+1}), \tag{7.4}$$

$$s_{j+1} = S(s_j, u_{j+1}). \tag{7.5}$$

Here the indices j and $j+1$ refer to the jth and $(j+1)$st steps, respectively, in the construction of the complex image. The variable b_{j+1} and the function $b(s_j, u_{j+1})$ assume values in the alphabet $\mathfrak{B}$ of terminal symbols. The variables s_j and s_{j+1}, and the function $S(s_j, s_{j+1})$ take on values in the alphabet $\mathfrak{S}$ of nonterminal symbols. The variable u_{j+1} has integer values. The functions (7.4) and (7.5) may naturally be undefined for some integer values of u_{j+1}. For every value of $s \in \mathfrak{S}$ we may define a subset $U(s)$ of the values of the control variable admissible for s, i.e., the subset of values of u for which the functions $S(s, u)$ and $b(s, u)$ are defined for a given s.

It is well known that a finite-state grammar has much in common with a finite automaton. This is because the sequence of terminal symbols generated by such a grammar can be realized as a string of output symbols of a finite automaton. The inner state of the automaton corresponds to a nonterminal symbol σ_k, the output symbols are the terminal symbols β_i, and the controls represent the input signals. It is clear that the equations (7.4) and (7.5) respectively define the output function and the transition function of the automaton. From now on we shall abandon the term "nonterminal symbol" and use the equivalent term "state," which is shorter and more expressive.

The operation of a finite automaton can be described by a transition graph. The states (nonterminal symbols) are represented by vertices, and the several controls by oriented edges. As many edges leave a vertex s as there are different values for the control u at this vertex. The edge issuing from the vertex s and corresponding to a value u goes to the vertex $S(s,u)$. This edge is marked with the output (terminal) symbol $b = b(s,u)$. To every concrete admissible sequence $\beta_{i_1}, \beta_{i_2}, \ldots, \beta_{i_n}$ there corresponds a definite path, consisting of edges with the tail of each joined to the head of its predecessor.

In many cases, it will be convenient to define the subset $\mathfrak{S}_I$ consisting of initial vertices of the graph and the subset $\mathfrak{S}_F$ of final vertices. Every admissible path in the graph must begin at one of the vertices $s_0 \in \mathfrak{S}_I$ and end at one of the vertices $s_m \in \mathfrak{S}_F$. The several different admissible paths correspond to the various images E composed from the elementary images $e(b_j)$. Let us look at an example of a simple grammar defining the images of all possible continuous curves on a retina with 8×4 cells [Figure 7.1(a)]. The alphabet $\mathfrak{B}$ contains 32 terminal symbols β_{xy}, where $x = 1, \ldots, 8$ and $y = 1, \ldots, 4$. To every β_{xy} there corresponds an elementary image $e(\beta_{xy})$ consisting of one black cell in column x and row y [Figure 7.1(b)]. The alphabet $\mathfrak{S}$ of nonterminal symbols contains 32 symbols of the form σ_{xy}, $x = 1, \ldots, 8$, $y = 1, \ldots, 4$, plus the initial symbol σ_0. The symbols σ_{81}, σ_{82}, σ_{83}, and σ_{84} are final and form the subset $\mathfrak{S}_F$. The grammar is defined by the graph shown in Figure 7.1(c). The path shown on the graph by thick lines corresponds to the image E shown in Figure 7.1(a).

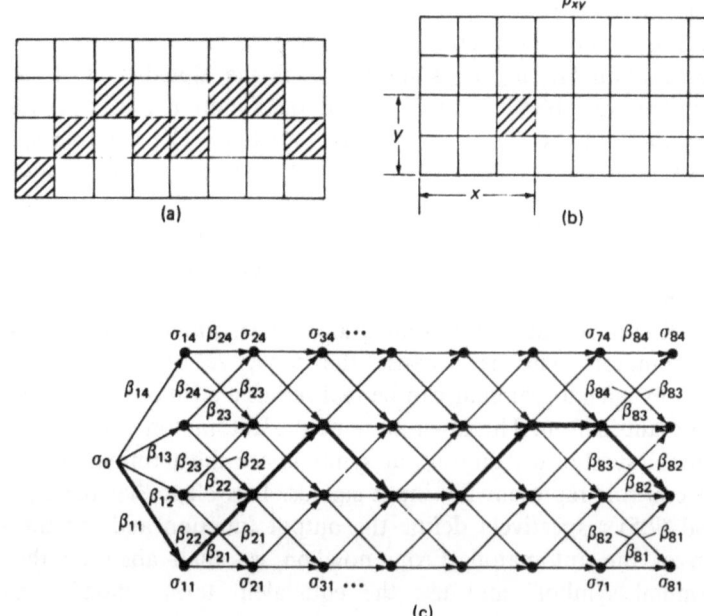

Figure 7.1 Graph defining the set of "continuous curves." (a) Example of a continuous curve; (b) elementary prototype; (c) graph.

In the sense of our present task, the graphs designed for the definition of a set of images cannot have either loops or cycles, since these would permit an infinite number of repetitions of the same elementary image, and this has no meaning for us. (Elementary images that differ by a translation are to be regarded as different and must be denoted by different terminal symbols.) We shall assume from now on that our graphs do not contain loops or cycles.

7.3 Solution of the Problem of Maximum Similarity

In the preceding section we set up a formalism that permits us to define sets of sequences of parameters b_j satisfying given constraints and corresponding sets of composite images with given properties. As we noted in Section 7.1, this formalism for composing complex images interests us primarily as a means for defining a set of prototypes. From now on we shall refer to a composite image as a *composite* prototype, and the elementary images that make it up will be called *elementary prototypes* or *elements*.

To solve the problem of the search for the composite prototype E most similar to a given image, we must express the similarity $g(v, E)$ of image and prototype in terms of the parameters b_j of the prototype E. The method we shall suggest is applicable when the overall similarity $g(v, E)$ can be expressed in terms of elementary similarities, i.e., similarities with the elementary prototypes $e(b)$. The overall similarity must depend monotonely on the elementary similarities; this happens, for instance, when the overall similarity is the sum or product of the elementary similarities, or the maximum, etc. We shall suppose, probably without loss of generality, that the overall similarity is the sum of the elementary similarities.

This requirement is met in the very important particular case when the similarity is expressed by the scalar product

$$g(v, E) = [v, E],$$

and the composite prototype is constructed by summing the elementary prototypes:

$$E = \sum_{j=1}^{m} e(b_j),$$

or, in component form:

$$E_i = \sum_{j} e_i(b_j), \qquad i = 1, 2, \ldots, N.$$

In fact, in this case

$$g(v, E) = \sum_{i=1}^{N} v_i E_i = \sum_{i=t}^{N} v_i \sum_{j=1}^{m} e_i(b_j)$$

$$= \sum_{j=1}^{m} \sum_{i=1}^{N} v_i e_i(b_j) = \sum_{j=1}^{m} g(v, e(b_j)).$$

Other cases are also of interest, however, namely when the criterion is the square of the Euclidean distance, or the Hamming distance, or more generally the logarithm of the likelihood function, or some other criterion. The requirement that the similarities be additive can be met by an arbitrary criterion that is expressible as a sum over the cells of the retina, by the following device.

For every value of the parameter b we define, apart from the elementary prototype $e(b)$, a so-called *window* $W(b)$ which is a subset of the retinal cells. The window is defined so that it contains the cells corresponding to the "essential" components of the elementary prototype $e(b)$. The rules defining the admissible sequences of values of the parameters b_j must be so constructed that the windows $W(b_j)$ for the members of an admissible sequence do not intersect. In the example given above, the window for each β_{xy} might consist of the vertical column x containing the single black cell corresponding to the elementary prototype $e(\beta_{xy})$.

We can use the windows to express an arbitrary criterion of similarity which is a sum over the retinal cells as a sum over the elementary images making up a composite prototype. We write

$$g(v, E) = \sum_{i=1}^{N} g_i(v_i, E_i), \tag{7.6}$$

where i is the cell index and N is the number of cells in the retina. Then we express the components E_i in terms of the components $e_i(b_j)$ of the elementary prototypes. For this we note that the procedure (7.2) for making up a composite prototype from elements can be represented in the following way by using nonintersecting windows:

$$\text{if } i \in W(b_j), \quad \text{then } E_i = e_i(b_j). \tag{7.7}$$

We resolve the sum in (7.6) into parts corresponding to the subsets $W(b_j)$, and we make the substitution (7.7) for each part:

$$g(v, E) = \sum_{j=1}^{m} \sum_{i \in W(b_j)} g_i(v_i, E_i) = \sum_{j=1}^{m} \sum_{i \in W(b_j)} g_i(v_i, e_i(b_j)).$$

The sum over $i \in W(b_j)$ on the right-hand side of this equation will be called an *elementary similarity* and denoted by

$$g^*(v, b_j) = \sum_{i \in W(b_j)} g_i(v_i, e_i(b_j)).$$

We note that we cannot regard it as a similarity $g(v, e(b_j))$ between the image v and the element $e(b_j)$, since $g^*(v, b_j)$ depends on the window $W(b_j)$ as well as on $e(b_j)$.

In accordance with (7.4), the parameter b_j is a function of the state s_{j-1} and the control u_j. Therefore an elementary similarity can be written in the form

$$g^*(v, b(s_{j-1}, u_j)) = g'(v, s_{j-1}, u_j)$$

$$= \sum_{i \in W(b(s_{j-1}, u_j))} g_i(v_i, e_i(b(s_{j-1}, u_j))), \qquad (7.8)$$

where the functions g_i, which may differ or be identical for different values of i, are terms in the given criterion of similarity (7.6). Then the overall similarity $g(v, E)$ can be written as a sum of elementary similarities:

$$g(v, E) = \sum_{j=1}^{m} g'(v, s_{j-1}, u_j), \qquad (7.9)$$

where the terms $g'(v, s_{j-1}, u_j)$ are defined by (7.8). The problem under consideration is to find the number of terms m and a sequence of control values $\{u_j : j = 1, 2, \ldots, m\}$ that will maximize the similarity (7.9) under the constraints (7.4) and (7.5), and under the additional condition that the value of s_0 belongs to the set of initial states and s_m to the set of final states.

The formulation of the image description problem just presented, and the technique for its solution that we are about to give, constitute the essence of the reference sequence method. The proposed technique is founded on the ideas of dynamic programming [6].

The problem can be most simply and clearly formulated in the language of graphs. We are given an antisymmetric graph without loops or cycles, whose vertices correspond to the states

$$s \in \mathfrak{S} = \{\sigma_k : k = 0, 1, 2, \ldots, (n_{\mathrm{NT}} - 1)\},$$

and whose oriented edges correspond to the pairs (s, u), where u is the control variable. The edge (s, u) issues from the vertex s and ends at the vertex $S(s, u)$. We are also given the initial subset $\mathfrak{S}_I$ and the final subset $\mathfrak{S}_F$ of vertices. We assign to every edge in the graph the conditional length $g'(v, s, u)$ equal to the similarity of the elementary prototype $e(b(s, u))$ with the image v within the boundaries of the window $W(b(s, u))$. The total length G of a path in the graph is defined as the sum of the elementary similarities $g'(v, s, u)$ corresponding to the several edges in it. We are required to find the path of maximum total length leading from any initial vertex to any final vertex whatever.

This is a particular case of the general dynamic-programming problem, and can be solved in the following way: A vertex not entered by any edge will be called a *source*, and a vertex from which no edges issue will be called a *sink*. We may assume that all the sources lie in the set $\mathfrak{S}_I$ of initial vertices and all the sinks in the set $\mathfrak{S}_F$, else there would be an edge not included in the set of admissible paths.

For computational convenience we also assume that all the final vertices are sinks. This causes no loss of generality, since if some final vertex σ_f happens not to be a sink, we attach to it an exit edge of length 0, label its other vertex a sink, and substitute it for σ_f in the set of final vertices.

We now introduce the notion of the *rank* of a vertex or state. We consider all paths leading from a given vertex s to one of the sinks, and we count the number of edges in each. The largest count so arrived at is called the *rank of the vertex s* or of the corresponding state. We denote it by $\Gamma(s)$.

The rank can be computed by the following simple algorithm, due to Ford [28]. We first set all $\Gamma(s) = 0$. Then we inspect all the vertices s in some fixed order, adopting a new value for $\Gamma(s)$ in accordance with the recursive relation

$$\Gamma'(s) = \max_{u \in U(s)} (\Gamma(S(s,u)) + 1), \tag{7.10}$$

where $\Gamma'(\cdot)$ is the newly adopted value and $\Gamma(\cdot)$ is the former value. The subset $U(s)$ and the function $S(s, u)$ are as defined earlier (cf. Section 7.2).

The vertices s are repeatedly inspected until we arrive at a situation when all the vertices s have been inspected in turn without changing at least one of the values $\Gamma(s)$. It is easy to see that the values $\Gamma(s)$ found in this way are the ranks of the vertices [28]. To find the path of maximum length we must introduce the notion of the *potentially maximal sum* $\hat{G}(s)$ for the vertex s, defined as follows: We consider all paths leading from s to some final vertex. We choose the one with the largest conditional length, i.e., the largest sum of the elementary similarities. We call the path the *final potentially optimal path*, or simply the potentially optimal path for s. We denote the length of this path as $\hat{G}(s)$.

The variable $\hat{G}(s)$ satisfies the recursive relationship

$$\hat{G}(s) = \max_{u \in U(x)} \left[g'(v, s, u) + \hat{G}(S(s, u)) \right]. \tag{7.11}$$

For, every path leaving s goes through one of the vertices $S(s, u)$ where $u \in U(s)$. To find the maximum length over all such paths we must inspect all the $u \in U(s)$ and, for each, inspect all the continuations leading from $S(s, u)$ to one of the final vertices. But the maximum over all the continuations is $\hat{G}(S(s, u))$ by definition of $\hat{G}(\cdot)$. Therefore the relation (7.11) defines the maximum length of the paths issuing from the vertex s.

The $\hat{G}(s)$, like $\Gamma(s)$, can be found by the Ford algorithm [28]. However, if the ranks of the vertices have already been computed, the process can be significantly simplified: if we compute according to (7.11) and inspect the vertices s in order of increasing rank, we can determine the $\hat{G}(s)$ one after the other, without backtracking over already inspected vertices. In fact, let us begin by setting $\hat{G}(s) = 0$ for all vertices for which $\Gamma(s) = 0$, i.e., for all sinks, since the length of paths issuing from these is zero. We have agreed that all sinks are final vertices. Next we compute $\hat{G}(s)$ for all vertices of rank 1. In the computation of $\hat{G}(s)$ by (7.11) we need to know the value of

$\hat{G}(S(s,u))$ for all the vertices reached by paths leaving from s. By the definition of the rank, all the edges leaving a given vertex must lead to vertices of lesser rank. Therefore when computing $\hat{G}(s)$ for vertices of rank 1, we need consider only vertices of rank 0.

After inspecting all the vertices of rank 1, we can investigate those of rank 2, and so on, until we reach the vertices of highest rank, which will be the sources.

Therefore, the use of (7.11) after the ranks have been computed will allow us to compute the values of $\hat{G}(s)$ for all vertices.

We note that the preliminary computation of the ranks is justified when the optimal path must be computed many times for the same graph with different edge lengths. Exactly this situation occurs in problems of image-recognition and structural-analysis: the configuration of the graph is determined by the rules for composing the prototypes, and is constant for all the images to be analyzed, since these act only on the conditional lengths of the edges. In the opposite case, $\hat{G}(s)$ is more easily computed by an immediate application of the Ford algorithm, that is, by repeated inspection of all the vertices and the assignment of new values to the variables $\hat{G}(s)$ by (7.11) until these values remain unchanged.

To find the optimal path we must find the maximum $\hat{\hat{G}}$ of the $\hat{G}(s)$ over all the initial vertices,

$$\hat{\hat{G}} = \max_{s \in \mathfrak{S}_I} \hat{G}(s),$$

and the corresponding initial vertex

$$\hat{\hat{s}}_0 = \arg\max_{s \in \mathfrak{S}_I} \hat{G}(s). \tag{7.12}$$

[We recall that the notation $\arg\max_x f(x)$ was introduced to represent any value of x for which the function $f(x)$ attains its maximum value.]

To be able to reconstruct the optimal sequence of controls $\{\hat{\hat{u}}_j\}$ corresponding to the path of maximum length, we must fix for each vertex s the *potentially optimal control** $\hat{u}(s)$ at the same time as we find the maximum in (7.11) and fix the value of $\hat{G}(s)$, i.e., we must find the value of u for which the maximum is attained:

$$\hat{u}(s) = \arg\max_{u \in U(x)} \left[g'(v,s,u) + \hat{G}(S(s,u)) \right]. \tag{7.13}$$

After all the $\hat{u}(s)$ and $\hat{\hat{s}}_0$ have been found, the optimal sequence is defined by the recursions

$$\left. \begin{array}{l} \hat{\hat{u}}_j = \hat{u}(\hat{\hat{s}}_{j-1}), \\ \hat{\hat{s}}_j = S(\hat{\hat{s}}_{j-1}, \hat{\hat{u}}_j) \end{array} \right\} \quad (j = 1,2,3,\ldots). \tag{7.14}$$

To construct the optimal path we must go from the vertex $\hat{\hat{s}}_0$ determined

---

* We shall mark potentially optimal quantities with the symbol "`^`" and optimal quantities with the double symbol "`^^`".

by (7.12) along the edge determined by the optimal control $\hat{u}_1 = \hat{u}(\hat{s}_0)$ to the vertex $\hat{s}_1 = S(\hat{s}_0, \hat{u}_1)$. We then find by (7.14) the next optimal control $\hat{u}_2 = \hat{u}(\hat{s}_1)$ and go to the vertex $\hat{s}_2 = S(\hat{s}_1, \hat{u}_2)$, and so on in turn until we reach one of the sinks.

As an example we shall solve the recognition problem for the very simple image depicted in Figure 7.2(b). The prototypes may be taken as all the sequences of adjacent black cells, one in each column of the retina. The set of all prototypes and the rule for constructing them were defined in the example in Section 7.2. The corresponding graph is shown in Figure 7.1(c).

To solve the problem we need as many pairs of memory cells as there are vertices in the graph. To make the solution visually observable, we distribute these memory cells so that they lie on the corresponding vertices. The graph shown in Figure 7.2(a) reproduces that of Figure 7.1(c); each pair of memory cells is depicted as a circle. We write the value of $\hat{G}(s)$ in each circle and draw an arrow beside it to fix the corresponding $\hat{u}(s)$, which determines the choice of an edge. We note that the column number in this example uniquely determines the rank $\Gamma(s)$ of the vertices in the corresponding column. To every edge in the graph there corresponds a given pair consisting of an elementary image $e(b)$ and window $W(b)$. The window for $b = \beta_{xy}$ is the column numbered x.

We take the Hamming distance as the similarity criterion:

$$g(v, E) = \sum_{i=1}^{8} \sum_{j=1}^{4} |v_{ij} - E_{ij}|,$$

where v_{ij} and E_{ij} are respectively the components of the image and the prototype corresponding to the cell (i, j) of the retina. The elementary similarity for the adopted set of windows is defined over a single column:

$$g^*(v, \beta_{xy}) = \sum_{j=1}^{4} |v_{xj} - e_{xj}(\beta_{xy})|.$$

Here $e_{xj}(\beta_{xj})$ is the (x, j)th component of the elementary image corresponding to β_{xy} (cf. Figure 7.1).

We compute the elementary similarity for all $e(\beta_{xy})$ with the image v depicted in Figure 7.2(b). We set the conditional lengths of the edges equal to the corresponding elementary similarities, as shown in Figure 7.2(a). (We put $g^* = 0$ for images identical inside the corresponding window column, and $g^* = 2$ for all others.) Since the likelihood is a monotone decreasing function of the Hamming distance [cf. (2.8)], we need to find the path of *minimum* length from the initial vertex to one of the final vertices. This means that we must replace max and argmax by min and argmin, respectively, in (7.11), (7.12), and (7.13).

In keeping with the rules we have already defined, we set $\hat{G}(\sigma_{81})$, $\hat{G}(\sigma_{82})$, $\hat{G}(\sigma_{83})$ and $\hat{G}(\sigma_{84})$ equal to 0, i.e., we write 0 in the circles in the rightmost column. Then we compute $\hat{G}(\sigma_{71})$, $\hat{G}(\sigma_{72})$, $\hat{G}(\sigma_{73})$, and $\hat{G}(\sigma_{74})$. To compute

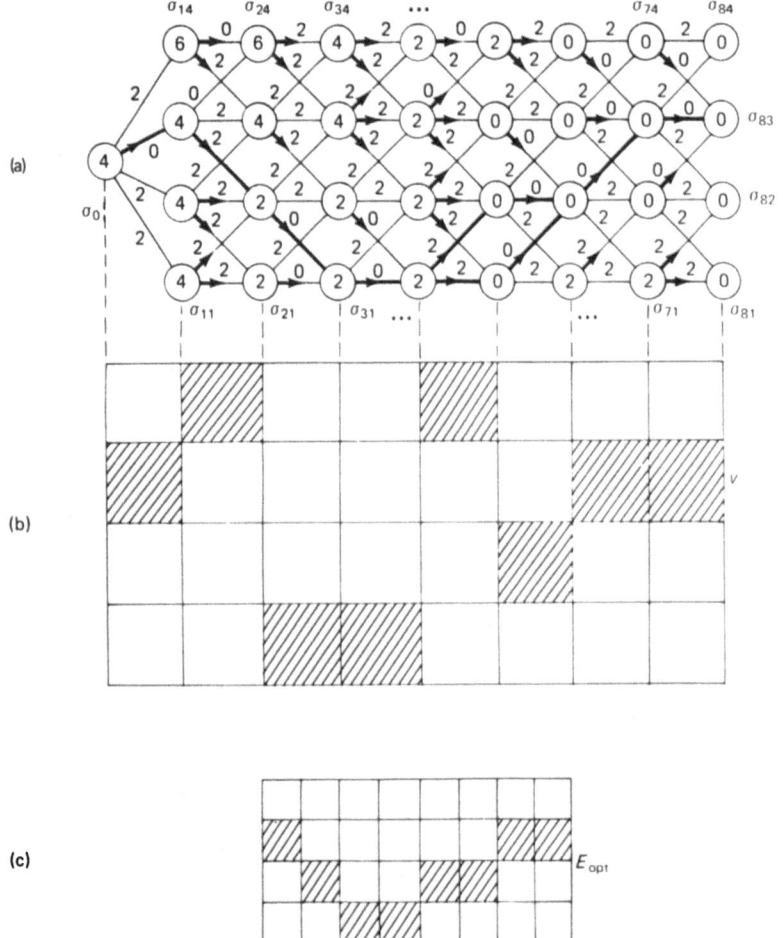

Figure 7.2   A recognition example. (a) Graph showing the values of the elementary similarities, potentially minimal sums, and the resultant optimal path (two variants); (b) the analyzed image; (c) the optimal prototype.

$\hat{G}(\sigma_{74})$, for instance, we go along the edges issuing from σ_{74} and find

$$g'(v, \sigma_{74}, 0) + \hat{G}(\sigma_{84}) = 2 + 0 = 2$$

and

$$g'(v, \sigma_{74}, 1) + \hat{G}(\sigma_{83}) = 0 + 0 = 0.$$

Then we choose the lesser of these values and mark the corresponding edge with an arrow attached to the circle.

We carry out a similar computation for all the vertices, in order of their increasing rank. The path of minimum length is traversed by moving from the initial vertex along the arrows attached to the circles. This path, which is marked in Figure 7.2(a) by a heavy line, corresponds to the prototype that is closest to the image. The prototype is shown in Figure 7.2(c) and the image in Figure 7.2(b). The value of $\hat{G}(\sigma_0)$ indicates that the Hamming distance between image and optimal prototype has the value 4.

7.4 Images on a Two-Dimensional Retina

We shall consider the case in which the components of the vectors v, $e(b)$, and E are not merely sets of independent quantities. For images, it is meaningful to speak of neighboring components and of a partial or complete ordering of the set of components. Having defined some of the components of the composite prototype E in the process of constructing it, we may go to its neighbors, and then to the neighbors of these, and so on. The construction of the prototype in this case is like a process that evolves in space.

We shall suppose that the retina cells are associated with the points of a discrete two-dimensional vector space R^2. This postulate is necessary so that we may define a composition operation on the retina cells to correspond to the translation of images. Then to every cell there corresponds a vector $r \in R^2$, with components that may, for instance, be a column number x and a row number y. (The rows are numbered from bottom to top, in order to conserve the usual directions of the coordinate axes.)

An arbitrary elementary prototype may be translated with respect to the retina, i.e., it may be located in various places in the retina. We assume that most of the components of such a prototype are equal to zero, and a translation is allowed only if all the components falling outside the retina have the value zero.

We shall refer to elementary prototypes that differ only by a translation as having the same *type*. It is then expedient to replace the parameter b of the elementary prototype $e(b)$ by two parameters: one, denoted by τ, defining the type of the prototype, and the other, $\rho \in R^2$, defining its location, i.e., the retina cell containing a definite point of the prototype. We call ρ the *origin* of the elementary prototype $e(\rho, \tau)$. Figure 7.3 displays an example of an elementary prototype of given type, and three positions of it in the retina. When we need to introduce the windows $W(b)$, they will be defined by the same two parameters and will be written as $W(\rho, \tau)$.

In most problems it is natural to suppose that the process of constructing prototypes is homogeneous, i.e., to suppose that the type of the elementary prototype following an already constructed portion of the prototype E will depend only on the types of the preceding elements, and will not depend on its position in the retina. On the other hand, the position of the newly added element depends only on the position of the end of the previously constructed portion. In some cases there may be a need to make a jump, i.e., to go ahead with the construction in a place

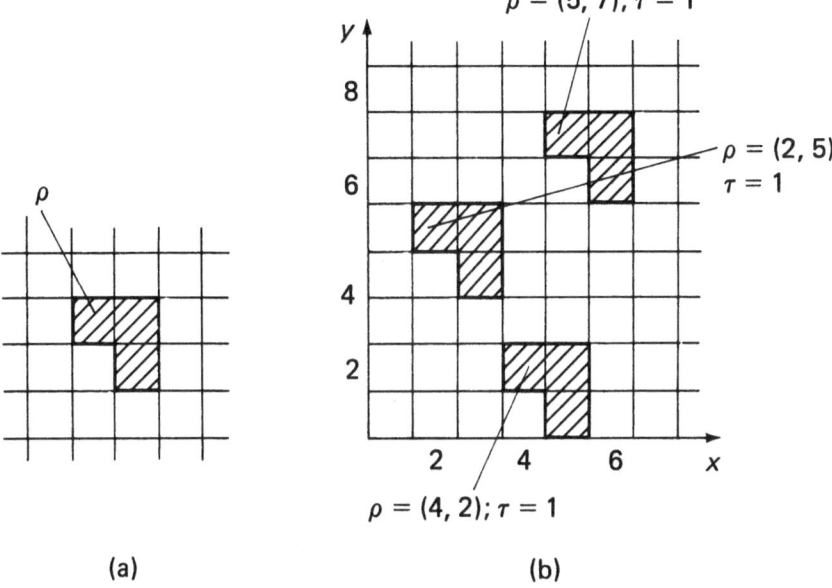

Figure 7.3   Elementary prototypes on a two-dimensional retina.

different from the end of the preceding construction. Then we may provide an elementary prototype with zero similarity which serves only to move the end of the existing construction to any desired retina cell.

With these assumptions, the state s in (7.4) and (7.5) may be defined by two independent variables. One of these, denoted by z, defines the successive values of τ, and the other, r, defines the values of ρ. The transitions between the states s are defined in the present case by graphs of a special kind, which we shall call *homogeneous*, defined as follows.

Suppose that the vertices of the graph have been indexed by the two discrete variables r and z. This means that to select a given vertex we need to specify the pair of variables (r, z). We shall call z the *type* of the state. The values of r, which we call the *location*, will be identified with the points in the discrete vector space R^2, which correspond to the retina cells. We write R_N^2 to denote the subset of the points of R^2 that correspond to the N cells in our retina.

We first assign to each edge of the graph a definite value of τ. Then we choose two arbitrary pairs of vertices in the graph $\{(r, z_1), (r + \Delta, z_2)\}$ and $\{(r_1, z_1), (r_1 + \Delta, z_2)\}$ with the same vector Δ in both pairs; i.e., the second pair is obtained from the first by a translation in the retina. All four vectors r, $r + \Delta$, r_1, and $r_1 + \Delta$ must belong to R_N^2. If for every oriented edge joining the vertices in the first pair we can find a corresponding edge for the second pair issuing from a vertex of the same type (z_1 or z_2) and marked with the same value of τ, and if this is true for every edge in the second pair, the graph is said to be *homogeneous in the variable* r.

The parameters ρ_{j+1} and τ_{j+1} of the elementary prototype $e(b_{j+1})$, being the components of b_{j+1}, are functions of s_j and u_{j+1}, by (7.4), and are therefore now functions of r_j, z_j, and u_{j+1}. (We recall that j is the index of the step that consists in adding the jth elementary prototype to the preexisting portion of the complex prototype E.) We shall consider only those rules for which ρ_{j+1} depends on r_j, z_j, and u_{j+1} in the following way:

$$\rho_{j+1} = r_j. \tag{7.15}$$

The definition of a homogeneous graph implies that τ_{j+1} does not depend on r_j, i.e.,

$$\tau_{j+1} = T(z_j, u_{j+1}). \tag{7.16}$$

For a homogeneous graph, (7.4) is to be replaced by (7.15) and (7.16).

It also follows from the same definition that the function f expressing the dependence of r_{j+1} on r_j must satisfy the condition $f(r_j + \Delta, z_j, u_{j+1}) = f(r_j, z_j, u_{j+1}) + \Delta$. In other words, when the point r_j is displaced by an arbitrary amount Δ, the point r_{j+1} must be displaced by the same amount. This means that

$$r_{j+1} = r_j + \Delta(z_j, u_{j+1}). \tag{7.17}$$

The variable z_{j+1} does not depend on r_j:

$$z_{j+1} = Z(z_j, u_{j+1}). \tag{7.18}$$

For a homogeneous graph Equation (7.5) is to be replaced by (7.17) and (7.18).

Let us look at the peculiarities of a homogeneous graph that will be used in specifying the rules for assembling elementary prototypes $e(\rho, \tau)$ into a composite prototype. The location denoted by r_j in (7.15) may be interpreted as the retina cell in which the jth step of the assembling process has ended, or, more precisely, the place from which the assembling is to be continued. The new elementary prototype $e(\rho_{j+1}, \tau_{j+1})$ which is to be added in the state (r_j, z_j) must have its origin at the point r_j. The point r_{j+1}, from which the new construction is to be continued, is displaced by the vector quantity $\Delta(z_j, u_{j+1})$. This, as well as the type z_{j+1} of the new state, is independent of the position. Thus a homogeneous graph, defined by the equations (7.15)–(7.18), defines a rule for constructing prototype images on a retina, under which the type and relative position of the elementary prototype to be attached to the already constructed portion of the prototype do not depend on the location of the end of that portion, but only on its configuration. In other words, the construction rule defined by a homogeneous graph is position-independent.

A homogeneous graph can be defined by much more economical and perspicuous methods than an arbitrary graph. It suffices to define the type transitions (7.18) by a special and often very simple graph, and to

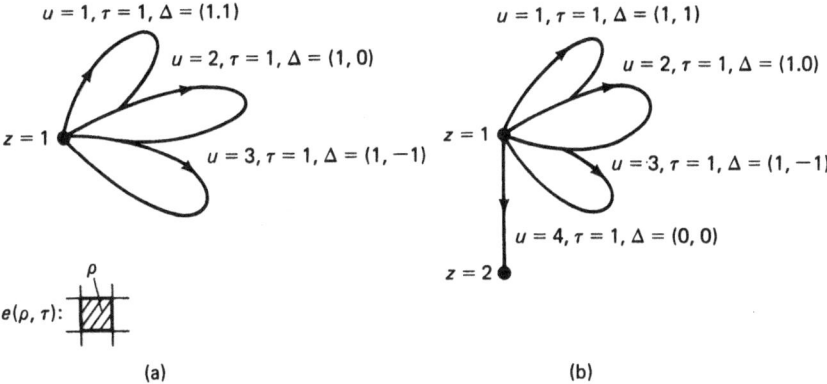

Figure 7.4   Type graph and elementary prototype for the example given in Figure 7.1: (a) with origin and end on the boundary of the retina; (b) with origin and end at arbitrary points.

determine for each edge of this graph the corresponding values of u, τ and Δ. For instance, the graph shown in Figure 7.1(c) may be easily made into a homogeneous graph if we replace the vertex σ_0 by four vertices $\sigma_{01}, \sigma_{02}, \sigma_{03}, \sigma_{04}$ forming a null column and placed like the vertices $\sigma_{11}-\sigma_{14}$ in the first column. On this graph all the vertices are of the same type. The transitions (7.18) can be defined by a very simple graph, as shown in Figure 7.4(a). The vector r takes on 32 values, corresponding to all the retina cells.

We shall refer to a graph corresponding to (7.18) as a *type graph*. As opposed to this, a graph whose vertices correspond to the pairs (r, z) will be called an *expanded graph*. The subsets of initial and final states may be variously defined in the case of a type graph. If the lines (or other details) of the prototype images being defined by a type graph must begin and end on the boundaries of the retina, the initial and final states of the corresponding expanded graph must be those sources and sinks which arise due to cutting its edges at the boundaries. This is a natural consequence of the fact that an expanded graph cannot contain an edge corresponding to an elementary prototype that lies entirely or partly outside the retina. On the other hand, it must contain edges corresponding to *all* the admissible elementary prototypes. Sometimes it is necessary to admit vertices lying outside the retina in order to meet this requirement. For instance, if we associate the vertices of the graph in Figure 7.1(c) with the cells in Figure 7.1(b), either σ_0 or the vertices $\sigma_{81}-\sigma_{84}$ will lie outside the retina. This awkwardness is easily avoided (for a rectangular retina) if we associate the vertices of an expanded graph with the nodes rather than the cells of the retina, i.e., with the vertices of the cells. This was done in Figure 7.2(a) and (b).

When we need to define a set of images whose outlines can begin and end in arbitrary cells, special vertices must be introduced into the type graph, at least for the final states. These vertices are sinks in the type graph. We do this for the reason given in Section 7.3: for computational convenience, all final states must be sinks, although the initial states need not be sources. For instance, in Figure 7.1, if the sequence of black cells beginning and ending in arbitrary cells of the retina are to be admissible, we must introduce the vertex $z = 2$ in the type graph and make it a sink. A graph of this kind is shown in Figure 7.4(b). In this case, the vertices of the graph may be associated indifferently with the cells or nodes of the retina.

Figure 7.1 shows that the type graph, for the variable z, may have loops. In general, it may also contain cycles. This, of course, does not prevent us from solving the problem of finding the longest or the shortest path, since the path is not drawn on the type graph, but rather on the expanded graph with the vertices (r, z), in which there are no loops or cycles.

The optimal path on a homogeneous graph is computed just as it is in the general case. The recursive relation for computing the potentially maximal sums for a homogeneous graph may be found by replacing the variable s in (7.11) with the pair of variables r and z. At the same time we must take account of the relations (7.17) and (7.18). The elementary similarity $g'(v, r, z, u)$ is computed as it was in the general case (7.8):

$$g'(v, r, z, u) = \sum_{i \in W(r, \tau)} g_i(v_i, e_i(r, \tau)), \qquad (7.19)$$

where, by (7.16), $\tau = T(z, u)$; the elementary prototypes $e(r, \tau)$, the windows $W(r, \tau)$, and the similarity $g_i(v_i, e_i)$ for the ith component are to be defined simultaneously with the graph and with the equations (7.16)–(7.18). The set $U(z)$ of controls for a state of type z is defined by the type graph. The fact that this set does not depend on r follows from the definition of a homogeneous graph. With all this said, we may now transform (7.11) into the form

$$\hat{G}(r, z) = \max_{u \in U(z)} \left[g'(v, r, z, u) + \hat{G}(r + \Delta(z, u), Z(z, u)) \right]. \quad (7.20)$$

In a similar way we transform (7.13):

$$\hat{u}(r, z) = \arg \max_{u \in U(z)} \left[g'(v, r, z, u) + \hat{G}(r + \Delta(z, u), Z(z, u)) \right]. \quad (7.21)$$

The ranks of the states are in general defined in the same way as before.

The computations begin with the assignment of $\hat{G}(r, z) = 0$ for all final states. After all the $\hat{G}(r, z)$ have been calculated, we find the initial state for which $\hat{G}(r, z)$ is maximal:

$$\hat{r}_0 = \arg \max_r \max_{z \in \mathcal{J}_I} \hat{G}(r, z); \qquad (7.22)$$

$$\hat{z}_0 = \arg \max_{z \in \mathcal{J}_I} \max_r \hat{G}(r, z). \qquad (7.23)$$

Here $\mathfrak{Z}_I$ is the set of initial types of the states. To re-create the optimal path on the expanded graph we go from the optimal initial state $(\hat{\vec{r}}_0, \hat{\vec{z}}_0)$ along the edges corresponding to the equations (7.21) of potentially optimal controls. The optimal sequence of states is defined by the following recursion relations:

$$
\left.\begin{aligned}
\hat{\vec{u}}_j &= \hat{u}(\hat{\vec{r}}_{j-1}, \hat{\vec{z}}_{j-1}), \\
\hat{\vec{z}}_j &= Z(\hat{\vec{z}}_{j-1}, \hat{\vec{u}}_j), \\
\hat{\vec{r}}_j &= \hat{\vec{r}}_{j-1} + \Delta(\hat{\vec{u}}_j).
\end{aligned}\right\} \quad (j = 1, 2, 3, \ldots). \qquad (7.24)
$$

Here the values of $\hat{\vec{r}}_0$ and $\hat{\vec{z}}_0$ are defined by (7.22) and (7.23).

7.5 Recognition of Lines with Restricted Change of Direction

Let us consider a simple special case of the general scheme we have just described. Suppose that we need to recognize and/or to define structural descriptions of lines having the property that the directions of arbitrary chords joining two points on a line lie in one of a given set of sectors. The number of sectors may in principle be arbitrary, and they may intersect or not. In our very simple example we shall divide all the directions lying within 180° limits (directions differing by 180° will be considered identical) into four nonintersecting sectors of 45° each. We first look at the process, corresponding to one of these sectors, of building approximately vertical lines, i.e., lines whose chords deviate from the vertical by no more than half the width of the sector. We shall have to take into account the specific nature of the digitized representation of images of lines. We shall deal with images on a retina with square cells forming vertical columns and horizontal rows (Figure 7.5). Thin lines are represented on such a retina by chains of adjoining black cells. The direction of a chord joining the centers of two cells that immediately adjoin each other may take on only four discrete values differing by 45°. Therefore the constraints described above, on the directions of the chords, can be applied only to sufficiently long chords. In our case, with inclinations of the order of 45°/2, we may confine our attention to chords of length 2, i.e., chords joining the centers of sequentially adjacent cells with indices j and $j + 2$. The maximum deviation from the vertical is then $\pm 27°$ (which is a little larger than we want), and the deviation from a line drawn at an angle of 45° is 18°. With tighter constraints we would need to consider longer chords.

The process of constructing a chain of black cells consists of sequential steps, each one adding a new black cell to the chain. A step is characterized by a vector issuing from the center of the last cell in the chain and ending in the center of its successor, i.e., the vector Δ in Equation (7.17).

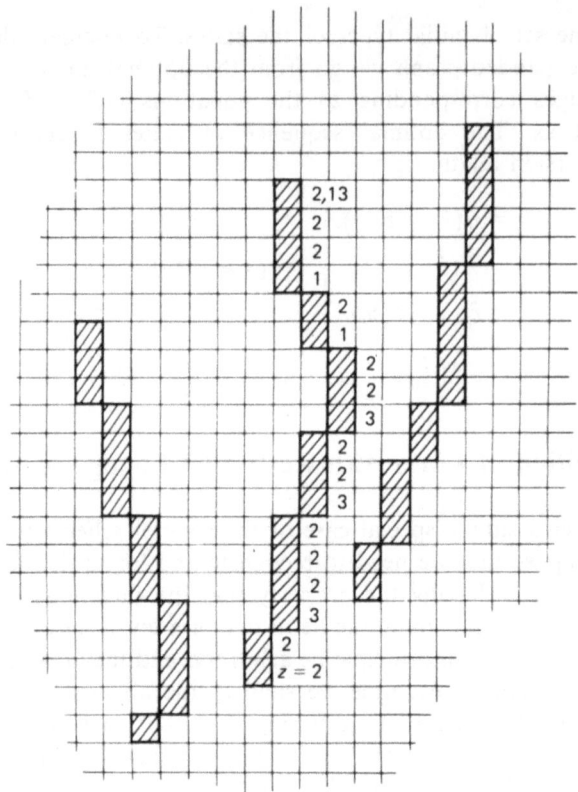

Figure 7.5   Examples of approximately vertical lines. The numbers indicate types of states (see the text).

To specify the stated constraints for a vertical sector the rules for constructing a chain of black cells must forbid the appearance of a sequence of two steps deviating from the basic direction—in this case the vertical. A similar prohibition applies in respect of other sectors. These rules are representable by the type graph shown in Figure 7.6. Each of the four petals in the graph corresponds to one of the four designated sectors. The circles designate the initial states, and the final state is marked by a solid disk. The components Δ_x and Δ_y of the vector Δ in (7.17) are shown beside each edge, enclosed in parentheses. The values of u and τ are omitted, since u can be chosen arbitrarily and the type τ of an elementary prototype is the same for all in this case: an elementary prototype consists of a single black cell which is its own origin ρ. The arrows on the edges in the diagram point in the direction of the vectors Δ, i.e., in the direction of the steps that construct the line. For instance, the approximately vertical lines shown in Figure 7.5 are obtained by sequential use of the vectors Δ with components $(0, 1)$, $(-1, 1)$, and $(1, 1)$, starting from an initial state of type $z = 2$. After the strictly vertical step $(0, 1)$ we are at the state $z = 2$, where any of the three step directions possible in this sector are permitted.

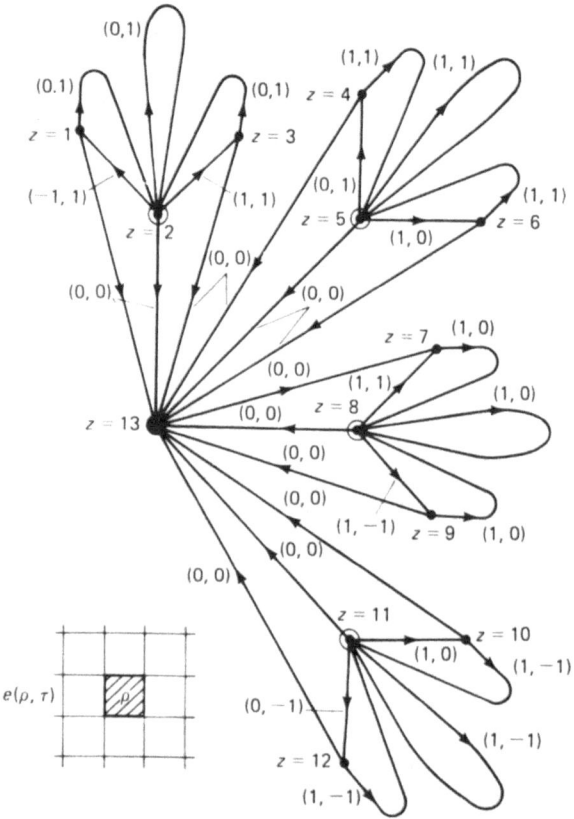

Figure 7.6 Type graph and elementary prototype for lines with slow change of direction (explanation in text).

However, after an inclined step $(-1, 1)$ or $(1, 1)$ we are in state $z = 1$ or $z = 3$. In these states only the step $(0, 1)$ is permitted, bringing us back to the state $z = 2$. The successive values of z are shown for one of the lines in Figure 7.5.

As a criterion of similarity we choose the Hamming distance $H(v, E)$. This is a sum over the retina cells, and as shown in Section 7.3, it can be represented as a sum of elementary similarities by the use of the corresponding system of nonintersecting windows.

However, there is another simpler method for finding this representation of the Hamming distance, without introducing windows. We need only express $H(v, E)$ as a scalar product, i.e., as a function linear in E, and then represent E as a sum of elementary prototypes.

Every function $f(x)$ of a binary variable x can be represented in the form

$$f(x) = xf(1) + (1 - x)f(0)$$

and therefore is expressible as a sum of a linear function and a constant.

The sums of such functions obviously have the same property. Therefore

$$H(v, E) = \sum_{i=1}^{N} \left[v_i(1 - E_i) + (1 - v_i)E_i \right]$$

$$= \sum_{i=1}^{N} v_i - \sum_{i=1}^{N} (2v_i - 1)E_i.$$

We use the criterion of similarity to find the optimal prototype. Therefore the first sum, which does not depend on the prototype, may be omitted, and we adopt the new criterion of similarity

$$\Phi(v, E) = \sum_{i=1}^{N} (2v_i - 1)E_i.$$

Our general scheme for solving the problem requires that the similarity be exhibited in the form of the sum of elementary similarities, as in (7.9). If we write $E = \sum_{j=1}^{m} e(\rho_j, \tau_j)$, and the elementary prototypes $e(\rho_j, \rho_j)$ that make up a single prototype do not overlap—i.e., have no common black cells—the similarity $\Phi(v, E)$ may be written as

$$\Phi(v, E) = \sum_{j=1}^{m} \sum_{i=1}^{N} (2v_i - 1)e_i(\rho_j, \tau_j). \qquad (7.25)$$

Since the elementary prototype $e_i(\rho_j, \tau_j)$ in our example has a single component, whose value is 1 (corresponding to the single black cell ρ), the summation over i contains only one term, of the form $(2v_i - 1) \times 1$, where v_i is the component of the image that corresponds to the cell ρ_j. We denote this component by $v(\rho_j)$. Then (7.25) becomes $\Phi(v, E) = \sum_{j=1}^{m} (2v(\rho_j) - 1)$. By (7.15) the origin ρ_j of the jth elementary prototype coincides with the location r_{j-1} of the preceding state: $\rho_j = r_{j-1}$. Then we find that an elementary similarity for our example is given by

$$g'(v, r_{j-1}, z_{j-1}, u_j) = 2v(r_{j-1}) - 1. \qquad (7.26)$$

The overall similarity is

$$\Phi(v, E) = \sum_{j=1}^{m} (2v(r_{j-1}) - 1). \qquad (7.27)$$

The task is as follows: For an arbitrary image v with binary components defined on our retina, to find a sequence of cells r_j ($j = 1, 2, \ldots, m$) which will satisfy the conditions (7.15)–(7.18) as described by the graph of Figure 7.6, and will maximize the similarity (7.27).

This task is to be accomplished in accordance with the general scheme described in the preceding section. We first determine the ranks of the states, for which we need not only the type graph (Figure 7.6), but also the expanded graph whose vertices correspond to the pairs (r, z). To each retina cell there correspond 13 vertices of the graph; the edges join vertices corresponding to neighboring cells as directed by the increment $\Delta(z,u)$ and the type graph (Figure 7.6).

We note first that the states for which $z = 13$ are sinks for all values of r, since as shown in Figure 7.6 no edges issue from these states. They are therefore of rank zero. To compute the ranks of other states, we must pay attention to the direction of the exit edges.

We are dealing with a rectangular retina made up of square cells distributed in horizontal rows and vertical columns. The columns are numbered by $x = 1, 2, \ldots, x_{max}$, and the rows by $y = 1, 2, \ldots, y_{max}$, from bottom to top. Every cell r has two coordinates (x, y). Every vertex in the expanded graph is determined by the variables (r, z) or equivalently by (x, y, z).

Let us first consider the states of types $z = 1, 2, 3$ in Figure 7.6. The edges that issue from these states have $\Delta_y = 1$ or $\Delta_x = \Delta_y = 0$. If $\Delta_y = 1$, the new location r_{j+1} is higher than r_j on the retina. Therefore, on the expanded graph, edges with $\Delta_y = 1$ cannot issue from a vertex (x, y, z) with $z = 1$, 2, or 3 and $y = y_{max}$. The expanded graph contains no vertices requiring such edges as inputs. Therefore, every state with $z = 1$, 2, or 3 has exactly one exit edge leading to the sink $(x, y_{max}, 13)$. Thus the rank of such states is 1. It is easy to see that for a state (x, y, z) with $z = 1$, 2, 3 the rank is $\Gamma = y_{max} - y + 1$. By a similar argument, we are led to find the ranks of all the states.

We must remember that the ranks need to be determined only once for a given graph. For the description or recognition of a new observed image, only the conditional lengths of the edges change, not the ranks of the vertices. Therefore the relatively tedious procedure for determining the ranks is not a part of the recognition algorithm.

After the ranks of the states have been determined, we can use (7.20) and (7.21) to compute the potentially maximal sum $\hat{G}(r, z)$ and the potentially optimal control $\hat{u}(r, z)$ for each state. The computation begins by setting $\hat{G}(r, 13) = 0$ for the final states $z = 13$ (Figure 7.6), for all r in the retina. The computation continues by the inspection of all values of r and z in order of increasing rank. For instance, to compute $\hat{G}(r, z)$ for the cell with the coordinates $x = 2$, $y = 5$, and for $z = 1$, [i.e., to compute $\hat{G}(2, 5, 1)$], we must carry out the following steps, in accordance with (7.20):

1. Define the set $U(z)$ of edges in the type graph (Figure 7.6) that issue from a vertex of the given type. For $z = 1$ there are two such edges: one has $\Delta = (0, 1)$ and the other $\Delta = (0, 0)$.
2. Compute the elementary similarity $g'(v, r, z, u)$ by (7.26). It will equal 1 if the cell r of the image with the given coordinates $x = 2$, $y = 5$ is black $[v(r) = 1]$, and will equal -1 if it is white $[v(r) = 0]$.
3. Now start with the first of the two edges we have in hand, i.e., the edge for which $\Delta = (0, 1)$, and compute the location $r + \Delta = (2 + 0, 5 + 1) = (2, 6)$ and the type $z = 2$ of the state to which it leads. Find (in the memory) the value, which should be already written down, of $\hat{G}(2, 6, 2)$ for this state.

4. Add the value of g' to the value of $\hat{G}$.
5. Repeat steps 3 and 4 for the second edge issuing from the vertex. (Since in our example g' does not depend on u, we need not repeat step 2 for the second edge.) We find $r = (2 + 0, 5 + 0) = (2, 5)$ and $Z(z, u) = 13$; we find in memory the value $\hat{G}(2, 5, 13) = 0$, since $z = 13$, which is a sink.
6. Choose the larger of the results obtained by step 4 for the two edges, and assign it to the target quantity $\hat{G}(2, 5, 1)$. Take $u = 1$ as the value of $\hat{u}(2, 5, 1)$ ($u = 1$ is the number of the edge that yields the maximum). Note that in Figure 7.6 the controls are omitted.

Figure 7.7 illustrates the application of this method to a concrete image. It shows a portion of the table of values of $\hat{G}(r, z)$ computed by the method we have described, for the four leftmost columns of the image in Figure 7.9(a) and for the states $z = 1, 2, 3$. This table simultaneously represents the portion of the image being processed, in which the black cells $v(r) = 1$ are outlined by heavy lines. The values of $\hat{G}(r, z)$ corresponding to each cell r, and to $z = 1, 2, 3$, are written inside this cell. The arrangement of the $\hat{G}(r, 1)$, $\hat{G}(r, 2)$, and $\hat{G}(r, 3)$ inside the cells is explained in Figure 7.8, which shows a portion of the expanded graph with vertices of the types $z = 1, 2, 3$. The numbers attached to the vertices in Figure 7.8 indicate the type z of the corresponding states. Vertices of type $z = 13$ and their input edges are omitted in Figures 7.7 and 7.8 ($\hat{G} = 0$ for all of these).

The numbers in Figure 7.7 show the value of the potentially optimal sums for the corresponding vertices, and are arranged as in Figure 7.8. The edges corresponding to the potentially optimal controls are marked by lines in Figure 7.7, and the other edges are omitted. For each vertex in Figure 7.7 *all* the potentially optimal edges are marked, corresponding to the values of u for which the maximum in (7.20) is attained. This is a deviation from the general scheme according to which only one of the optimal edges was fixed by Equation (7.21); it allows us to see the nonuniqueness of the optimal path.

In the computation of the $\hat{G}(r, z)$ the cells are inspected in order of increasing rank $\Gamma = y_{max} - y + 1$, from left to right and from top to bottom, beginning in the upper left corner. We have already seen that the computations for (7.20) do not require backtracking to previously processed states. Therefore we need to execute (7.20) about $n_{ts} \times N$ times, where n_{ts} is the number of different state types, excluding the final states, and N is the number of cells in the retina.

To find the optimal control sequence $\{\hat{u}_j\}$ we have to find the maximum value of $\hat{G}(r, z)$ over all the initial states, or, in our example, over the states of type 2. There are three vertices in Figure 7.7 for which $\hat{G}(r, z)$ attains its maximum $\max \hat{G}(r, z) = 6$. Therefore the optimal path and the optimal prototype are not uniquely defined for the given image. (A unique solution could be obtained if we were to assign a lower *a priori* weight to an inclined step than to a vertical step.) Next we must start from one of the optimal initial states $(\hat{r}_0, \hat{z}_0)$ and move along potentially optimal edges. In

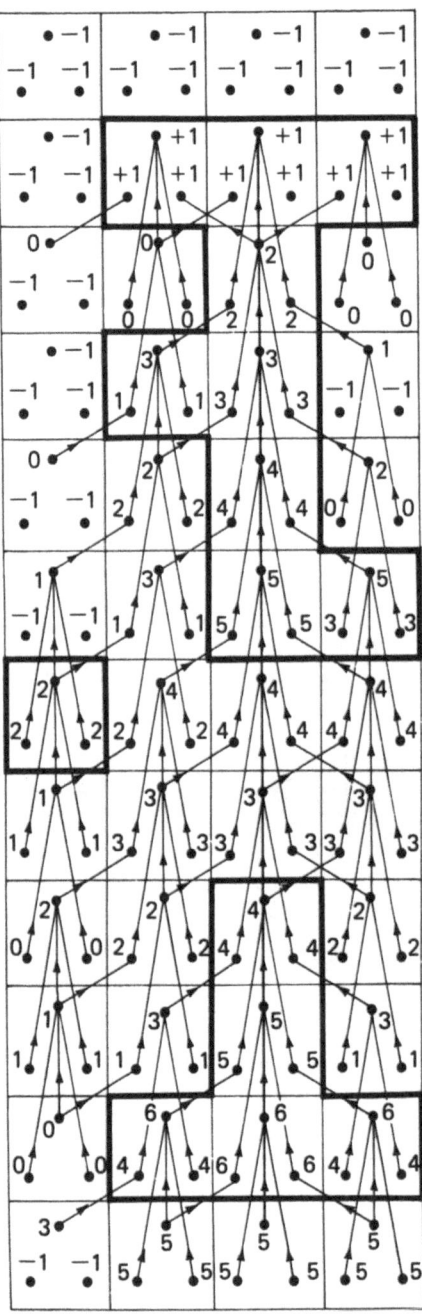

Figure 7.7   Example of the recognition of a vertical line (see text).

this way we establish an optimal sequence of states, as defined by the recursive procedure (7.24). This procedure is to be continued until we reach a final state. One of the optimal paths is marked with heavy lines in Figure 7.7.

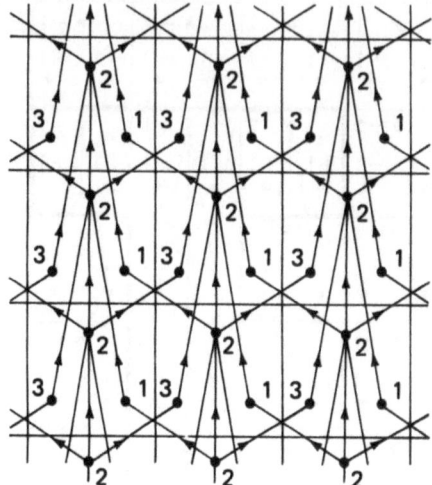

Figure 7.8 Portion of the expanded graph for an approximately vertical line (see text).

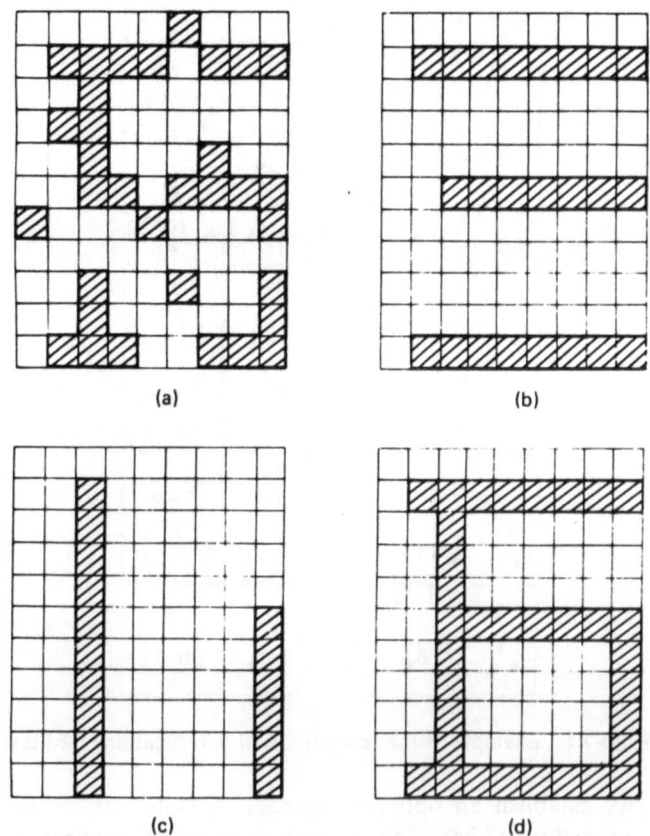

Figure 7.9 (a) Image distorted by noise; (b) description of it by horizontal lines; (c) description by vertical lines; (d) restored image.

Figure 7.9 shows an example of a noise-distorted image together with the horizontal and vertical lines selected and described by our algorithm (the computations were done by hand). Once a line giving the largest value of $\Phi(v, E)$ was chosen, the corresponding black elements of the image were erased and the next line in the same direction was searched for. To find lines of another direction, the original image was used again.

7.6 Recognition of Handwritten Characters

The algorithm used in the preceding section for the description of "straight" lines is usable as the basic part of a more complex algorithm designed for the structural description and recognition of various classes of hand-printed characters. We will consider only those characters that can be made with straight lines and without lifting the pen. Letters of this kind are outlined in Figure 7.10. The process for drawing them without regard to any constraints on the length of the segments can be represented schematically by graphs of the change of direction, as shown in Figure 7.10. These graphs display the order in which the direction of the successive straight lines may change. To the end of a segment drawn in a given direction we attach the origin of the next segment, drawn in the next following direction. Each segment is constructed by the rule defined in the preceding section, i.e., according to a type graph like one of the four petals displayed in Figure 7.6. For instance, the very simple graph of directions defining the character Б , shown in Figure 7.11(a), corresponds to the type

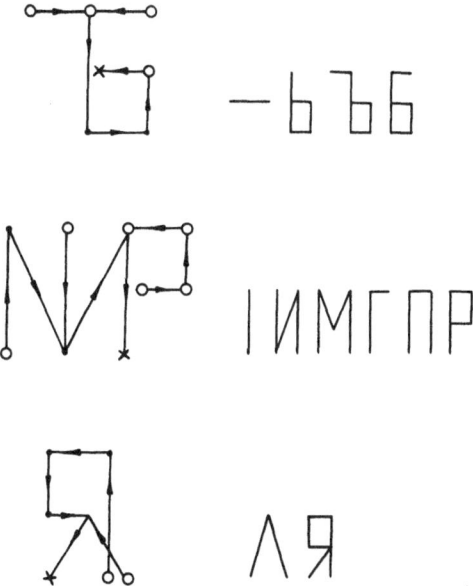

Figure 7.10   Sequences of directions for constructing character prototypes.

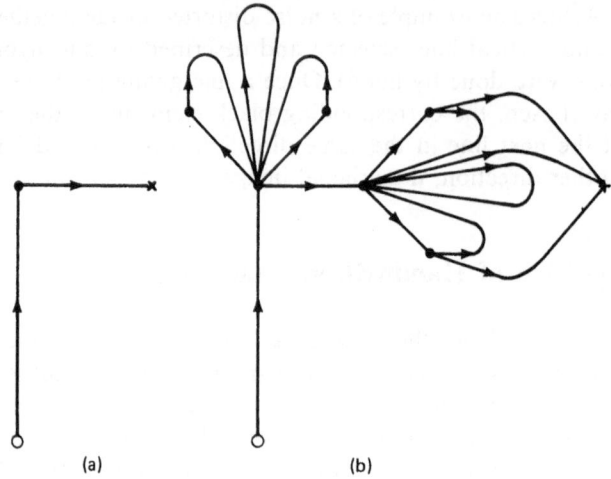

(a)   (b)

Figure 7.11   (a) A very simple direction scheme; (b) the corresponding type graph.

graph shown in Figure 7.11(b). Here, as in the graph of Figure 7.6, a definite value of the components Δ_x and Δ_y of the vector Δ corresponds to each edge. The type graphs of more complex images are constructed in the same way. It is worth while to use eight directions rather than four, since in constructing the outlines shown in Figure 7.10 we must be able to construct a segment in either direction, e.g., to traverse a horizontal segment either from left to right or right to left.

Each of the direction graphs in Figure 7.10 has several initial vertices, marked by circles, and one final vertex, marked by a cross. As can be seen from the figure, not all the initial vertices are sources. To construct an admissible prototype for a character, we must traverse the corresponding graph from an initial state to a final state.

Experiments in the description and recognition of characters by means of this algorithm have been carried out by V. M. Šarypanov. Images of characters drawn with a pencil were fed to the Minsk-2 computer via the image converter described earlier in Section 5.5. Figure 7.12(a) shows the digitized image as it was given to the computer, and Figure 7.12(b) and (c) show the prototypes of the characters Б, P, and П nearest to this image. The maximum value of the similarity $\Phi(v, E)$ is displayed next to each prototype. The time required for recognizing a single character corresponds to the time required for executing 250,000 two-address commands. On the Minsk-2 computer this amounts to about 50 seconds.

In the first stage some fifty such experiments were tried, with no intention of accumulating error statistics. The images were chosen for their special difficulty, in order to discover the weaknesses of the algorithm. These turned out to be: the invariant thickness of the lines in the prototype, often not at all compatible with the varying thickness of the lines in the image; the very great freedom in the inclinations of the constructed straight line segments with respect to the basic direction; and

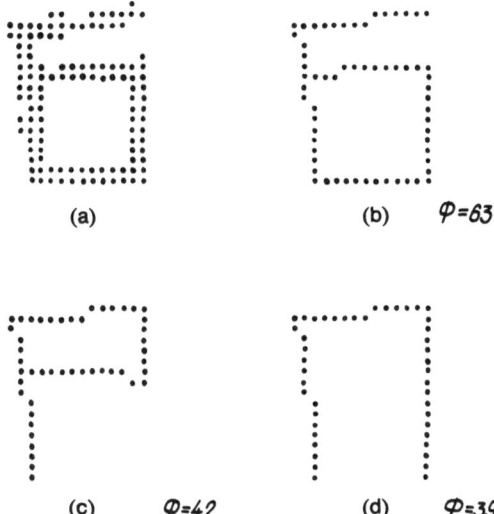

(a)   (b) $\varphi = 63$
(c) $\varphi = 42$ (d) $\varphi = 39$

Figure 7.12   (a) Image as fed to the computer; (b), (c), (d) the maximum similarity prototypes as constructed.

the absence of constraints specifying the proper proportions of the sizes of the various parts of the characters.

The first two of these failings, and in part the third, were eliminated in the second round of trials. The rules for constructing a complex prototype were changed as follows: For vertical and horizontal lines all deviations from the basic directions were forbidden, i.e., the states of the types $z = 1$, 3, 7, and 8 were excluded from the type graph in Figure 7.6. The existing deviations were retained for slanting lines. The line width was taken into account by defining as admissible prototypes all the images derivable from the initial prototype, which consists of thin lines, by blackening some of the cells that touch it. This amounts to saying that these cells are neutral, i.e., the blackness of the corresponding cells in the image has no effect on the similarity.

The third failing—the violation of proportions—is not easy to overcome, since the introduction of the corresponding constraints would sharply increase the required memory space and computing time. It was eliminated in part by imposing a lower bound for each straight line segment, so that it must contain at least a minimum number of cells, say five. Furthermore, after the discovery of the prototype with maximum similarity to the input image, the proportions of its parts were tested, and if they failed to satisfy some predetermined constraints, the decision was made to reject. If the constraints were satisfied, however, the prototype as found was in fact the solution of the constrained problem. Thus, neglect of the constraints in computing the prototypes increased the rejection probability to some extent, but not the error probability.

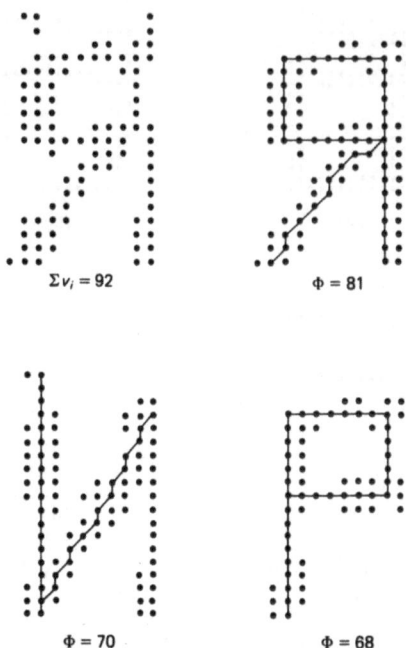

$\Sigma v_i = 92$ $\Phi = 81$

$\Phi = 70$ $\Phi = 68$

Figure 7.13   Example of recognition using the improved algorithm.

The second-stage experiments, with the above improvements, gave good results. Figure 7.13 shows an example of a digitized image of the character "Я" and the three nearest prototypes, together with the values of the similarity. It can be seen from the figure that the similarity for the prototype "Я" is significantly higher than for the others.

Experiments on the recognition of characters with an improved algorithm have also been tried by Šarypanov, using very ingenious programs. He and M. I. Šlezinger later on developed this line of research, and produced a very fast and noise-resistant method for analyzing particle tracks in photographs resulting from bubble-chamber experiments [68].

7.7 Conclusions

The application of dynamic programming to the image recognition problem shows great promise in the case where the images to be recognized cannot be satisfactorily approximated by a small number of convex sets. The use of a grammar, or of the corresponding graph on a rectangular retina of N cells, can yield a set of prototype images containing at least $(\min_s |U(s)|)^{\sqrt{N}}$ members, where $\min_s |U(s)|$ is the minimum number of edges leaving a vertex. The quantity $\sqrt{N}$ appears as an estimate of the number of elementary prototypes that will compose each prototype image.

If we assume that to each prototype image there corresponds a convex set of noise-distorted images in the space V, the total class of images that can be recognized is approximated by the union of a large number $(\min_s |U(s)|)^{\sqrt{N}}$ of convex sets.

Though the image classes have a very complex structure, the recognition problem requires for its solution only a comparatively small memory size, equal to the number $|\mathfrak{S}|$ of vertices in the expanded graph. Given a homogeneous graph on a retina of N cells, this number is equal to $N|\mathfrak{Z}|$, where $\mathfrak{Z}$ is the number of types of the different states. The tasks for which the grammar is not too complex yield a value of $|\mathfrak{Z}|$ not exceeding a few tens or at most a few hundreds. The main point is that as N increases the required memory space increases only as the *first power* of N. The number of operations required is proportional to $N|\mathfrak{Z}||\overline{U}|$, where $|\overline{U}|$ is the mean number of edges leaving a vertex, and the coefficient of proportionality is of the order of 10, i.e., about 10 operations are needed per vertex-edge pair. Therefore, the number of operations and the memory size are proportional to N, while the number of variant prototype images depends on N exponentially. The reference-sequence method therefore yields an economical means for solving complex recognition problems.

In this chapter we have considered a formulation of the problem of structurally describing and recognizing images making use of the maximum-likelihood method. It is not hard to see that the reference-sequence method used to solve this problem can also be used in the Bayesian case.

In fact, when we compute the total similarity of the image v with some prototype E corresponding to a certain path on the graph, we are computing the logarithm (or some other monotone function) of the conditional probability $p(v|E)$. If now we specify the conditional probability $p(u_j|s_{j-1})$ of a transition from the state s_{j-1} to another state $S(s_{j-1}, u_j)$, we can compute the prior probability of each path $\{u_j : j = 1, 2, \ldots, m\}$ on the graph, and so the joint probability of the image v and the path $\{u_j\}$:

$$p(v, \{u_j\}) = \prod_{j=1}^{m} p(u_j|s_{j-1}) \cdot p(v_j|s_{j-1}, u_j).$$

Let us assume now, for the sake of simplicity in our reasoning, that we are given a separate graph for each class k together with the transition probabilities $p(u_j|s_{j-1}, k)$. Then we can write down the conditional probability

$$p(v, \{u_j\}|k) = \prod_{j=1}^{m} p(v, u_j|s_{j-1}, k).$$

The factors in this product are expressed in terms of known probabilities

$$p(v, u_j|s_{j-1}, k) = p(v_j|s_{j-1}, u_j, k) \cdot p(u_j|s_{j-1}, k). \tag{7.28}$$

The probability $p(v|k)$, which we need to compute in order to solve the Bayesian problem, can be written as

$$p(v|k) = \sum_{\{u_j\}} p(v, \{u_j\}|k).$$

This sum can be computed by the device we used in Chapter III, Section 3.3. We need a recursion formula like (7.11), with $\max_{u \in U(s)}$ replaced by a summation over u and the summation replaced by a product. The role of the potentially maximal sums $G(s)$ falls to the conditional sum

$$F(s,k) = \sum_{u \in U(s)} p(v,u|s,k) \cdot F(S(s,u),k),$$

where the conditional probability $p(v,u|s,k)$ is defined by (7.28).

We calculate $F(s,k)$ sequentially for the vertices in order of increasing rank and arrive finally at the initial state s_0 with

$$F(s_0,k) = p(v|k).$$

These quantities must be computed for all classes $k = 1, 2, \ldots, n$. Given the prior probabilities $p(k)$, we can now solve the Bayesian recognition problem.

As we know [44], the class of Bayesian decisions is complete, i.e., the optimal solution of every statistical decision problem is a Bayesian decision of some other problem. This means that for an arbitrary statistical problem there exists a prior distribution of the recognition parameters such that the solution of the Bayesian problem is also the solution of the given problem. Therefore if a method for finding the prior distribution $p(k)$ and the conditional distribution $p(u|s,k)$ can be determined for a statistical problem that interests us, the solution of the problem can be reduced to the method we have just described for solving the Bayesian problem. Thus the class of problems soluble by one or other modification of the reference-sequence method is very wide.

An essential limitation on the capabilities of this method arises from the necessity of representing a two-dimensional image as a one-dimensional sequence of elementary prototypes. For instance, this constraint prevents us from solving the recognition problem for those images that cannot be traced with a single stroke of the pen and are not in the form of a tree, e.g., images containing a closed curve. To recognize images of this kind we need a generalization of our method, to *two-dimensional grammars* which describe sets of two-dimensional tables rather than the one-dimensional chains dealt with by the customary one-dimensional grammars. Dynamic programming cannot serve for the development of such a two-dimensional generalization of the reference-sequence method. The formulation and solution of this problem are presented in the papers [89] by M. I. Šlezinger.

CHAPTER VIII

The Recognition of Sequences of Images

The recognition of composite images consisting of strings of elementary images is of great theoretical and practical interest. Lines of typewritten characters provide an example.

The difficulties of separating a line into distinct characters come up in the automatic reading of typewritten documents. With print of ordinary quality there are often no separating blank spaces between characters, yet at the same time breaks in the line may introduce false blanks. The very simple method of separation by the presence of white spaces is therefore applicable in practice only when the spaces between symbols are artificially widened and the print quality is high.

Another method for separating characters is the following: A delimiting window frames a portion of the image the size of which corresponds to a single symbol. The window is displaced continuously along the line. Whenever the image in it coincides with a prototype (or more generally, satisfies some condition for recognition), the corresponding signal is accepted for processing. This method was described by V. I. Zaĭcev and A. A. Savin [27] as early as 1962. However, errors can arise in practice because portions of two neighboring images falling in the window simultaneously may closely imitate a third symbol. For instance, vertical lines belonging to two neighboring characters with serifs above and below may form an image of the letter "Π" [cf Figure 8.3(a)]. The neighboring characters "O" and "C" may form an image reminiscent of the character "X", and so on.

For these reasons we need information about the neighboring characters before we can make decisions about the single symbols. In other words we must recognize whole lines rather than individual characters.

To recognize a line means to name the characters in it in the right order. A process of recognizing a line by comparing it with all possible prototype lines can only be an imaginary one. It is practically impossible, since a line containing 50 characters from an alphabet of 50 symbols can have 50^{50} different variants. (Even if we take account of redundancy in the language, the number of variants is still of the order of 10^{50}.) It is easy to see that so many variants cannot be inspected in a reasonable time span by the fastest of computers. Nevertheless the line recognition problem can be formulated and solved by the methods of dynamic programming [35]. Here we shall regard it as a particular case of the general reference-sequence method.

As for any recognition problem, the formulation of the line recognition problem should begin with the construction of a mathematical model describing all the signals that may present themselves for recognition. In our case, these signals are images of lines of typewritten characters.

8.1 Mathematical Model of a Typewritten Line, and Formulation of the Problem

Consider the simplest model of a line, for which the prototype image of a line is composed of prototype images of single characters. We shall use a retina which is a long narrow rectangle of the smallest dimensions sufficient to include any image of the typewritten lines to be recognized. This retina is divided into small square cells forming vertical columns and horizontal rows. We take the length of the side of a cell as our unit of measurement, and we introduce a coordinate system having its origin at the lower left corner of the retina. In this system the abscissae of the vertical lines separating the retina columns are equal to integer numbers

$$x = 0, 1, 2, \ldots, N_h.$$

An elementary prototype is the prototype image of a character in the chosen alphabet, which is located in a definite place on the retina. The characters include letters, digits, punctuation marks, etc. An elementary prototype is characterized by various parameters: its name, or class k, the abscissa ρ of its leftmost edge, and others that we will collectively denote by the single symbol γ, which may include a vertical displacement, line width, contrast, etc. We denote the elementary prototype by $e(\rho, k, \gamma)$. The abscissa ρ takes integral values, i.e., it is the abscissa of the leftmost edge of the group of adjoining retina columns in which the components of the elementary prototype are defined. The width q of this group of columns is uniquely defined by the class k, i.e., for every k we are given the width $q = q_e(k)$. The components of the elementary prototype are not defined outside this group of columns. There is an elementary prototype for a blank, consisting of a white column; a blank of arbitrary width can be constructed from these prototypes.

The prototype E for the line is constructed according to the condition (7.7), from elementary prototypes with the aid of nonintersecting windows so that within the jth window the components of the prototype E coincide with the components of the jth elementary prototype.

The window $W(\rho, q)$ with $q = q_e(k)$ represents a subset of the retinal cells for which the components of the elementary prototype $e(\rho, k, \gamma)$ are defined. These cells occupy several neighboring columns of the retina lying between the abscissae ρ and $\rho + q$. In other words, the window $W(\rho, q)$ is a rectangle having the same height as the retina and width q, with ρ as the abscissa of its left edge. The window for a blank occupies a single column.

The process for constructing a composite prototype from elementary prototypes consists in covering the retina with windows, from left to right, each containing an elementary prototype. The windows must touch along their vertical edges, i.e., no column may be omitted and no windows may overlap. No other constraint is imposed on the parameter values of the elementary prototypes. The advantages and disadvantages of this choice of constraints are discussed in Section 8.6.

It is assumed that the images observed in the same retina arise from random distortions of prototypes of the line just described. Then we may introduce the similarity criterion $g(v, E)$ (cf. Chapter V) of the image v and the prototype E. The similarity can be exhibited as a sum (7.6) over all the retinal cells, at least in the case when the noise in the several cells is independently distributed. Then, as shown in Section 7.3, the similarity is also the sum of elementary similarities, each corresponding to an elementary prototype. In the present case, the elementary similarities are given by

$$g^*(v, \rho, k, \gamma) = \sum_{i \in W(\rho, q_e(k))} g_i(v_i, e_i(\rho, k, \gamma)). \tag{8.1}$$

Here the functions g_i, which may be the same or different for different i, are the similarities for the ith component. They are defined by the noise distribution and are assumed known.

The task of recognizing an image v consists in finding an admissible sequence of elementary prototypes for which the sum of the elementary similarities (8.1) with the image is maximal. An admissible sequence of elementary prototypes must begin with a prototype for which

$$\rho_1 = x_0 = 0.$$

The sequence must satisfy the condition $\rho_{j+1} = \rho_j + q_e(k_j)$, and the last (i.e., the mth) elementary prototype must satisfy the equation

$$\rho_m + q_e(k_m) = N_h.$$

The sum of the elementary similarities for such a sequence has the form

$$g(v, E) = \sum_{j=1}^{m} g^*(v, \rho_j, k_j, \gamma_j). \qquad (8.2)$$

The formal statement of the problem is as follows:

We are given a method for computing the function (8.1) for parameter values satisfying the conditions

$$\rho \in X = \{0, 1, 2, \ldots, N_h\},$$

$$k \in K = \{1, 2, \ldots, n\},$$

$$\gamma \in B_e, \qquad \rho + q_e(k) \leqslant N_h,$$

where $q_e(k)$ is a function mapping K to X and the set B_e is such that for all fixed ρ and k we can find the maximum of (8.1) over $\gamma \in B_e$. The value of v in (8.1) is supposed given. No other constraints are imposed on (8.1).

We are to find the number m and a sequence of m triples

$$(\rho_j, k_j, \gamma_j), \qquad j = 1, 2, \ldots, m$$

such that

$$\sum_{j=1}^{m} g^*(v, \rho_j, k_j, \gamma_j) = \max$$

under the conditions

$$\rho_1 = 0$$

$$\rho_{j+1} = \rho_j + q_e(k_j), \qquad j = 1, 2, \ldots, m - 1,$$

$$\rho_m + q_e(k_m) = N_h.$$

8.2 Solution of the Problem

We solve the problem, as formulated, by the general reference-sequence method that we developed in Chapter VII. The process that we have just described in the preceding section, for constructing a sequence of elementary prototypes, can be defined with the aid of a homogeneous graph. Since all the parameters of the elementary prototype, except the parameters ρ, are independent, the state of a partially filled retina is completely characterized by the abscissa x of the right-hand edge of the completed portion. In fact, if this portion ends at the point x, any continuation beginning at this point is admissible. The variable x characterizes the *location* of a state; in the general case it was denoted by the variable r (cf. Section 7.4). Here it is one-dimensional, and to every value $x = 0, 1, 2, \ldots, N_h$ there corresponds a vertex on the graph. All the vertices represent states of a single type, and we may therefore omit the variable z.

Suppose that the constructed portion of a complex prototype contains j elementary prototypes (including the blanks) and that the abscissa of its right-hand end has the value x_j. Then the $(j + 1)$st elementary prototype to be added, $e(\rho_{j+1}, k_{j+1}, \gamma_{j+1})$, must satisfy (7.15):

$$\rho_{j+1} = x_j.$$

After this prototype is added, the state x_j is changed to

$$x_{j+1} = x_j + q_e(k_{j+1}). \tag{8.3}$$

In the graph, an edge runs from x_j to x_{j+1}, and this edge corresponds to the elementary prototype

$$e(\rho_{j+1}, k_{j+1}, \gamma_{j+1}).$$

An example of a sequence of elementary prototypes on a retina is shown in Figure 8.1(a), and the corresponding vertices and edges of the expanded graph are shown in Figure 8.1(b).

Let us now look at the task of finding the optimal path in the graph. We note first that in Chapter VII our first step in finding an optimal path was to define for each vertex a *final* potentially optimal path, i.e., an admissible path leading from the given vertex to a final vertex, along which the sum of the elementary similarities was maximal. With no substantial change this method can find an optimal path by using *initial* potentially optimal paths, which lead from the initial vertex to every other given vertex. In the general case the use of initial paths is less convenient, since it requires us to define the inverses of the functions (7.4) and (7.5) as well as the functions themselves. In our present case we must use initial paths, since we shall be studying the recognition of lines of unbounded length, where a final

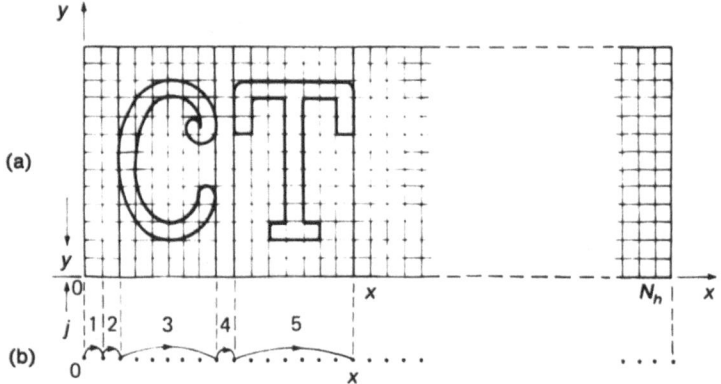

Figure 8.1   (a) Sequence of elementary prototypes; (b) corresponding edges in the graph.

decision on the initial portion of the line is reached before the line is scanned to the end.

The search for an initial potentially optimal path leading to a given vertex in the homogeneous graph uses a recursive relation like (7.20), differing in that the value of $\hat{G}$ for the given vertex is computed by reference to its values at the *preceding* vertices connected to it by oriented edges, rather than at those that follow it. As before, the elementary similarities are computed for every edge that connects the given vertex with another. However, since during the computation of $\hat{G}(x)$ we fix the vertices lying at the termini of the considered edges, it is more convenient to regard the elementary similarity as a function of the terminus of an edge rather than of its origin as before. Then after omitting the variable z, as explained earlier, the formula (7.20) becomes

$$\hat{G}(x) = \max_{u \in U} (g'(v,x,u)) + \hat{G}(x - \Delta(u)). \qquad (8.4)$$

Here the values of the control u correspond to edges *entering* the vertex x. The set U of values of u is the same for all vertices, since all vertices have the same type.

The parameter u in this case could be represented by the pair (k, γ) defining the type τ of an elementary prototype.* This would imply that the graph would contain a number of edges originating and terminating at the same vertices. To be rid of this inconvenience we add a small supplement to the general scheme described in Chapter VII. It is convenient to begin our search for the optimal path by choosing for each pair of vertices connected by a number of edges the one bearing the greater similarity, and only after this resorting to the procedure (8.4). By (8.3), elementary prototypes having the same wdith $q_e(k)$ are matched by edges having a common origin and terminus, and each of these edges is matched by an elementary prototype $e(\rho,k,\gamma)$ with $k \in K(q)$, where $K(q)$ is the set of classes k for which the elementary prototypes have width q. Therefore we shall characterize an edge by the three parameters q,k,γ, where q defines the choice of the left vertex (the origin) while $k \in K(q)$ and γ dictate only the choice of the elementary prototype from among those having width q.

Accordingly, Equation (8.4) becomes

$$\hat{G}(x) = \max_{q \in Q} \max_{k \in K(q)} \max_{\gamma} (g'(v,x,q,k,\gamma) + \hat{G}(x - q)). \qquad (8.5)$$

Here Q is the set of values of the width q of the elementary prototypes. In this equation the similarity $q'(v,x,q,k,\gamma)$ refers to an edge entering the vertex x. Therefore it is to be computed for the elementary prototype having x as the coordinate of its *righthand* edge. This is the prototype

---

* The replacement of u by τ is not always permissible, since the relation between u and τ is not one-to-one when a single value of τ corresponds to transitions into several different states, e.g., as in the graph of Figure 7.1(c).

$e(x - q, k, \gamma)$ and by $(8, 1)$ the corresponding elementary similarity is

$$g'(v, x, q, k, \gamma) = g^*(v, x - q, k, \gamma)$$

$$= \sum_{i \in W(x - q, q_e(k))} g_i(v_i, e_i(x - q, k, \gamma)). \qquad (8.6)$$

Use of the set $K(q)$ allows us to simplify (8.5). We note that the second term on the right does not depend on the parameters k and γ. Thus

$$\hat{G}(x) = \max_{q \in Q} \left(\max_{k \in K(q)} \max_{\gamma} g'(v, x, q, k, \gamma) + \hat{G}(x - q) \right).$$

We write

$$g_M(x, q) = \max_{k \in K(q)} \max_{\gamma} g'(v, x, q, k, \gamma) \qquad (8.7)$$

and

$$k_M(x, q) = \arg \max_{k \in K(q)} \max_{\gamma} g'(v, x, q, k, \gamma). \qquad (8.8)$$

Then

$$\hat{G}(x) = \max_{q \in Q} (q_M(x, q) + \hat{G}(x - q)). \qquad (8.9)$$

The potentially maximal controls are defined for each x by

$$\hat{q}(x) = \arg \max_{q \in Q} (g_M(x, q) + \hat{G}(x - q)),$$

$$\hat{k}(x) = k_M(x, \hat{q}(x)). \qquad (8.10)$$

For optimization over the paths leaving the initial vertex, the rank of a vertex is defined as the maximum number of edges leading from the initial to the given vertex (cf. Section 7.3). It is easy to see that in our current graph the rank of the vertex x is equal to x. Therefore the computations in accordance with (8.9) and (8.10) should be performed sequentially for $x = 0, 1, 2, \ldots, N_h$.

For a given image v the quantities $g_M(x, q)$ and $k_M(x, q)$ characterize the set of edges leaving the vertex $x - q$ and entering the vertex x. This means that we have reduced the former task to the simpler process of finding the optimal path in a graph in which each pair of vertices is joined by no more than a single edge. In this graph as many edges enter (or leave) a vertex as there are values of the width q of the elementary prototypes. An edge in the new graph is characterized by a control $q \in Q$, a similarity $g_M(x, q)$, and a parameter $k_M(x, q)$. The sequence of values of $k_M(x, q)$ for edges in the optimal path obviously solves the problem initially posed. The new type graph corresponding to the example given in Figure 8.1 is shown in Figure 8.2. It contains three edges, since the width q in the example has three different values.

The optimal path is found in accordance with our general scheme by use

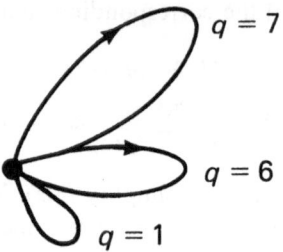

Figure 8.2   Simplified type graph for the line recognition problem ($Q = \{1, 6, 7\}$).

of the potentially optimal controls $\hat{q}(x)$ and $\hat{k}(x)$ [cf. (8.10)], beginning with the right-hand end of the line $\hat{x}_t = N_h$.

$$x_{j-1} = \hat{x}_j - \hat{q}(\hat{x}_j) \qquad (j = m, m-1, \ldots, 3, 2). \tag{8.11}$$

The values

$$\hat{k}_j = \hat{k}(\hat{x}_j), \qquad j = 1, 2, \ldots, m \tag{8.12}$$

identify the characters making up the prototype that has the greatest similarity to the given image v of the line, i.e., the sequence $\{\hat{k}_1, \hat{k}_{2\odot}, \ldots, \hat{k}_t\}$ is the result of recognizing the line. If the criterion of similarity $g(v, E)$ is some monotone function of the likelihood, as we recommended in Chapter V, then the values of the $\hat{k}_j$ represent the maximum-likelihood sequence of characters for the line in question.

Let us look at an application of this method. Figure 8.3(a) shows an enlarged photograph of a group of typewritten characters, in which we can clearly discern a false image of the letter "Π". Figure 8.3(b) shows a graph of the corresponding functions $g_M(x, q)$ and $\hat{G}(x)$. The width of the window in this example has two values: $q = 1$ for the blank prototype and $q = 5$ for character prototypes. The size of the digitization step on the x-axis has been greatly increased in order to cut down the amount of computation. The values of the similarities $g_M(x, 1)$, $g_M(x, 5)$ and of the parameter $k_M(x, 5)$ are displayed in Table 8.1. The computation of these functions in the course of recognition of the line may be envisioned as follows: We move two windows along the line from left to right (in the general case, of course, we have as many windows as there are values of the width q of the elementary prototypes for the given alphabet). For each window, and for each value x of the abscissa of its right-hand edge, we compute the similarity of the portion of the image falling inside the window with all the elementary prototypes having the proper width and a position corresponding to the current position of the window. The maximum similarity over all these prototypes defines the value of $g_M(x, q)$,

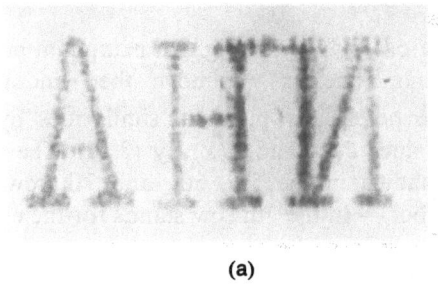

(a)

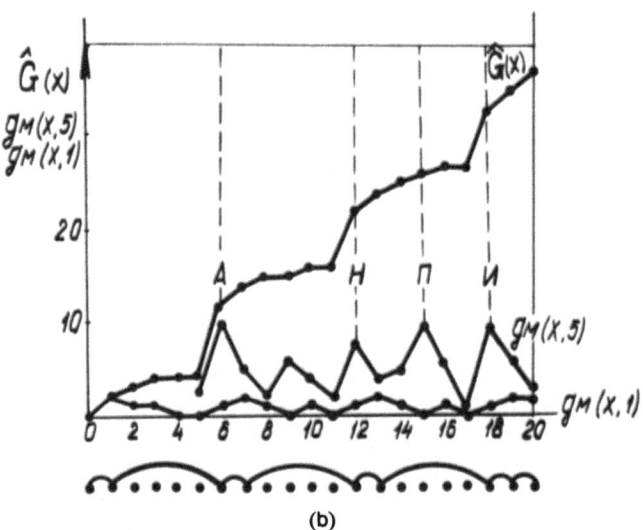

(b)

Figure 8.3 Example of the recognition of a sequence: (a) false image of "Π"; (b) diagrams of the similarities.

Table 8.1

Row	Variable	Value																				
1	x	0	1	2	3	4	5	6	7	8	9	10	11	12	13	14	15	16	17	18	19	20
2	$g_M(x,1)$	—	2	1	1	0	0	1	2	1	0	1	0	1	2	1	0	1	0	1	2	2
3	$g_M(x,5)$	—	—	—	—	—	3	10	5	2	6	4	2	8	4	5	10	6	1	9	6	3
4	$k_M(x,5)$	—	—	—	—	—	—	A	—	—	—	—	—	H	—	—	Π	—	—	И	—	—
5	$\hat{G}(x)$	0	2	3	4	4	4	12	14	15	15	16	16	22	24	25	26	27	27	33	35	37
6	$\hat{q}$	(x)	—	1	1	1	1	1	5	1	1	1	1	1	5	1	1	5	1	1	5	11
7	$\hat{k}(x)$	—	—	—	—	—	—	A	—	—	—	—	—	H	—	—	Π	—	—	И	—	—
8	x	**0**	1	2	3	4	5	**6**	7	8	9	10	11	**12**	**13**	14	15	16	17	**18**	**19**	20

and the class k of the prototype yielding this maximum gives the value of $k_M(x,q)$. At the same time as we move the window we compute the sum $\hat{G}(x)$ of the potentially maximal similarities by (8.9) and the potentially optimal values $\hat{q}(x)$ and $\hat{k}(x)$ by (8.10). The values of $\hat{G}(x)$, $\hat{q}(x)$, and $\hat{k}(x)$ are shown in the 5th, 6th, and 7th rows of Table 8.1, respectively. The symbol — in the 7th row stands for the elementary blank prototype.

After the window reaches the end of the line, the formulae (8.11) and (8.12) are used to compute the optimal sequences $\hat{\hat{x}}_j$ and $\hat{\hat{k}}_j$. The values of x are repeated in the 8th row. The values of $\hat{\hat{x}}_j$ that are printed in boldface and joined by edges represent the optimal sequence of vertices in the graph. The corresponding $\hat{\hat{k}}_j$ in row 7 form the maximum-likelihood sequence of names of the elementary prototypes.

8.3 Solution of the Problem with a Correlation Criterion for the Similarity

The correlation criterion described in Chapter V is one of the most effective similarity criteria for images. It can be successfully applied to the recognition of sequences of images, and in particular to lines of printed characters. However, in using a criterion of similarity developed for simple images to recognize composite images, we must test each of our assumptions for adequacy and if necessary make corrections.

An assumption basic to the correlation criterion was the hypothesis that the contrast and the darkening of the image varied uniformly over the whole retina. This hypothesis hardly holds for composite images. It is more natural to assume it holds within a window corresponding to an elementary prototype. But this assumption leads to a model of the total image that is more complex than the one we developed in Chapter V. We now proceed to study the new model.

We shall show that the similarity criterion $g(v, E)$ corresponding to this model is the sum of the *squares* of the correlations, compounded with the weighted sum of squares of the mean gray shades, rather than the sum of the correlation coefficients themselves as we might have expected.

We shall suppose that the parameter γ of the elementary prototype $e(\rho, k, \gamma)$ contains three components: a vertical displacement y and two optical parameters α and β (cf. Section 5.4), on which it depends linearly:

$$e(\rho, k, \gamma) = \alpha e'(\rho, k, y) + \beta I(\rho, k).$$

Here $I(\rho, k)$ is an image for which all the components lying in the window $W(\rho, q_e(k))$ are equal to 1. Then the ith component of the jth elementary prototype (if it is not the blank prototype) is given by

$$e_i(\rho_j, k_j, \gamma_j) = \alpha_j e_i'(\rho_j, k_j, y_j) + \beta_j. \tag{8.13}$$

We take $k_j = 0$ for the blank prototype; the parameter α has no meaning here, and its components in the window $W(\rho, 1)$ are

$$e_i(\rho_j, 0, \gamma_j) = \beta_j,$$

i.e., we may simply suppose that

$$e'_i(\rho_j, 0, y_j) \equiv 0. \tag{8.14}$$

The parameters α_j, β_j, and y_j are assumed to be independent for different j, i.e., if there is a certain constraint imposed on α_j, β_j, and y_j, it does not depend on the values of these parameters with different subscript value.

As before, we shall assume that the observed line images v (with fixed E) are realizations of a multidimensional random variable with a spherically symmetrical distribution. This means that the probability density $p(v|E)$ is a monotone decreasing function of the square of the Euclidean distance

$$D^2 = (v - E)^2.$$

Since it is more convenient to use a similarity that is an increasing function of the likelihood $p(v|E)$, we write

$$g(v, E) = -(v - E)^2 = -\sum_i (v_i - E_i)^2.$$

Noting that the equation

$$E_i = e_i(\rho_j, k_j, \gamma_j)$$

holds within the jth window, where $i \in W(\rho_j, q_e(k_j))$, we represent the similarity as the sum of m elementary similarities

$$g(v, E) = -\sum_{j=1}^m \sum_{i \in W(\rho_j, q_e(k_j))} (v_i - E_i)^2$$

$$= -\sum_{j=1}^m \sum_{i \in W(\rho_j, q_e(k_j))} (v_i - e_i(\rho_j, k_j, \gamma_j))^2.$$

We substitute (8.13) in the above and write the expression for the elementary similarity, omitting the index j as

$$g^*(v, \rho, k, y, \alpha, \beta) = - \sum_{i \in W(\rho, q_e(k))} (v_i - \alpha e_i(\rho_i, k, y) - \beta)^2.$$

Next, as in Section 8.2, we single out the subsets $K(q)$ of classes k, each subset having a fixed value q equal to the width $q_e(k)$ of the window, and we compute the elementary similarity and maximize its value over all the edges having a common origin at $x - q$ and common terminus at x:

$$g_M(x, q) = \max_{k \in K(q)} \max_y \max_{\alpha, \beta} \left(- \sum_{i \in W(x - q, q)} (v_i - \alpha e_i(x - q, k, y) - \beta)^2 \right).$$

We find the maximum over the optical parameters by using the assumption that they are independent as we did in Section 5.3:

$$\max_{\alpha, \beta} \left(- \sum_{i \in W(x - q, q)} (v_i - \alpha e_i(x - q, k, y) - \beta)^2 \right)$$

$$= - \sum_{i \in W(x - q, q)} v_i^2 + \left(\sum_{i \in W(x - q, q)} v_i e_{0i}(x - q, k, y) \right)^2$$

$$+ \frac{1}{N(q)} \left(\sum_{i \in W(x - q, q)} v_i \right)^2,$$

where $e_{0i}(x - q, k, y)$ is the ith component of the prototype for the class k with the vertical component y, normalized and neutralized (cf. Section 5.4) within the window $W(x - q, q)$, and $N(q)$ is the number of cells in a window of width q. For the blank prototypes ($k = 0$) we find by (8.14) that the second term vanishes. When we sum the elementary similarities over j, the terms $\sum_{i \in W_j} v_i^2$—where $W_j = W(x_j - q_e(k_j), q_e(k_j))$—sum to $\sum_{i \in R_N^2} v_i^2$; the sum extends over the whole retina R_N^2, and the result does not depend on the prototype E. Therefore this term may be removed, and we have

$$g_M(x, q) = \frac{1}{N(q)} \left(\sum_{i \in W(x - q, q)} v_i \right)^2$$

$$+ \max_{k \in K(q)} \max_y \left(\sum_{i \in W(x - q, q)} v_i e_{0i}(x - q, k, y) \right)^2. \quad (8.15)$$

This quantity is to be computed for each $q \in Q$ and for every position of the window $W(x - q, q)$ along the line to be recognized.

8.4 Recognition of Sequences of Unbounded Length

The algorithm given in Section 8.2 for the recognition of sequences of images (typewritten lines) yields an effective solution for problems that cannot be solved by recognizing individual elementary images. However, it demands a relatively large amount of memory: for every state we must remember the potentially optimal control $\hat{u}(x)$ [or the components $\hat{q}(x)$ and $\hat{k}(x)$] until the recognition is completed for the entire sequence. Other data also must be remembered, but they usually demand much less memory volume. In fact, the values of $g_M(x,q)$ need not be stored, since they are used as soon as they are computed, during the movement of the window along the line. As regards $\hat{G}(x)$, when $\hat{G}(x+1)$ is computed we need only the values of $\hat{G}(x)$ for those vertices of the graph that lie between $x - q_{max}$ and $x + 1$, where $q_{max} = \max_{q \in Q} q$ is the maximum value of the width q.

The amount of memory needed to store the control values $u(x)$ grows without limit as the length of the line increases. There is a simultaneous increase in the delay time for recognizing the elementary images at the beginning of the sequence. It is very important from the point of view of application to study the means and the conditions under which the memory size and the delay can be limited.

Aside from these purely utilitarian considerations, there is a theoretical interest in knowing how far one portion of a composite image can reach to influence a decision on another part. It seems intuitively obvious that a decision on a given part of a line of typewritten characters should be influenced only by the immediately adjacent portions. After the latter have been inspected, we should be able to make a decision about the given part, and throw away the data respecting it. This would permit a substantial reduction in the delay in reaching a decision and in the memory size required.

If these intuitive propositions are correct, then after having inspected a sufficiently large part of the line, from the beginning to the point x, and having calculated $\hat{G}(x)$ and $\hat{u}(x)$ for all the inspected vertices, we should be able to identify those of the inspected vertices that lie on the optimal path. This decision should be independent of any results obtained by inspecting subsequent sections of the graph. Clearly this is impossible in the general case, when arbitrary values of the elementary similarity can be attached to the edges of the graph. However, we can formulate a necessary and sufficient condition under which some initial portion of the optimal path can be specified during the inspection process; i.e., under this condition we can specify at each stage of the process the vertex through which the optimal path must pass, with a guarantee that this vertex will remain unchanged, no matter what elementary similarities may be found during the rest of the process. Together with this vertex, its initial potentially optimal path (that is, the path having the maximal sum of the elementary similarities among the paths leading from the initial vertex to the chosen one) is also contained in the final optimal path.

We shall call this the *condition of optimality*. It will appear as a theorem applying not only to the recognition of sequences of images, but also to the general problem of finding an optimal path on a graph satisfying its hypotheses.

We consider an antisymmetric graph [28] with one source and one sink. We assign a conditional length to each edge; in the line-recognition case, this is the corresponding elementary similarity. We find the rank of each vertex, for instance with respect to the source, and we denote by $\Delta\Gamma_{max}$ the greatest difference in the ranks of two vertices that are joined by an edge. The rank of the source is taken as zero, and the rank of the sink will be denoted by Γ_{max}. As before, the potentially optimal path for the vertex s is defined as the path leading from the source to s and having the largest sum of the lengths of its edges. Then the following assertion is true:

Theorem on the Condition of Optimality.   *Let a be an integer not exceeding* Γ_{max}. *If for all the vertices, in a given graph, whose ranks* $\Gamma(s)$ *satisfy the inequality*

$$a - \Delta\Gamma_{max} < \Gamma(s) \leqslant a, \tag{8.16}$$

their potentially optimal paths pass through a vertex s^*, *then the optimal path also passes through* s^*.

PROOF.   First we show that if $\mathfrak{S}_a$ is the subset consisting of *all* vertices s whose rank $\Gamma(s)$ satisfies (8.16) for some given value of a, the optimal path passes through one of the vertices in $\mathfrak{S}_a$. By definition of the rank (cf. Section 7.3), it varies monotonely along every path. The rank of a vertex on the optimal path increases monotonely from 0 at the source to Γ_{max} at the sink. Therefore if we assume that the optimal path does not go through one of the vertices in $\mathfrak{S}_a$, there must exist an edge in the optimal path for which the rank increases from a value not exceeding $a - \Delta\Gamma_{max}$ to a value greater that a. But this contradicts the definition of $\Delta\Gamma_{max}$. Thus the optimal path necessarily goes through one of the vertices $s \in \mathfrak{S}_a$.

It follows from Bellman's optimality principle [6] that if the optimal path goes through a vertex s, the potentially optimal path to s is part of the optimal path. But according to the hypothesis of the theorem, all the potentially optimal paths for the vertices $s \in \mathfrak{S}_a$ go through the vertex s^*. Then the optimal path also goes through this vertex, which is what we set out to prove.

This proves the *sufficiency* of the condition of optimality. It is *necessary* in the following sense: If we want to guarantee that under arbitrary weights (conditional lengths) of those edges whose termini have rank greater than some integer a, the optimal path must go through a vertex s^* of rank $\Gamma(s^*) < a - \Delta\Gamma_{max}$, then the hypothesis of the theorem must hold. For, if the potentially optimal path for some vertex $s \in \mathfrak{S}_a$ does not go through s^*, it can happen that exactly its continuation to the vertices of rank greater than a will appear optimal, and therefore the optimal path will not go through the vertex s^*. $\square$

This theorem generalizes a sufficient condition of optimality discovered by V. G. Kalmykov* for the line recognition problem: if for as many as $q_{max} - 1$ sequential values of x the potentially optimal control has the value $\hat{q}(x) = 1$, which corresponds to passing $q_{max} - 1$ adjacent elementary

---

* Kalmykov. V. G., Avtoreferat dissertacii, IK AN USSR, Kiev, 1974. (Author's review of his dissertation, Institute of Cybernetics, Ukrainian SSR.)

blanks, then the vertex

$$x^* = x - q_{max}$$

lies on the optimal path.

The theorem provides a basis for the method of recognizing the inspected portion of a composite image. The idea, as applied to line recognition, is as follows: We first remind ourselves that in this case the rank of a vertex x equals x. On the other hand, $\Delta\Gamma_{max}$ is equal to the maximum width of an elementary prototype:

$$\Delta\Gamma_{max} = q_{max} = \max_{q \in Q} q.$$

For brevity, we shall refer to vertices on the potentially optimal path leading to some vertex x as *related to* x. If it turns out during the calculation of $\hat{G}(x)$ for some vertex x that there exists a vertex $x^* < x$ which is related to all the vertices lying between $x - q_{max}$ and x, we may conclude that x^* lies on the optimal path. Therefore the potentially optimal path for x^* is part of the optimal path. The subsequent search for the optimal path can be conducted as though x^* were the initial vertex. This means in particular that from then on we need only inspect vertices lying to the right of x^* when looking for vertices related to some further vertex x.

We now define an algorithm for line recognition, using a test of the optimality condition that we have just described. This test is based on the following concepts. For every vertex x_j related to the current vertex x we must count the number of those vertices to which the vertex x_j is related. We count only within an uninterrupted sequence of adjacent vertices terminating at x. We shall denote this number by $\lambda_1(x_j)$. If $\lambda_1(x_j)$ reaches the value of $\Delta\Gamma_{max} = q_{max}$, then the condition of optimality is met for the vertex x_j, and thus it is included in the optimal path. To compute $\lambda_1(x_j)$ we need only know the corresponding number $\lambda_2(x_j)$ for the vertex $x - 1$. The vertices x_j related to x are defined only for the part of the graph lying to the right of some point ϑ which represents the boundary of the portion of the line already recognized and which moves to the right when a decision is taken with respect to a new portion. The vertices related to the running vertex x form a list X_1. In another list X_2 we keep the vertices related to $x - 1$, the predecessor of the running vertex.

The following version of this algorithm is convenient for presentation but does not economize on memory space or number of operations. A more economical version can be achieved by proper coding of the lists of vertices and proper organization of the memory for the values of $\lambda_1(x)$ and $\lambda_2(x)$,

Our version has the following structure.

Begin. Set $x = 0$; clear the list X_2; set $\vartheta = 0$.

  Step. Increment x by 1. Compute $\hat{G}(x)$, $\hat{q}(x)$, and $\hat{k}(x)$. If x is final, i.e., $x = N_h$, set $x^* = x$ and go to "Output".

List. Enter in the list X_1 all vertices x_j related to x and lying to the right of ϑ (including x). For each x_j test whether it is in the list X_2 corresponding to $x - 1$. If it is, go to "Count", else set $\lambda_1(x_j) = 1$ and go to "Continue".

Count. Read the number $\lambda_2(x_j)$ calculated in the preceding execution of "Step". If $\lambda_2(x_j) = q_{max} - 1$, set $x^* = x_j$ and go to "Output", else set $\lambda_1(x_j) = \lambda_2(x_j) + 1$.

End Count.

Continue. Go to the next vertex in X_1; repeat until X_1 is exhausted.

End List. Copy the vertices from X_1 into X_2; set $\lambda_2(x_j) = \lambda_1(x_j)$. Go to "Step".

End Step.

Output. Enter the vertex x^* and all related vertices lying to the right of ϑ in the list of vertices for the optimal path together with the corresponding values of $\hat{k}(x)$. If $x^* < N_h$ set $\vartheta = x^*$ and go to "Step", else stop.

End Output.

End Algorithm.

An analysis of the algorithm shows that we need an amount of memory proportional to the difference $x - x^*$. If the assigned memory is limited, an uninterrupted execution of the algorithm requires that the condition of optimality should be met before the memory is full. Clearly, if we know only the topology of the graph and some nonrigorous constraints on the lengths of the edges, we cannot predict when the condition will be met, or whether it will be met at all. This is a major defect, from the point of view of one searching for the optimal path on a graph, but it is not a defect for line-recognition purposes.

In fact, if, after inspecting a sufficiently large segment of an image, containing a number of characters, one still cannot reach a unique decision regarding at least some of them before going on to inspect the rest of the line, then the images are highly illegible and seriously distorted by noise. In this case the line, or a part of it, should be rejected.

It can be shown [29] that under given realistic assumptions on the images the probability of such an ambiguous decision decreases rapidly as the length of the inspected portion $x - x^*$ increases. Therefore we can choose the length of the portion to be inspected, and the corresponding amount of memory, to be large enough to guarantee any required probability of correct recognition of long sequences.

8.5 Examples and Experiments

An example of the use of the above algorithm is given in Table 8.2, for the problem already solved in Table 8.1. The upper portion of Table 8.2 repeats the data in Table 8.1. The list of vertices related to x is constructed

Table 8.2

x	0	1	2	3	4	5	6	7	8	9	10	11	12	13	14	15	16	17	18	19	20
$\hat{G}(x)$	0	2	3	4	4	4	12	14	15	15	16	16	22	24	25	26	27	27	33	35	37
$\hat{q}(x)$	—	1	1	1	1	1	5	1	1	1	1	1	5	1	1	5	1	1	5	1	1
$\hat{k}(x)$	—	—	]	]	]	]	A	]	]	]	]	]	H	]	П	]	]	и	]	]	]
x	0	1	2	3	4	5	6	7	8	9	10	11	12	13	14	15	16	17	18	19	20
$\dfrac{x_i}{\lambda(x_j)}$	—	$\frac{1}{1}$	$\frac{2}{1}$	$\frac{3}{1}$	$\frac{4}{1}$	$\frac{5}{1}$	$\frac{6}{1}$	$\frac{7}{1}$	$\frac{8}{1}$	$\frac{9}{1}$	$\frac{10}{1}$	$\frac{11}{1}$	$\frac{12}{1}$	$\frac{13}{1}$	$\frac{14}{1}$	$\frac{15}{1}$	$\frac{16}{1}$	$\frac{17}{1}$	$\frac{18}{1}$	$\frac{19}{1}$	$\frac{20}{1}$
			$\frac{1}{2}$	$\frac{2}{2}$	$\frac{3}{2}$	$\frac{4}{2}$		$\frac{6}{2}$	$\frac{7}{2}$	$\frac{8}{2}$	$\frac{9}{2}$	$\frac{10}{2}$	$\frac{12}{2}$	$\frac{12}{2}$	$\frac{13}{2}$	$\frac{10}{1}$	$\frac{15}{2}$	$\frac{16}{2}$	$\frac{13}{1}$	$\frac{18}{2}$	
				$\frac{1}{3}$	$\frac{2}{3}$	$\frac{3}{3}$			$\frac{6}{3}$	$\frac{7}{3}$	$\frac{8}{3}$	$\frac{9}{3}$			$\frac{12}{3}$	$\frac{9}{1}$	$\frac{10}{2}$	$\frac{15}{3}$	$\frac{12}{2}$	$\frac{13}{2}$	
					$\frac{1}{4}$	$\frac{2}{4}$					$\frac{6}{4}$	$\frac{7}{4}$	$\frac{8}{4}$			$\frac{8}{1}$	$\frac{9}{2}$	$\frac{10}{3}$		$\frac{12}{2}$	
						$\frac{1}{5}$					$\frac{6}{5}$	$\frac{7}{5}$					$\frac{8}{2}$	$\frac{9}{3}$		$\frac{2}{2}$	
																		$\frac{8}{3}$			
x^*	—	0	0	0	0	0	1	1	1	1	6	7	7	7	7	7	7	7	7	7	20
Optimal path	0	0	0	0	0	0	0	0	0	0	0	0	0	0	0	0	0	0	0	0	0
							1	1	1	1	1	1	1	1	1	1	1	1	1	1	1
										6	6	6	6	6	6	6	6	6	6	6	6
											7	7	7	7	7	7	7	7	7	7	7
																					12
																					13
																					18
																					19
																					20
ϑ	0	0	0	0	0	1	1	1	1	1	6	7	7	7	7	7	7	7	7	7	—

by using the values of $\hat{q}(x)$ and (8.11). The list X_1 for x is given in the corresponding column. The values of $\lambda_1(x_j)$ are shown for all vertices in the list, and are displayed below the vertex number, separated by a horizontal bar. The list X_2 is given in the preceding column, from which the values of $\lambda_2(x_j)$ are taken for the computations. The value of ϑ for completion of column x is the value of x^* for the preceding column. If after computing all the $\lambda_1(x_j)$ we find the value of x^* unchanged, it is copied into the current column from the preceding one, as is the list of vertices lying in the optimal path. When a new vertex x^* is detected, it is added to the list. The values of $x_j = x^*$ are printed in boldface. The final vertex $x = 20$ lies on the optimal path, by definition. Therefore we must take $x^* = 20$ for $x = 20$, without regard to the value of $\lambda_1(x_j)$.

This example also illustrates the amount of information stored in memory. To complete the column $x = 19$, which is marked by a dashed line in the table, we need the information contained in the area enclosed in solid lines. This is the maximum amount of information that must be stored for this example.

A trial of the algorithm was run by V. G. Kalmykov on the Minsk-2 computer. The input consisted of selected sequences of typewritten characters, chosen to be especially difficult to separate. They were typed and then fed to the scanner incorporated in the character reader (cf. Section 9.3). The image of a word as it appeared after digitization for input to the computer is shown in Figure 8.4. The diagrams of the functions $g_M(x, 9)$ and $\hat{G}(x)$ are shown below it. The similarity criterion used was the one given in (8.15). All the elementary prototypes for characters had the same width, $q = 9$. The diagram of $g_M(x, 1)$ is not shown. The row of letters and hyphens under the graphs indicates the values of $\hat{k}(x)$. Each value of $\hat{k}(x)$ is the name of the elementary prototype most resembling the image in the window whose right-hand edge has an abscissa equal to x; the hyphens denote the blank prototype.

A row of values of $\hat{q}(x)$ is shown under the row for $\hat{k}(x)$; beneath that the edges of the optimal path are shown. The peaks of the broken line mark the sequence of values $\hat{x}_j$. It is clear from the figure that the corresponding values of $k(\hat{x}_j)$ are correct.

The recognition of similar images by means of the local algorithms mentioned at the beginning of this chapter runs into substantial difficulties. There are not always blank spaces between characters; moreover, false symbols may be encountered. Thus, in the word shown in Figure 8.4, an "X" can be falsely formed between the first "O" and the succeeding "C"; its image as seen from the diagram of $g_M(x, 9)$ in the figure resembles the X-prototype more closely than the image of the "C" resembles its own prototype. A local algorithm makes a wrong decision in this case. Nevertheless, the algorithm based on the reference-sequence method has correctly recognized all the images used in all the experiments made.

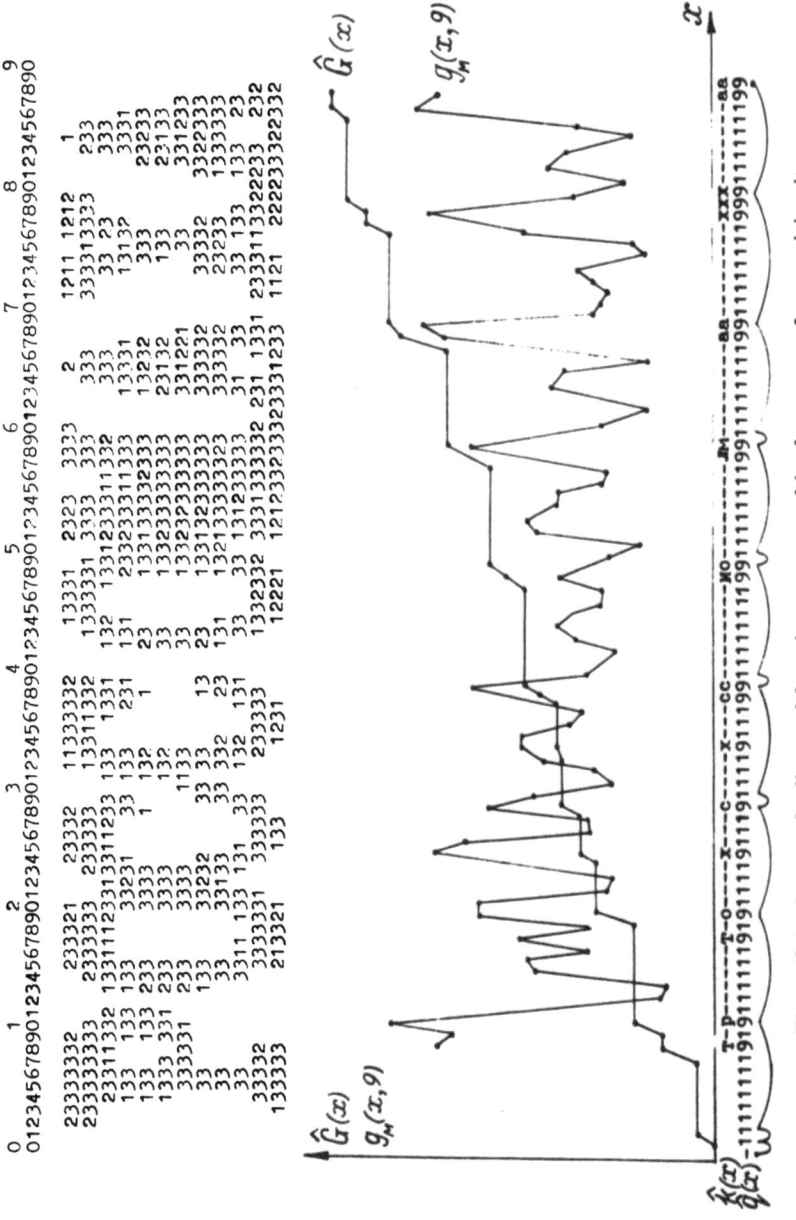

Figure 8.4   Image of a line and functions computed in the course of recognizing it.

8.6 Scope of the Algorithm and Possible Generalizations

The algorithm we have described is founded on the assumption that all the parameters of the elementary prototypes are independently restricted, except ρ, which defines the origin of an elementary prototype. The graph defining the corresponding rule for constructing a composite prototype is extremely simple. Therefore the task we have considered illustrates most perfectly the basic idea in the optimal recognition of a sequence of images. Nevertheless, despite the simplification we have made in the assumptions, the results are fully applicable for the solution of practical problems. In fact, if we neglect both context and the mutual dependence of vertical displacements, we thus suppose the parameters of the elementary prototypes to be mutually independent. The set of admissible prototypes for lines is expanded in this case, since some sequences of letters are not found in real text and the characters in a line do not ordinarily jump up and down in a chaotic manner.

This extension of the set of admissible prototypes for a line can seriously increase the error probability when the prototypes in the extended set for one class closely resemble the observed images belonging to another class. To decide whether such an extension is permissible, we must conceive of a recognition problem in which the images are generated by the expanded set of prototypes. If the problem is soluble in principle under these conditions with sufficient reliability (that is, if the probability that doubtful images will appear is not much greater than in the original case), then the extension may be accepted.

In our present case, it seems obvious that with the ordinary quality of typescript, for which every individual letter can be correctly recognized without regard to its context, chaotic lines can be recognized almost as well as orderly lines. What we lose when supposing the lines chaotic is that the redundancy of the text is not used (there is none for a sequence of numbers), nor is any information on the probably vertical displacement of a character succeeding one with a known displacement.

When we need very high reliability and the noise is also strong, we must apply a more complex model. The general scheme outlined in Chapter VII allows us to state rules for constructing composite prototypes that will take account of all form of mutual dependence among the elementary prototypes: as to context, vertical displacement, and others. To state such a rule we must construct a graph having some tens of vertices for each column of the retina. The corresponding recognition algorithm may require some thousands of memory cells for its implementation, and this is acceptable within the current state of computing technology.

Interesting possibilities arise when we consider rules that let the windows cover less than the full retina. The uncovered portion does not influence the similarity of the image and the prototype, and therefore the parts of the image in this portion may be arbitrary without changing the result of the recognition. Thus we can make the results independent of the presence of extraneous lines and spots on the retina that happen to be close to the printed line but do not intersect the outlines of the characters themselves.

The formal statement of the corresponding task presents no difficulty if the total area of the windows is fixed. We may for instance define windows corresponding to the elementary prototypes of the characters in the line, having a height less that the height of the retina and exactly equal to the height of the corresponding character. All windows, including the window for the elementary blank, must be of the same height. Then the rule for constructing composite prototypes can be defined so that an arbitrary component can appear outside the windows. In this case the optimal prototype will be the one whose components outside the windows coincide with the components of the image. Let us assume that the maximum total similarity attained for a given area when image and prototype coincide completely will depend only on the magnitude of the area and not on the look of the image. This property is possessed, for instance, by a similarity computed as the number of cells in which the values of the components agree, or as the Euclidean distance, or the Hamming distance. Then the maximum total similarity for the area lying outside the windows does not depend on the location of the windows which do not intersect. Therefore it may be omitted, and we maximize only the total similarity within the windows.

Clearly, this problem must be solved with account taken of the mutual dependence of the vertical displacements of neighboring windows.

An essentially different formulation admits a variable total area of the windows containing the elementary prototypes. In this case, proceeding from the same kind of considerations, we establish a threshold for the elementary similarity, depending on the area of the corresponding window. A composite prototype is constructed from non-intersecting windows covering the *whole* retina. A window may contain an elementary prototype; then the elementary similarity is computed as usual. However, a window may also be empty, or indeterminate, i.e., it may contain no elementary prototype, not even the blank. The elementary similarity for an empty window, independently of the corresponding portion of the image, is set equal to the given threshold value, proportional to the area of the window. Thus an empty window is essentially different from a window containing a blank, for which the similarity depends on the image.

Given an image, we want to construct the composite prototype for which the total similarity is maximal. Clearly, for the portions of the image that are of poor quality, where no elementary prototype yields a similarity above the threshold, the optimal prototype will contain empty windows. Here the current case is different from our earlier one, in that the region covered by empty windows depends on the image.

In precisely this case, in which thresholds are assigned to the elementary similarities, it makes sense to construct a graph in which the admissible paths may begin and end in arbitrary retinal cells. In the opposite case, without thresholds and with an always positive similarity, an arbitrary portion of a path may only have a total similarity less than that of the whole path. Therefore it makes no sense in that case to solve the problem with arbitrary beginnings and endings of paths. A particular case of the problem with thresholds for the similarities is provided by a recognition task in which the elementary similarities may be either positive or negative, and the threshold is set at zero. Such a problem was solved in Section 7.4.

8.7 Conclusions

The reference-sequence method defined in Chapter VII allows us to obtain an exact solution to the problem of finding the maximum-likelihood prototype for sequences of elementary images. Typewritten lines are a special case of such sequences. Thus we have succeeded in solving the important and difficult problem of recognizing the image of a line that has not been resolved into separate characters.

For immediate application of the reference-sequence method we need a memory containing as many cells as there are columns in the retina that covers the line. For typewritten lines of 60 characters, with 20 columns per character, this amounts to 1200 cells. A memory of this size can be included without difficulty in a character reader. However, from many points of view, it is of interest to improve the algorithm arising from the reference-sequence method so that the optimal recognition of symbols in the early portions of the line can be accomplished before the whole line has been inspected. Not only is this improvement important for economy of memory space; we also want to know how far the statistical influence of one portion of the image of the line extends to another.

The problem of making the optimal decision with respect to the part of the sequence already inspected is solved on the basis of the "condition of optimality" formulated and proved in this chapter. This condition permits us to improve not only the algorithm for recognizing sequences of images, but also the general algorithm for finding the optimal path in a graph.

Future improvements in the algorithm for recognizing a sequence may apparently be made by taking into account the probability that the uninspected portion of the line will contain images which might alter the potentially optimal decision taken with respect to the inspected portion. We may expect that an optimal algorithm will be developed and justified, which will require a relatively small memory necessary for storing the sufficient statistics for three or four adjacent characters in the line.

CHAPTER IX

The "ČARS" Character Reader

Some of the foregoing theoretical results were applied in the design of the reading automaton ČARS. A reading machine, or character reader, is a contemporary device for feeding alphanumeric information to a computer. As opposed to the traditional input devices, which use punched cards or perforated tape, the reader allows the immediate input of documents printed on an ordinary typewriter. (Some readers also accept handwritten characters.) The use of readers permits a significant reduction of the amount of manual labor required in the preparation of documents for input.

The ČARS [4, 5, 16, 17, 30, 33], which we are about to describe, was designed for the mechanical input of multiline documents typed on standard sheets of typing paper measuring 210×297 mm. It recognizes Russian capital letters, digits, punctuation marks, and arithmetical and other auxiliary symbols; in all, 53 characters (cf Section 9.5). The requirements for registration of the material on the paper are minimal and easily met; for instance, there are lower bounds on the margin width and the separation between lines. Perhaps the only unusual requirement is that each line to be read by the machine must be tagged by a marker. The marker consists of several minus signs, typed in the left-hand margin of the paper.

We describe the ČARS reader here with the aim of illustrating the practical results of the theory of image recognition. Therefore we focus less on a detailed technical account of its construction and more on the considerations that led to the choice of algorithms and the methods for implementing them. These are described separately, that is, we first show *what* needed to be done with the signals, and then show *how* it was done, and by what means. This mode of exposition seems most suitable, since otherwise it might turn out (and often does) that the fundamental ideas are buried in a mass of inessential technical detail.

9.1 The Operational Algorithm for a Character Reader

An automatic reader must deal with a mass of documents without requiring human intervention. Its flow chart is therefore complicated, including such operations as extracting a document from the input stack, locating the next line to be read on a document, scanning (digitizing) its image, resolving the image into separate symbols and then recognizing them. It must also handle illegible characters semiautomatically, and do many other auxiliary tasks.

Some of these operations are based on informal and heuristic considerations, since no theory to support them has been developed. For instance, one such is the pickup and transport of papers from the input stack. These operations imitate the actions of a human reader. Others, such as the resolution of line images and recognition of characters, must be based on a formal recognition method. They cannot imitate the corresponding human actions, about which almost nothing is known. The results of theoretical work on recognition have also been applied to the development of algorithms for finding lines, digitizing the gray shades of images, and choosing the parameters of the scanning process.

The choice of the line-finding algorithm was based on the following considerations. The algorithm most resistant to noise and to variations in the distance between lines would be like the one described in Chapter VIII for resolving a line into characters. Such an algorithm is usable for resolving pages into lines if all the lines are parallel to one another and if their slopes are known in advance. Failing these conditions, the task becomes much more complex. However, the lines in documents are usually separated by fairly wide and distinguishable blank spaces (which is not true of characters in a line), and simpler methods can be used.

In order to be able to detect lines containing only a few characters and skip lines containing information meant for human consumption only, a decision was made to base the search for the lines on the use of markers located in the margin. The markers must be produced by the typewriter on which the document is typed, and simultaneously with the text. The algorithm for finding a marked line is as follows: The left margin of the document is scanned from top to bottom by a small moving field of view, which accepts the image of a single marker. The similarity (e.g. the correlation coefficient) of the image in the field with the template of a marker is computed for every position of the view field. When a marker appears and occupies a predetermined position in the field of view, the similarity exceeds a preset threshold, and the movement stops. The view field then moves to the right, beginning the scan of the image of the new line to be read.

To simplify the search for the position of maximum similarity between template and marker, the marker symbol should exhibit little change of the similarity measure under a translation perpendicular to the direction of motion of the field of view; then there is no need to inspect several horizontal translations in the marker recognition process. Vertical translations occur naturally in the scan. Any image containing one or several horizontal lines will meet this requirement, e.g., the minus or the equal sign. To avoid putting rigid constraints on the position of the marker with respect to the document edge, it was decided that several sequential minus signs would be used.

The sampling algorithm is basically obvious; we need only choose the parameters for it: the sampling step and the horizontal and vertical dimensions of the retinal cells (or in general the parameters of the point lattice consisting of the centers of all the retinal cells and the parameters of the weight function $\omega(x - x_i, y - y_i)$, which characterizes the distribution of the incident light or the sensitivity of the light receptor for the ith cell). The sampling steps and the cell dimensions need not be the same, but if they are not, there will be unused gaps between the cells or the cells will overlap. In order to detect thin lines, i.e., those with width less than the length of the sampling step, it is useful to make the length of the sampling steps equal to the cell dimensions, so that the cells do not overlap and there is no unused gap between them. Some quantitative arguments supporting this choice of the sampling parameters are given in [37], which is concerned with the optimal choice of the sampling and quantization parameters.

The choice of the number of retinal cells for the ČARS was dictated by various factors connected with its design and manufacture [16], and was therefore not optimal. The retina contains 20 columns and 18 rows. Fifteen of the rows fit into the height of the tallest character.

When we solved the problem of the optimal choice of templates in Chapter VI, we contemplated a retina with 15 such rows. It turned out, however, that for the overwhelming majority of templates one of the bounding rows contained only white elements, i.e., it contributed nothing of value to the recognition. For simplicity, the body of the template was reduced to $20 \times 14 = 280$ components, not $20 \times 15 = 300$ as stated in Chapter VI.

The cells are 0.135 mm wide by 0.31 mm high. These unusual proportions were forced rather than chosen, and led to different resolving powers for vertical and horizontal lines. The deficient resolving power for horizontal lines caused some trouble in distinguishing the characters "H" and "Π", which differ only in their horizontals. The deficiency had little effect on the recognition of other characters.

The parameters for the quantization algorithm, which preprocesses the images, were optimized according to the criterion of the **EPA**, which was shown in Chapter VI to be related to the error probability. At the outset, two different quantization algorithms were compared. Both compared the gray shade of a given cell with a threshold dependent on the gray shades of several neighboring cells. In the first algorithm, the threshold was proportional to the average gray shades of fifteen neighboring cells:

$$\vartheta_{mean}(x, y) = \gamma \sum_{\eta=-m}^{m} \sum_{\xi=-l}^{l} \tilde{v}(x + \xi, y + \eta) + \vartheta_0, \qquad m = 1, \quad l = 2, \quad (9.1)$$

where $\tilde{v}(x, y)$ is the gray shade of the cell in column x and row y.

The threshold in the second algorithm was proportional to the maximum of three quantities obtained from the average gray shades in three horizontal strips, the middle one containing the given cell and the other two abutting on it:

$$\vartheta_{max}(x, y) = \max\left\{\left(\gamma \max_{\eta=-m, m} \sum_{\xi=-l}^{l} \tilde{v}(x + \xi, y + \eta) + \vartheta_0\right), \vartheta_{min}\right\}. \quad (9.2)$$

Here the constant ϑ_{min} defines the minimum value of the threshold for values of $v(x, y)$ near zero. The quantization rule in both cases is as follows: if the gray shade $v(x, y)$ of the given cell exceeds its threshold value, the cell is assigned the quantized value 1; otherwise the value is 0.

Several values of γ, ϑ_0, and ϑ_{min} were chosen and the decision rules for the separation of closely similar characters (3 and Э, also H and П) were optimized for all parameter values and for both algorithms; the optimal value of **EPA** was also computed. The parameter values were chosen to maximize **EPA** [14].

The most crucial and difficult decision was the choice of the recognition algorithm. The considerations set forth at the beginning of Chapter VI led to a choice of an algorithm implementing the piecewise linear decision rule (6.36), with the similarity maximized over the translation parameters. The peculiarities of this algorithm, and the method for optimizing its parameters, were explained in detail in Chapter VI.

The choice of the algorithm for resolving a line into characters is especially interesting. An optimal algorithm for this purpose was described in Chapter VIII, based on the method of maximum likelihood. The memory required for implementing it amounts to only a few hundred cells, and in the current technology of electronic computers this presents no difficulty. Nevertheless, in order to lower the cost of the machine, a simpler and suboptimal algorithm was adopted; this algorithm was proposed by A. G. Semenovsky [4] and improved by V. G. Kalmykov [29, 30]. Named the "line start algorithm", it gives good results when the noise level is low enough, and consists of the following: Two windows move along the line, as in the optimal algorithm of Chapter VIII. One of these has width $q = q_b$ corresponding to the step movement of the typewriter carriage, and the same for all characters. The second has the width of a single column, i.e., $q = 1$.

Two quantities are computed at each position x of the right-hand edge of the window: the similarity $g_M(x, 1)$ with the prototype column of a blank character, and two quantities similar to those appearing in (8.7) and (8.8):

$$g_M(x, q_b) = \max_k \max_\tau \max_\eta g'(v, x, q_b, k, \tau, \eta), \tag{9.3}$$

$$k_M(x, q_b) = \arg\max_k \max_\tau \max_\eta g'(v, x, q_b, k, \tau, \eta). \tag{9.4}$$

The first of these is the maximum similarity of the part of the image v that falls within the window of width q_b and right-hand edge at x, with all of the templates $\mathcal{T}_\eta c(k, \tau)$ subjected to various vertical translations $\mathcal{T}_\eta$ parametrized by η. The templates $c(k, \tau)$ are used instead of the elementary prototypes of the characters, as explained in Chapter VI, Section 6.4. The value of (9.4) represents a potential decision on the current character.

The quantities (9.3) and (9.4) are processed by the suboptimal algorithm as follows: We store in the memory three quantities, which we call the *potentially maximal similarity* $\hat{G}$, the *potentially optimal abscissa* $\hat{x}$ of the right-hand edge of the character, and the *potentially optimal decision* $\hat{k}$. After the decision is made that a character has been recognized for $x = x^*$, the value of $g_M(x, q_b)$ is determined for $x = x^* + q_b$ and the following assignments are made:

$$\hat{G} = g_M(x, q_b), \qquad \hat{x} = x, \qquad \hat{k} = k_M(x, q_b). \tag{9.5}$$

Then the window is moved to the next position $x = x^* + q_b + 1$ and the inequality

$$\hat{G} + m < g_M(x, q_b) + g_M(x - q_b, 1) \tag{9.6}$$

is tested. Here m is the maximum value attainable by the similarity of one column of the image with a column of any of the existing templates.

If (9.6) is true, we put into the memory the new values of $\hat{G}$, $\hat{x}$, and $\hat{k}$ according to (9.5). If not, the window is moved on, i.e., x is assigned the succeeding integer values and for each the inequality

$$\hat{G} + m(x - \hat{x}) < g_M(x, q_b) + \sum_{\xi = \hat{x} - q_b + 1}^{x - q_b} g_M(\xi, 1) \tag{9.7}$$

is tested. Whenever it is satisfied, we fix the new values given by (9.5). If it does not fail once for $(q_b - 1)$ successive values of x $(x = \hat{x} + 1, \hat{x} + 2, \ldots, \hat{x} + q_b - 1)$, then the decision $\hat{k}$ is taken as final, the abscissa x^* is given the value $x^* = \hat{x}$, and the process begins again with $x = \hat{x} + q_b = x^* + q_b$.

In essence, this algorithm chooses the one of two composite prototypes (cf. Chapter VIII) which has the greatest similarity with the portion of the image lying between the abscissa x^* and the running abscissa $x \geqslant x^* + q_b$. One of the compared prototypes, the potentially optimal one, contains a template for one of the characters; to its left there are white columns, and to its right there are columns each having maximum similarity (equal to m) with the corresponding column of the image.

The potentially optimal prototype has the form shown in Figure 9.1. The central portion contains the template of the class $\hat{k}$ exhibiting maximum similarity equal to $\hat{G}$ at $x = \hat{x}$. The columns on the left with abscissae from $x^* + 1$ to $\hat{x} - q_b$ are white, i.e., they form the prototype image of a blank between characters. The columns with abscissae from $\hat{x} + 1$ to x, to the right of the template, are assumed to be those columns of the existing templates that have maximum similarity with the corresponding columns of the image. They are introduced with the purpose of obtaining an upper bound for the potentially maximal similarity.

The second prototype competing with the potentially optimal one for a given value of x, consists of some other template with the abscissa x for its right-hand edge, together with white columns to its left. The inequality (9.7) contains only those terms of the similarity functions that differ for the two prototypes being compared.

The algorithm just described was simulated on a computer and showed good results. As will be seen later, it was also successful in the reader.

The algorithm for the semiautomatic input of rejected characters is also worth mentioning. It has no relationship to the recognition theory, but is an essential part of the total flow chart of the machine. During the reading process some characters will fail of reliable recognition because of some defect in the image. The machine rejects them, and the corresponding character codes must be supplied manually by a human operator. For this purpose the operator must see the image of the illegible character in its context, i.e., together with a few neighboring characters.

A peculiarity of the algorithm [16, 17] is that it was designed for a mode of operation in which the line scan is not interrupted when an illegible character appears. The codes for the recognized characters in a single line are stored in a buffer memory, along with the corresponding coordinate x.

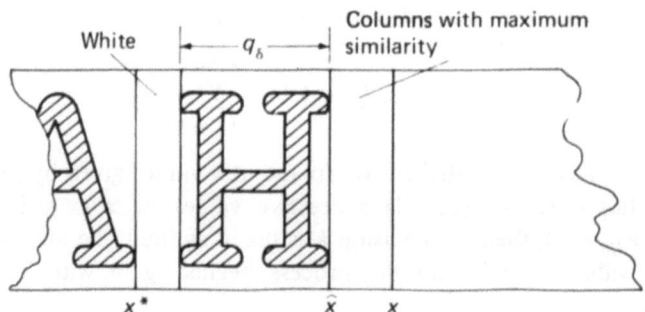

Figure 9.1   Potentially optimal prototype constructed during the recognition of the portion of the line from x^* to x.

When an illegible character appears a special rejection symbol is recorded for it, along with its coordinate.

When the line scan is completed the contents of the memory are scanned, beginning with the first character in the line. If a rejection symbol is detected, an audible alarm is given and a special optical sighting device is aimed at the point with the coordinate x, recorded along with the rejection symbol. The operator looks at the illegible character in its context, recognizes it, and keys its code into the buffer, which stores it in place of the rejection symbol. The scan of the buffer then resumes, and all illegible characters in the line are thus correctly interpreted one by one. After this, the search for the next line, and the recognition process, are again begun.

9.2 The Technical Implementation of the Line Recognition Algorithm

In most cases a given algorithm can be implemented in more than one way. The choice of one method among all those that meet the requirements is to a large extent determined by the intuition and tastes of the person working on the implementation. Nevertheless, the implementer must constantly keep in mind the advantages and disadvantages of the different processes. We shall now look at various possible methods for implementing the most important parts of the flow chart for the machine, and at the considerations that led to the choice of a method.

It is clearly unnecessary to describe in detail the method for separating documents from the input stack and transporting them to the reader, since these are not an essential part of the recognition process. On the contrary, the digitization of images, and the search for a line, are inseparable parts of the whole image recognition problem. The technical implementation of these tasks is essentially determined by the method chosen to implement the central task—the resolution of the line into characters and the recognition of these, i.e., the recognition of the line. Therefore we begin by looking at methods for accomplishing the latter task.

Any method for technical implementation of the line recognition algorithm is subject to fairly severe speed requirements. To achieve a scanning speed of some v characters per second, a window (i.e., a field of view) having a width q_b must move along the line at a rate of vq_b retina columns per second, where q_b is the number of columns contained in the width of a character. After each displacement of the window by one column, the next value of (9.3) must be computed. The maximum with respect to k, τ, η can be found by enumeration only. Therefore the similarity $g'(v, s, q_b, , \tau, \eta)$ must be computed as many times for a given x as there are values of the parameter triplet (k, τ, η).

Let us denote the number of templates for the various classes by n' (as opposed to the number n of different classes), and the number of vertical displacements by m'. Then the total number of additions and multi-plications per second comes to

$$v_v = vq_bn'm'2N,$$

where N is the number of components in a template. If we set $v = 200$ characters per second, $q_b = 20$, $n' = 72$, $m' = 5$, and $N = 300$, we find

$$v_v = 200 \times 20 \times 72 \times 5 \times 300 = 432 \times 10^6$$

operations per second.

It is very difficult to execute such a large number of operations sequentially in one second. We therefore need to look for a technical solution that will permit parallel computation of the similarity of a portion of the image with all templates; that is, all the similarities, and all the terms in the similarities that correspond to different components of the image, are computed simultaneously.

There are four known methods for meeting this requirement; they are the following:

1. *Incoherent optical correlation.* A continuous analogue of the scalar product of image and template may be implemented by projecting an image with the brightness function $v(x, y)$ on a plate whose transmittance is defined by the function $c^{(k)}(x, y)$. Then the total light flux transmitted through the plate is

$$\int \int v(x, y)c^{(k)}(x, y)dx\,dy.$$

This flux is picked up by a photomultiplier, transformed into electric current, and measured. By subtracting the outputs of two such optical correlators one can model a function $c^{(k)}(x, y)$ with alternating sign, which is needed for the correlation method and for the piecewise linear decision rule studied in Chapter VI. To use an optical correlator for the computation of similarities, one must translate the template with respect to the image. The horizontal translation (along the lines of the text) can be accomplished mechanically, but the vertical translation must occur a hundred times faster than the number of characters recognized per second, i.e., at a rate of some tens of kilohertz. It would be hard to do this mechanically, by moving either the plate or some optical component. One could prepare several templates for each class, differing only as to vertical placement, but this would complicate the construction of the correlator.

A new and different method, still rather complex, uses an electron-optical transducer; it is described in [18].

There is also another and well-known method for optical computation of the correlation function. The equipment for it is sketched in Figure 9.2. It is not difficult to see that the illumination at the various points of the principal focal plane $\mathscr{P}$ of the lens L_2 is proportional to the value of the

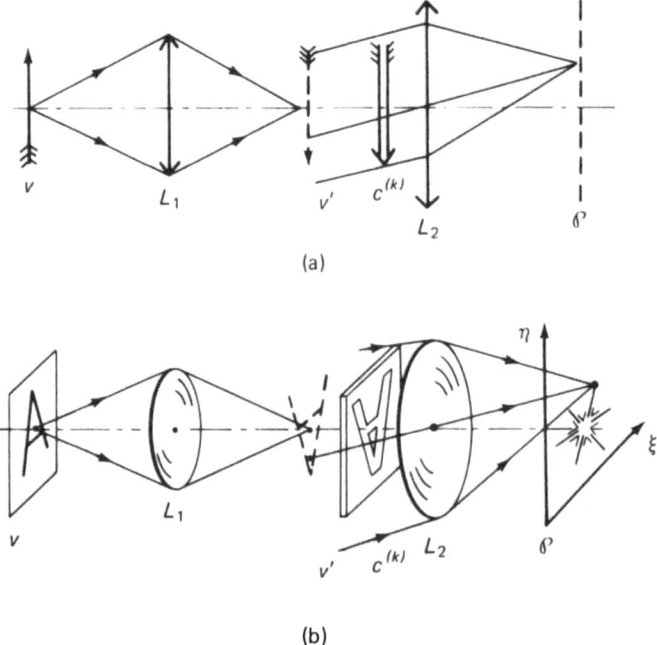

(a)

(b)

Figure 9.2   Incoherent optical correlator, which computes the similarity between image and a single template, as a function of the translation parameters ξ and η. (a) diagram of the optics; (b) physical configuration.

similarity for various values of the translations ξ and η:

$$g^{(k)}(\xi,\eta) = \int\int v(x,y)c^{(k)}(x-\xi, y-\eta)dx\,dy. \qquad (9.8)$$

Vertical translations can be implemented by measuring the brightness at the various points of the plane $\mathscr{P}$ with several light-sensitive elements (photomultipliers) or with some suitable scanning apparatus. Thus, whether we use an optical correlator or some other method for computing the similarity, we cannot dispense with a scanner, or an equivalent apparatus consisting of a row of light-sensitive elements.

The advantage of the optical correlator is the simplicity with which it generates a signal proportional to the similarity. There is no need to digitize the image.

The disadvantages are the following:

a.   It is difficult to construct and adjust the optical system for several tens of templates.

b.   The use of many photomultipliers requires a powerful and stable high-voltage supply, which is technically inconvenient. If relatively insensitive photodiodes are used to replace the photomultiplier, the image must be very brightly lighted.

c.   Instabilities and noise fluctuations in the light-sensitive devices (the photomultipliers) make it difficult to attain the necessary precision, i.e., within 2–3%.

d.   It is difficult to implement templates, as optimized by a computer, with the necessary accuracy. As shown in Chapter VI, one cannot dispense with the optimization of the templates.

2. *Coherent optical correlator.*   The use of holography appears at first glance to have substantial advantages over the use of incoherent light correlators, because with coherent light it is easy to compute the Fourier transform of the image. Given the Fourier transform of both image and templates, we can simplify the computation of the similarity as a function of the translation parameters. In fact, the values of the correlation function, for all the values of the translation parameters being considered, are given by its two-dimensional spectrum, which can be obtained by a *single* multiplication of the two-dimensional spectra of image and template. In the absence of the Fourier transform, the integral (9.8) must be evaluated many times, in fact as many times as there are distinct values of the two-dimensional translation parameter.

However, to solve the recognition problem we need the inverse Fourier transform, which converts the spectrum of the correlation function for each kth template into the corresponding correlation function $g^{(k)}(\xi, \eta)$. Without it, we cannot find the maximum similarity and reach a correct decision. The inverse transform is as expensive, in terms of the complexity and difficultness of the implementing equipment, as the computation of the correlation using incoherent light. Thus the apparent advantage of holography vanishes.

Another and highly essential shortcoming is the impossibility of using light reflected from the image, due to the fact that light reflected from the paper is incoherent. The coherent light method can be used only for images on film, and this is most unsuitable for the purposes of a character reader.

3. *A mosaic of light-sensitive cells.*   The image is projected, as onto a retina, on a mosaic. This method permits the simultaneous transformation of the image into a collection of voltages proportional to the components v_i of the sampled image, and the modeling of the scalar product by an electrical current. The components of the templates are modeled by the conductivity of resistors attached in a star formation to the amplified outputs of the light-sensitive elements [Figure 9.3 (a)]. To each template corresponds its own cluster of resistors. In this, as in the two preceding schemes, the horizontal translation of the image relative to the templates can be accomplished mechanically. A commutator can be used for the vertical translation, to connect the resistors to different amplifier outputs [Figure 9.3 (b)]. This method for implementing the translations is simpler and faster than scanning the plane of the correlation function in the optical correlation methods.

The mosaic method has two merits, as compared to the optical methods: the technologically superior process for preparing the templates, and the

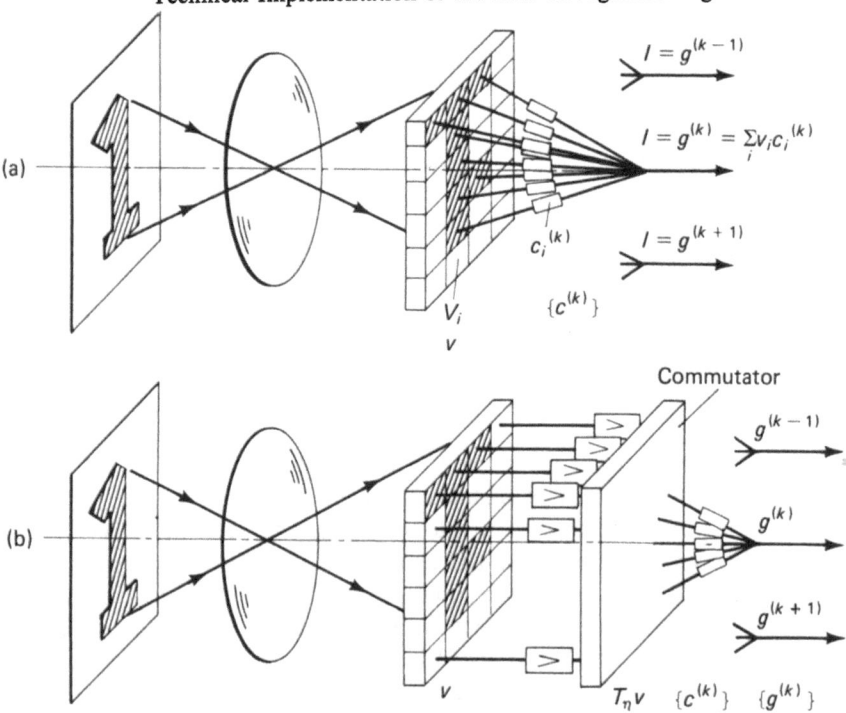

Figure 9.3 Computation of the similarities using a mosaic of light-sensing elements and stars of resistors.

greater precision attainable. In fact, let us suppose that in both cases we use light-sensitive elements with the same transducer error, i.e., relative accuracy in the conversion of the light flux to an electric signal, and that the errors in the individual elements are statistically independent. Then when we sum the currents in accordance with the scheme shown in Figure 9.3 we add the mean values and the variances of the currents generated by the N elements. The relative error in the total current is the ratio of the standard deviation (the square root of the variance) to the mean total current, and is therefore smaller by a factor $\sqrt{N}$ than the relative error of the currents from individual elements, which is equal to the transducer error. In an optical correlator we are transforming light fluxes that are proportional to the similarity. Therefore the relative error in the similarity is equal to the transducer error.

A shortcoming of the mosaic system is the need for constructing a large number of amplifiers of measurement quality; these are complex devices, requiring careful adjustment.

4. *The shift register.* If we write the gray shades of the retina cells into a memory whose cells are arranged in the form of a matrix like the retina, we can materially decrease the number of light-sensors and amplifiers, as compared to the number required for the mosaic. We need only a single column of sensors and amplifiers, which we move along the line being

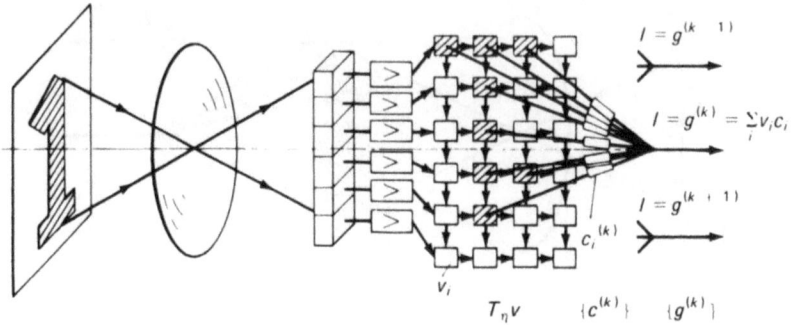

Figure 9.4   Computation of the similarity with a shift register.

read, writing the output signals into memory column by column. When the matrix is full, it will contain signals characterizing the gray shade of all the cells in the portion of the image into which the character being recognized will fit. To renew the stored image as the sensing column moves along the line, the memory cells must be so connected that each row of the matrix forms a shift register. When a new value of the gray shade is written into the leftmost column of the matrix (Figure 9.4), the contents of all the other columns must be shifted one place to the right. Then the matrix will always contain information characterizing the image falling inside a window of the required width as it moves along the line.

If the memory cells provide a voltage signal at the output which is proportional to the stored quantity, we can attach resistors to the outputs, with conductivity proportional to the components of the templates. Thus, as in the mosaic, we can obtain currents proportional to the similarities.

To implement a vertical translation, the columns of the matrix must also represent shift registers. All the necessary vertical translations of the stored image must occur in the interval between horizontal translations. Since flip-flops provide the best storage medium to meet the requirements just described, the signals to be stored must be quantized, i.e., transformed into coded values. The number of quantization levels may differ. With four or more levels, the quantization consists simply in converting the gray shade into a binary code. For two levels, it is best to use an adaptive method in which the quantization threshold depends on the gray shade of some neighboring cells.

As in our other methods, the shift-register method permits the similarity with all templates to be computed simultaneously and practically instantaneously. Time is required only for transfer of the information in the shift registers and for measuring the maximum value of the similarity.

The speed requirements are estimated as follows. The number of vertical translations per second is

$$\nu_c = \nu q_b m' = 200 \times 20 \times 5 = 2 \times 10^4 \text{ sec}^{-1}.$$

Thus one shift takes 50 microseconds. Allowing for the fact that the rate of $\nu = 200$ char/sec is an average value, and that there will inevitably be losses of time in moving the document, searching for lines, etc., we must count on allowing no more than 25 to 30 microseconds for a shift. We must measure the maximum value of the similarity during the same time interval. Such speeds are easily attainable with modern computer technology.

The shift-register technique for computing the similarity meets all the requirements for speed and manufacturing technology, and is simpler than the mosaic method with respect to the amount of hardware needed. It was therefore chosen for the ČARS reader. One disadvantage is that the gray shade of the image must be quantized, and this means some loss of information and therefore a higher error probability. However, by an optimal choice of the parameters in the quantization algorithm we can keep the increase to an acceptable level. The method employed, i.e., optimization according to the **EPA** criterion, was briefly described in the preceding section.

We have considered the processes for computing the similarity $g'(v, x, q, k, \tau, \eta)$ between the portion of the image in a window of width q_b and the several templates. The actual reading of the continuous lines in a text requires us to choose a technical method for implementing the suboptimal algorithm that we described earlier, which processes the values of the similarity as the window moves along the line. In principle we could apply the generally accepted method of computing technology: convert the values of the similarity with all the templates into codes, and work on it with a digital processor. However, we can also use a more economical method, based on the notion of the compensating extremum detector, which was proposed by K. A. Netrebenko [54, 55] and improved by A. G. Semenovskii [62]. In this method, the coding of certain analogue quantities and the search for their maximum (or minimum) value can be combined in one apparatus and carried out with the same precision as the coding of the analogues. The corresponding diagram is shown in Figure 9.5.

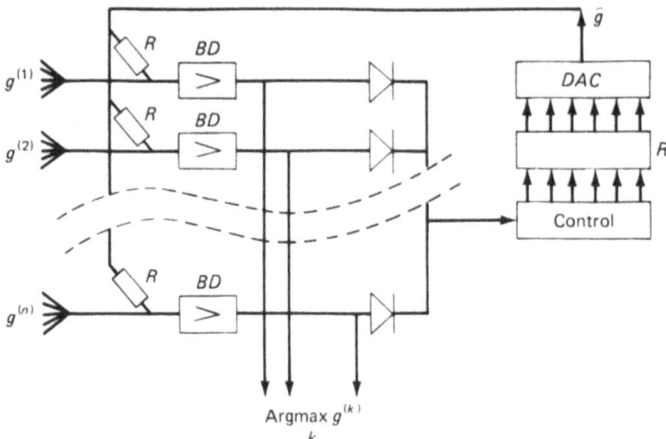

Figure 9.5 Diagram of an extremum detector based on sequential compensation. BD: Balance detectors; DAC: digital-to-analogue converter.

The operating principle is as follows: Suppose that all the input voltages $g^{(k)}$ whose maximum is being sought are positive. The initial value of the feedback voltage $\hat{q}$ at the output of the digital-to-analogue converter DAC is zero. Each of the balance detectors BD emits a unit signal if $g^{(k)} > \hat{g}$. In the initial state all the signals from the balance detectors have the value 1. The control block increases the value of $\hat{q}$, digit by digit, beginning with the most significant binary digits in the register R. If, when a given digit is increased, all the inequalities $g^{(k)} > \hat{g}$ are violated, this digit is returned to a zero value and a trial is made to see whether the digit of next lower order can be increased while at least one of the inequalities is preserved.

At the end of the process the register R will hold the code of the largest value of $\hat{g}$ for which at least one of the inequalities holds. Therefore, to within the precision of the least significant digit,

$$\hat{g} = \max_{k} g^{(k)}.$$

The output signal from any balance detector for which

$$g^{(k)} > \hat{g}$$

will have unit value. Therefore the unit signals at the outputs of the balance detectors serve as markers for the inputs of the circuit representing the set $\arg\max_{k} g^{(k)}$.

V. G. Kalmykov [29, 30] has constructed a digital-to-analogue device, using this concept, to implement his suboptimal algorithm for line recognition. The diagram is shown in Figure 9.6.

This scheme tests the inequality (9.7), which is more conveniently

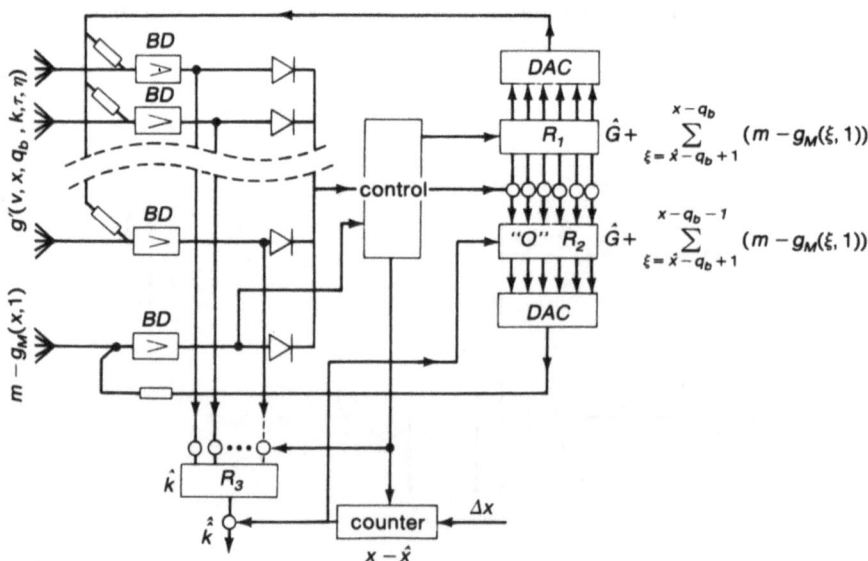

Figure 9.6 Apparatus for implementing the "line-start algorithm".

rewritten as

$$\left[\hat{G} + \sum_{\xi=\hat{x}-q_b+1}^{x-q_b-1} (m - g_M(\xi, 1))\right] + m - g_M(x - q_b, 1) < g_M(x, q_b).$$

The quantity in square brackets is contained in the register R_2, where it is transferred from R_1, after each measurement. The quantity $m - g_M(x, 1)$ is realized by a special star of resistors connected to the last column of the shift register (the lowest of the stars in Figure 9.6). The value of $g_M(x, q_b)$ is the maximum value of the signal over all the other stars. The measurements are made by the register R_1, using a compensation method like the one in the extremum detector (cf. Figure 9.5). The result of the measurement is the quantity

$$\hat{G} + \sum_{\xi=\hat{x}-q_b+1}^{x-q_b} (m - g_M(\xi, 1)),$$

if (9.7) is not satisfied, or $g_M(x, q_b)$ if it is. In both cases the result of the measurement is transferred to the register R_2. In the second case, the index $\hat{k}$ of the input showing the highest value of the similarity is written into the register R_3, and the counter C containing the value of $x - \hat{x}$ is set to zero, which is equivalent to assigning the value x to $\hat{x}$. Thus, the assignments (9.5) are made when the inequality (9.7) is satisfied. If it is never satisfied in the course of $q_b - 1$ steps, the counter C overflows, and this initiates the output of the final decision $\check{k}$ and the reset of R_2. The process begins again, making new assignments (9.5) with the next measurement.

The diagrams in Figure 9.4 and 9.6 specify on the whole the hardware implementation of the ČARS reader. The remaining units in the machine follow the customary computer technology.

9.3 The Choice of the Hardware for Finding and Scanning the Lines

Use of the shift-register method for comparing images and templates requires that the images be sampled and converted to electrical signals. This process is called scanning. There are three known basic methods for implementing it: mechanical, mosaic, and by the use of a cathode-ray tube (CRT). The last is the most popular, but it suffers from three essential shortcomings:

1. The resolving power of most of the existing CRTs is too low for the scanning of a document 200 mm wide, while details of the image down to a size of 0.1 mm must be revealed without essential loss of contrast. So far as is known, no transmission tubes meeting this requirement have been produced. Tubes for flying-spot scanners

have the needed resolving power of the order of 2000 lines, but with this number of distinguishable lines the contrast on the screen is lower by an order of magnitude than the maximum contrast of the screen. This means that thin and weak lines in the image may be lost during scanning.

2. The edges of the light spot on the screen are not sharp, and the spot has an unstable size and shape; it is therefore difficult to obtain by means of a CRT a lattice with sharply outlined nonoverlapping cells.

3. A CRT is an awkward, unstable, and short-lived device, demanding special additional facilities such as a stable high-voltage power supply, a precision deflection and focusing system, amplifiers and generators for the deflection signals, a dark room for reading the documents, etc.

The mosaic system described above (Figure 9.3) is free of these defects and most resembles the human eye; however, with the current state of the art of amplifier production and adjustment it requires too much equipment and can therefore be used only for retinas with a small number (a few tens) of cells.

Mechanical scanning systems are the simplest, the most precise, and the longest-lived. They are based on the use of rotating disks with apertures or slits, rotating mirrors, or mechanical movement of the documents. There is a widely held view that a mechanical scanning system cannot attain the necessary speed. This view, however, is incorrect. An electric motor can drive a disk at better than 30,000 rpm, i.e., more than 500 revolutions per second. With a hundred apertures in the disk, we can achieve a scanning rate of 50 kilohertz (50,000 columns per second), which yields a reading speed of 2500 characters per second (for 20 columns per symbol).

We can also use mechanical means for scanning along the line of characters and for moving from one line to another. However, the synchronization of various mechanical units presents real difficulties. These do not arise if the fastest unit—providing vertical scanning of the columns of the image—is replaced by a mosaic consisting of one column of light-sensing photodiodes. The horizontal scanning can be done mechanically, and the vertical scanning can be synchronized with it by pulses generated in the horizontal scanning mechanism.

The mechanical scanning of the line can be accomplished with a rocking mirror, with a rotating reflecting drum, or by displacing the document itself. The rocking mirror loses much time in its return motion, and the rotating drum is necessarily very clumsy if the optical system is to have a sufficient aperture.

These defects are overcome with scanning by moving the document. If the document is attached to a rotating drum, with the lines running around the circumference, the movement from the end of one line to the beginning of the next can be accomplished without reciprocal motion. This method also allows us to put the reading head close to the document and to get a wide aperture with optical components of small size. the ČARS reader uses

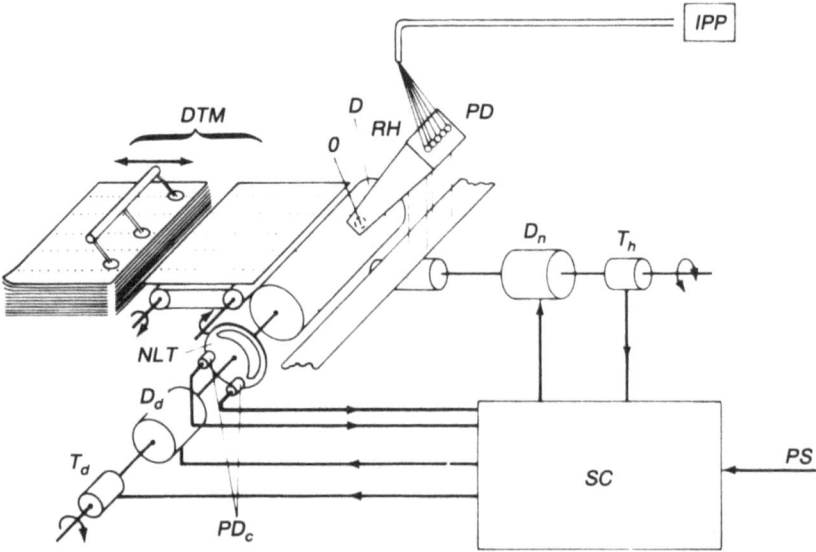

Figure 9.7   Sketch of the scanner.

a system of this type, with a rotating drum and a column of photodiodes (cf. Figure 9.7).

The documents to be read are automatically fed to the rotating drum D by the document feeding mechanism DTM and are held in position by suction. A small portion of the document, containing a single character (letter or digit), is strongly illuminated and projected through the objective O onto the row of photodiodes PD contained in the reading head RH and oriented perpendicular to the line of text. Each photodiode measures the gray shade of the corresponding cell, and the row of them simultaneously measures the gray shades in each cell of one column of the retina. As the drum rotates, the images of the characters move past the column of photodiodes. By reading the values of the gray shade at discrete instants in time, corresponding to equal tranlations of the image, we obtain values of the gray shade corresponding to all the cells in the retina.

The signals from the photodiodes arrive at the image preprocessor IPP, which amplifies them and executes the adaptive quantization process (cf. Section 9.1). As indicated in Section 9.2, the line search is conducted by inspecting the left margin of the document, where markers have been typed (Figure 9.11). The margin containing the markers extends along the axial direction on the drum; therefore, after each line is recognized the drum D must halt in a predetermined position and wait during the search for a new line.

The start-stop control for the drum is optimal with respect to time, under the following constraints: The maximum rotational speed ω_{max} is limited by the speed of the recognizer. The least time for a single revolution is obtained by bringing the drum to the speed ω_{max} with maximum acceleration ε, and stopping it with maximum deceleration $-\varepsilon$ at the end of the rotation. It is best to adopt the policy of accelerating and decelerating the drum while the reading head is opposite the marginal fields of the document, keeping the angular velocity constant while the line is being read, else it is difficult to track the line.

At the end of the rotation, the drum must be stopped in minimum time and held in a sharply defined position. Optimal control of this process is achieved by comparing two signals: one from a tachometer generator T_d, and the other from a special nonlinear transducer NLT, which emits a signal that has an absolute value proportional to the square root of the angular distance to the stopping point, where the signal changes its sign on transit. The transducer consists of two special optical masks that rotate with the drum, and two photodiodes PD_c. The signal of one photodiode is subtracted from the other.

A special low-inertia motor D_d, chosen to drive the drum, is a direct-current device with a smooth rotor, capable of high angular acceleration and deceleration for starting and stopping. The reducing gear (not shown in Figure 9.7) is a friction drive without free play.

The exact centering of the symbols is accomplished in the ČARS by going through all possible positions of the symbol relative to the templates. However, to keep the enumeration process from being too lengthy, a preliminary rough guidance along the line is necessary. At the beginning of the line it is achieved by a system that locates the reading head RH with respect to the marker. The reading head cannot be held stationary while the line is being read, since the line may be tilted and may pass entirely out of the field of view of a stationary reading head. It is impossible to enlarge the height of the field so that tilted lines will not leave it, since to do so would increase the volume of the equipment and decrease the reading speed.

Therefore a tilt compensator was developed, using a special line-tracking system. The reading head is moved, during the process of tracking the line, by the same drive (D_h, T_h) that is used in the search for a marker. The mismatch signals for control of the drive arrive from the recognition system.

The signals giving the position of the character with respect to the center of the view field are generated in the following way: The number of vertical steps needed to produce maximum similarity is recorded as the image of the character moves in the shift register. This number is used to generate a discrete mismatch signal. However, these signals appear at discrete times and with a significant delay slightly greater than the scanning time of a character. Furthermore, the line-tracking system is constrained by the fact that the reading head cannot move with high velocity in the direction normal to the line. If the head is moved too rapidly, the image written in the shift register will be distorted because the succeeding columns will suffer a relative vertical displacement among themselves. In this connection the rotational speed of the drum must be kept constant, else the maximum admissible speed of movement of the reading head, required to obtain the minimum performance time for the mismatch signal, must vary with the rotation speed of the drum to avoid distorting the image.

Like the stopping system for the drum, the control of the motion of the reading head during the line tracking is performed by a speed-optimal method. A signal proportional to the velocity is output by a tachometer T_h. The position signal is generated by a nonlinear digital-to-analogue converter, which converts the code generated by the recognizer and specifies the position of the character into a corresponding voltage which is compared with the voltage generated by the tachometer. The converter also takes into account the correction for the delay in the position signal.

While reading a document the machine must not only scan the lines in the horizontal and vertical directions, but also locate the lines. This can be done mechanically, by displacement in a direction perpendicular to the lines. It is more convenient to move the reading head, which contains the row of photodiodes, the objective lens, and the light source, than it is to move the document, which is affixed to the rotating drum.

A displacement of about 8.5 mm, which corresponds to double-spaced lines, can be accomplished within 50 milliseconds when applying an acceleration of about 10 m/sec^2, i.e., $1g$. Thus we can achieve a very fast line change without subjecting the reading head to a significant overload.

We have already described the algorithm for finding a marker, in some detail. Two basic problems had to be solved before it could be implemented: how to compute the similarity of the marker image with its template, and how to control the movement of the reading head so that it halts in the right place with sufficient precision.

We have noted that a linear decision rule can be quite simply implemented by an incoherent optimal correlator if the number of classes is not too large and if a practicable translation process can be found. There are only two classes in the recognition of a marker—namely, marker or no marker. Only one template is needed. The light reflected from the paper can be wholly focused on one light sensor. Because the light flux is strong, we can use a photodiode instead of a photomultiplier; this greatly simplifies the construction of the correlator. Since the marker has the form of a fairly long horizontal black bar, there is no need for horizontal translation. The vertical translation is accomplished by moving the field of view along the document margin during the search. Therefore no supplementary means for accomplishing the translation are needed. The correlator is constructed as shown in Figure 9.8. (a).

We may use the same light source LS and objective L_1 that we use in the basic character-reading optical system. The diaphragm D and the prism P form the positive and negative templates for the marker [cf. Figure 9.8 (b)]. Light passing through D but not through P is focused by the lens L_2 on the photodiode PD_1, and light passing through P is deflected so that it falls on PD_2. An inverting amplifier A at the input of the balance detector BD

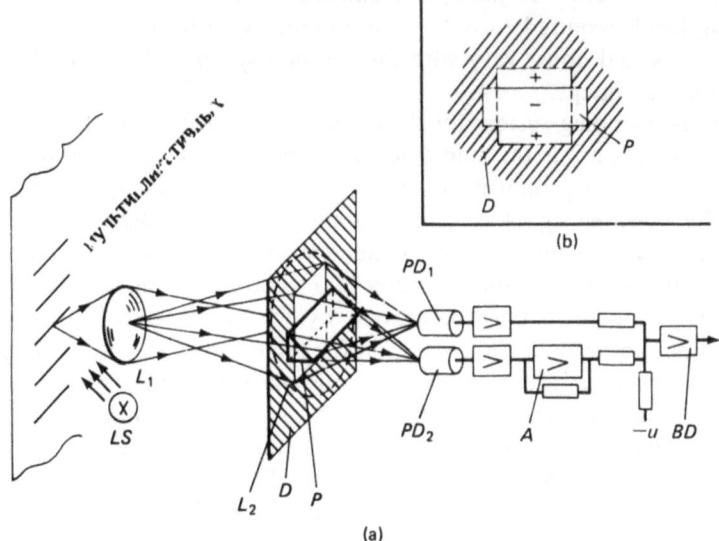

Figure 9.8   Optical correlator used to locate the markers.

forms the difference of the currents from the two photodiodes. Thus the template has what amounts to a negative component in its central portion, covered by the prism. The balance detector is activated only when the image of a black bar is projected onto the prism and a bright field is seen by the remainder of the slit in the diaphragm.

Let us consider the method for controlling the motion of the reading head during the search for a marker. Perhaps the best method for rapid searching would be the following: impose an acceleration $+a$ during the first half of the distance, and a deceleration $-a$ during the last half. However, it would be very difficult to build a pick-up that would put out a signal proportional to the distance to the marker. Moreover, this distance becomes known at the moment when the image of the marker is detected by the optical correlator. Then it is equal to the constant distance by which the projection of the template of the marker is offset from the optical axis of the reading head. This information may be used in a control system with constant length at the braking pass, equal to the offset. In this system using a constant deceleration requires that the velocity be constant and known when the braking begins.

The head is therefore accelerated to a fixed velocity of 24 cm/sec, which is maintained by the scan control block SC (cf. Figure 9.7) with the aid of signal from the tachometer T_h up to the start of the braking. The system settles on the marker with a precision of ± 0.7 mm. The transit time between double-spaced lines is about 60 msec. To increase the overall speed of the machine the braking of the reading head occurs in 24 msec during the acceleration of the drum, and the acceleration of the reading head occurs during the braking of the drum, also taking 24 msec.

The return of the head to its initial position after reading a whole document is under no speed constraint. As is the case for the drum halt, the head must reach a fixed position. This is accomplished by a tachometer and a nonlinear transducer like the one used for braking the drum (not shown in Figure 9.7). During the return the head is displaced by about 280 mm in 0.32 sec. The acceleration during startup and braking does not exceed 12 m/sec², which is safe for both the optics and the incandescent lamp used as the light source.

These technological solutions of the problems of scanning, line tracking, search for a marker, and return of the head are the main determinants of the construction of the document scanning unit. Ths remaining elements of the unit employ the customary methods of optics and computing technology.

9.4 Block Diagram of the ČARS Reader

The technical decisions described above, which form the basis for the two principal components of the reading machine, represent the means for implementing the algorithm for reading multiline documents. We now look at the block diagram of the total machine and the simultaneous working of all its components, in order to connect together all of the material we have been describing, and make a coherent whole.

The ČARS consists of three units: the scanner (S), the recognizer (R), and the buffer memory(B). The external appearance of the machine is shown in Figure 9.9. Each of the three units is made up of many blocks,

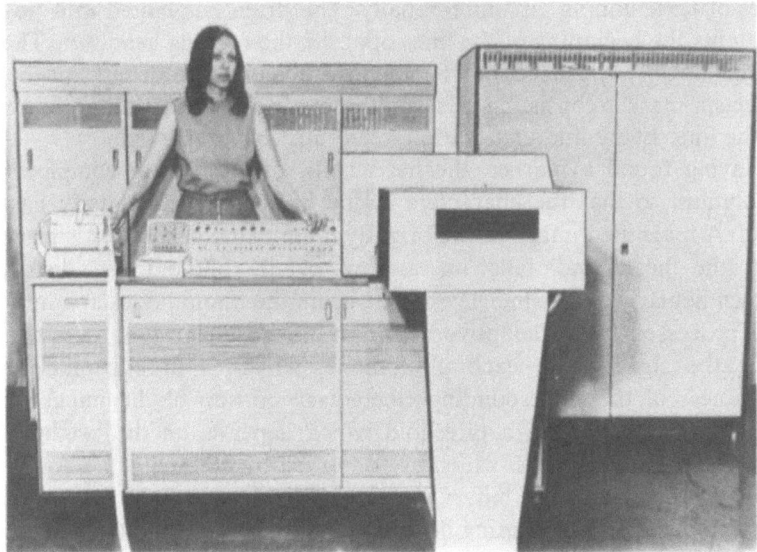

Figure 9.9   General appearance of the ČARS character reader.

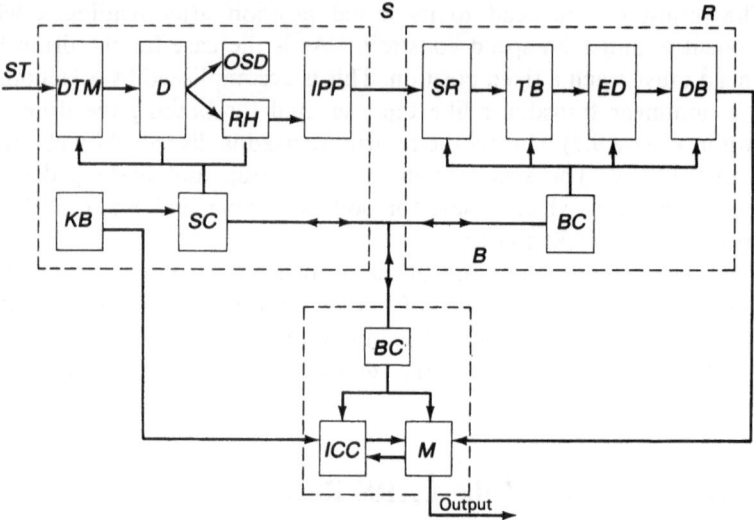

Figure 9.10   The block diagram of the ČARS character reader.

connected as shown in the block diagram in Figure 9.10. The machine functions as follows:

The stack *ST* of sheets (documents) with text to be read is placed in the input hopper. On a signal from the control block the document transfer mechanism (*DTM*) removes the top sheet from the stack, by suction, and transfers it to the vacuum drum *D* (see also Figure 9.7). The document is automatically seized and held to the surface of the rotating drum, with the lines of text running circumferentially. The drum has halted in a position that puts the beginning of the lines opposite the reading head *RH*. The line search begins; the head moves lengthwise along the drum axis until it detects a marker consisting of several minus signs written at the beginning of the line. Every line that is to be read must be so marked.

Having found a marker, the head halts and the drum completes one revolution, so that the characters in the line move sequentially past the head. A magnified image of the brightly illuminated characters is projected into the head and falls on a row of 18 photodiodes distributed perpendicularly to the line. The signals from the photodiodes are amplified and processed by an adaptive quantizer in the image preprocessor *IPP*. Here the signal from each photodiode, which is proportional to the brightness of the corresponding elementary portion of the image (retina cell), is compared with a threshold which depends on the brightness of several neighboring cells, which are observed by 18 auxiliary photodiodes in the reading head. The binary signals emitted by the quantizer are sent to the recognizer *R*. The reading head is not stationary during the line scan; it is capable of moving slightly, under the control of a signal from the scan control block *SC*, across the line in order to compens..te for a possible tilt.

The line is recognized during a single revolution of the drum. If one or more illegible characters are found, the drum makes another revolution, at lesser speed, and stops at a position that puts the first illegible character in the view field of the optical sighting device OSD which is fixed to the reading head. The operator sees the character that the machine has rejected, recognizes it either from its context or on the basis of prior information about the document, and presses the corresponding key on the keyboard *KB*. The character code is sent from the keyboard through the illegible character corrector block *ICC* to the memory *M* in the buffer *B*. The drum rotates to the next illegible character, or to the end of the line after all illegible characters have been corrected.

The drum halts in its initial position, and the head begins the search for the next line and continues the process. When it reaches the end of the document, it returns to its initial position. At this time the document on the drum is being changed. The document that has just been read is transferred to one of two receiving pockets, depending on whether or not illegible characters were found in it.

In the recognizer *R*, the binary signals from the image preprocessor *IPP* are sent to the two-coordinate shift register *SR*, where they are shifted vertically and horizontally. The transfer of these signals to the shift register is synchronized with the rotation of the drum, as is the whole action of the recognizer. The set of signals in the columns of the register form an image of the character. Several vertical shifts of the image as a whole are executed in the interval between successive transfers of new signals to the shift register. After each such shift the similarities with 72 templates stored in the template block *TB* are computed by analogue methods, and the template showing maximum similarity is selected. The computation of the similarity executes the following operations:

$$g'(v,x,q_b,k,\tau,\eta) = \sum_{i=1}^{N} v_i'(x,\eta)c_i(k,\tau) + c_0(k,\tau).$$

Here $v_i'(x,\eta)$ is the ith component of the image in the register when the abscissa of the scanning column of photodiodes is x and the vertical translation is η; $c_i(k,\tau)$ is the ith component of the kth template of type τ; $c_0(k,\tau)$ is its bias, or null component; $N = 20 \times 14 = 280$ is the number of retina cells in the window, which has the same width for all characters, namely $q_b = 20$.

The components $v_i'(x,\eta)$ of the image are represented by voltages read from the flip-flops of the register; the components $c_i(k,\tau)$ of the templates are conductances of resistors. The register is shifted every 20 microseconds. After each shift, 72 currents appear at the outputs of the template block; they are proportional to the 72 similarities of the image with the templates. These currents are applied to the inputs of the extremum detector *ED*, which finds the maximum similarity over the values of k, τ, and η.

The extremum detector *ED* and the decision block *DB* jointly implement the suboptimal line recognition algorithm described in Sections 9.1 and 9.2.

The decision block *DB* generates the six-bit binary code of the decision *k* for the successive characters in the line. These codes are transmitted from the recognizer *R* to the buffer *B*. If a character in the line turns out to be illegible, a special rejection code is written in place of the code *k*, and the buffer control block *BC* records the presence of an illegible character. This signal transfers the machine to the correction routine already described. Control passes to the illegible-character corrector block *ICC*, housed in the buffer unit.

9.5 Tests of the Reader

The ČARS reader, as developed according to the block diagram outlined above, was tested against the requirements initially laid down for it. Aside from the environmental tests and tests of the reliability of the apparatus,

```
—      0 I 2 3 4 5 6 7 8 9 0 I 2 3 4 5 6 7 8 9 0 I 2 3 4 5 6 7 8 9 0
—      000I0203040506070809I0III2I3I4I5I6I7I8I9202I222324252627282930
—      3I323334353637383940414243444546474849505I52535455565758596061
—      626364656667686970717273747576777879808I82838485868788899091 92
—      9394959697989900010203040506070809I0III2I3I4I5I6I7I8I9202I2223
—      24252627282930313233343536373839404142434445464748495051525354
—      5556575859606162636465666768697071727374757677787980818283 8485
—      868788899091929394959697989900010203040506070809I0III2I3I4I5I6
—      I7I8I9202I2223242526272829303132333435363738394041424344454647
—      48495051525354555657585960616263646566676869707172737475767778
—      798081828384858687888990919293949596979899000I0203040506070809
—      I0III2I3I4I5I6I7I8I9202I2223242526272829303I323334353637383940
—      4I4243444546474849505I52535455565758596061626364656667686970 7I
—      72737475767778798081828384858687888990919293949596979899000I02
—      03040506070809I0III2I3I4I5I6I7I8I9202I2223242526272829303I3233
—      34353637383940414243444546474849505I525354555657585960616263 64
—      65666768697071727374757677787980818283848586878889909I92939495
—      969798990001020304050607080 9I0III2I3I4I5I6I7I8I9202I2223242526
—      2728293031323334353637383940414243444546474849505I52535455 5657
—      585960616263646566676869707172737475767778798081 82838485868788
—      89909I929394959697989900010203040506070809I0III2I3I4I5I6I7I8I9
—      202I2223242526272829303132333435363738394041424344454647484950
—      5I525354555657585960616263646566676869707I72737475767778798081
—      82838485868788899091929394959697989900010203040506070809I0III2
—      I3I4I5I6I7I8I9202I2223242526272829303I3233343536373839404I4243
—      4445464748495051525354555657585960616263646566676869707I727374
—      75767778798081828384858687888990919293949596979899000I02030405
—      06070809I0III2I3I4I5I6I7I8I9202I2223242526272829303I3233343536
—      37383940414243444546474849505I525354555657585960616263646 56667
I23II—      68697071727374757677787980818283848586878889909I92939495969798
```

Figure 9.11   Sample of test document from the numerical array.

```
IB.X.----   0 I 2 3 4 5 6 7 8 9 + - / , . ( ) x = % ? § " А Б В Г Д Е Ж З
     ----   И К Л М Н П Р С Т У Ф Х Ц Ч Ш Щ Ы Ь Э Ю Я 0 I 2 3 4 5 6 7 8 9
     ----   000I02030405060708090+0-0/0,0.0(0)0x0=0%0?0§0"0А0Б0В0Г0Д0Е0Ж0З
     ----   0И0К0Л0М0Н0П0Р0С0Т0У0Ф0Х0Ц0Ч0Ш0Щ0Ы0Ь0Э0Ю0Я1О1I1I2I3I4I5I6I7I8I9
     ----   I+I-I/I,I.I(I)IxI=I%I?I§I"IАIБIВIГIДIЕIЖIЗIИIКIЛIМIНIПIРIСIТIУ
     ----   IФIХIЦIЧIШIЩIЫIЬI9IЮIЯ202I22232425262728292+2-2/2,2.2(2)2x2=2%
     ----   2?2§2"2А2Б2В2Г2Д2Е2Ж2З2И2К2Л2М2Н2П2Р2С2Т2У2Ф2Х2Ц2Ч2Ш2Щ2Ы2Ь2Э2Ю
     ----   2Я303I32333435363738393+3-3/3,3.3(3)3x3=3%3?3§3"3А3Б3В3Г3Д3Е3Ж
     ----   3Э3И3К3Л3М3Н3П3Р3С3Т3У3Ф3Х3Ц3Ч3Ш3Щ3Ы3Ь3Э393Ю3Я4О4I42434445464748
     ----   494+4-4/4,4.4(4)4x4=4%4?4§4"4А4Б4В4Г4Д4Е4Ж434И4К4Л4М4Н4П4Р4С4Т
     ----   4У4Ф4Х4Ц4Ч4Ш4Щ4Ы4Ь494Ю4Я505I52535455565758595+5-5/5,5.5(5)5x5=
     ----   5%5?5§5"5А5Б5В5Г5Д5Е5Ж535И5К5Л5М5Н5П5Р5С5Т5У5Ф5Х5Ц5Ч5Ш5Щ5Ы5Ь5Э
     ----   5Ю5Я606I62636465666768696+6-6/6,6.6(6)6x6=6%6?6§6"6А6Б6В6Г6Д6Е
     ----   6Ж636И6К6Л6М6Н6П6Р6С6Т6У6Ф6Х6Ц6Ч6Ш6Щ6Ы6Ь6Э636Ю6Я7О7I7273747576 77
     ----   78797+7-7/7,7.7(7)7x7=7%7?7§7"7А7Б7В7Г7Д7Е7Ж737И7К7Л7М7Н7П7Р7С
     ----   7Т7У7Ф7Х7Ц7Ч7Ш7Щ7Ы7Ь737Ю7Я80808I82838485868788898+8-8/8,8.8(8)8x
     ----   8=8%8?8§8"8А8Б8В8Г8Д8Е8Ж838И8К8Л8М8Н8П8Р8С8Т8У8Ф8Х8Ц8Ч8Ш8Щ8Ы8Ь
     ----   898Ю8Я909I92939495969798999+9-9/9,9.9(9)9x9=9%9?9§9"9А9Б9В9Г9Д
     ----   9Е9Ж939И9К9Л9М9Н9П9Р9С9Т9У9Ф9Х9Ц9Ч9Ш9Щ9Ы9Ь939Ю9Я+0+I+2+3+4+5+6
     ----   +7+8+9++-+/+,+.+(+)+x+=+%+?+§+"+А+Б+В+Г+Д+Е+Ж+З+И+К+Л+М+Н+П+Р
     ----   +С+Т+У+Ф+Х+Ц+Ч+Ш+Щ+Ы+Ь+Э+Ю+Я-0-I-2-3-4-5-6-7-8-9-+---/-,-.-(-)
     ----   -x-=-%-?-§-"-А-Б-В-Г-Д-Е-Ж-З-И-К-Л-М-Н-П-Р-С-Т-У-Ф-Х-Ц-Ч-Ш-Щ-Ы
     ----   -Ь-Э-Ю-Я/0/I/2/3/4/5/6/7/8/9/+/-///,/./(/)/x/=/%/?/§/"/А/Б/В/Г
     ----   /Д/Е/Ж/З/И/К/Л/М/Н/П/Р/С/Т/У/Ф/Х/Ц/Ч/Ш/Щ/Ы/Ь/Э/Ю/Я,0,I,2,3,4,5
     ----   ,6,7,8,9,+,-,/,,,.,(,),x,=,%,?,§,",А,Б,В,Г,Д,Е,Ж,З,И,К,Л,М,Н,П
     ----   ,Р,С,Т,У,Ф,Х,Ц,Ч,Ш,Щ,Ы,Ь,Э,Ю,Я.0.I.2.3.4.5.6.7.8.9.+.-./.,...(
     ----   .).x.=.%.?.§.".А.Б.В.Г.Д.Е.Ж.З.И.К.Л.М.Н.П.Р.С.Т.У.Ф.Х.Ц.Ч.Ш.Щ
     ----   .Ы.Ь.Э.Ю.Я(0(I(2(3(4(5(6(7(8(9(+(-(/(,(.((()(x(=(%(?(§("(А(Б(В
     ----   (Г(Д(Е(Ж(З(И(К(Л(М(Н(П(Р(С(Т(У(Ф(Х(Ц(Ч(Ш(Щ(Ы(Ь(Э(Ю(Я)0)I)2)3)4
И0903----   )5)6)7)8)9)+)-)/),).))))x)=)%)?)§)")А)Б)В)Г)Д)Е)Ж)З)И)К)Л)М)Н
```

Figure 9.12 Sample of test document from the mixed array.

trials were run to estimate the error and rejection probabilities. Three types of test document were used: (1) documents prepared in advance, by the development team; (2) documents typed on various typewriters with the same type, with text chosen by direction of the committee running the trials; and (3) a few documents prepared by groups of people not connected with the developer. Samples of the test documents are shown in Figures 9.11–9.13.

The test documents were written by operators without special training, who were merely familiarized with the instructions for preparing the documents. An ordinary medium-inked ribbon was used. Typing errors were unavoidable, and were corrected by erasing with a rubber eraser or by overpasting a small piece of paper bearing the correct character. A comparatively small number of documents were rejected, mainly because the markers were out of place or because the paper was of nonstandard

kovalevsky pat recog ch ix s 9.5 rus p 315   lx.49

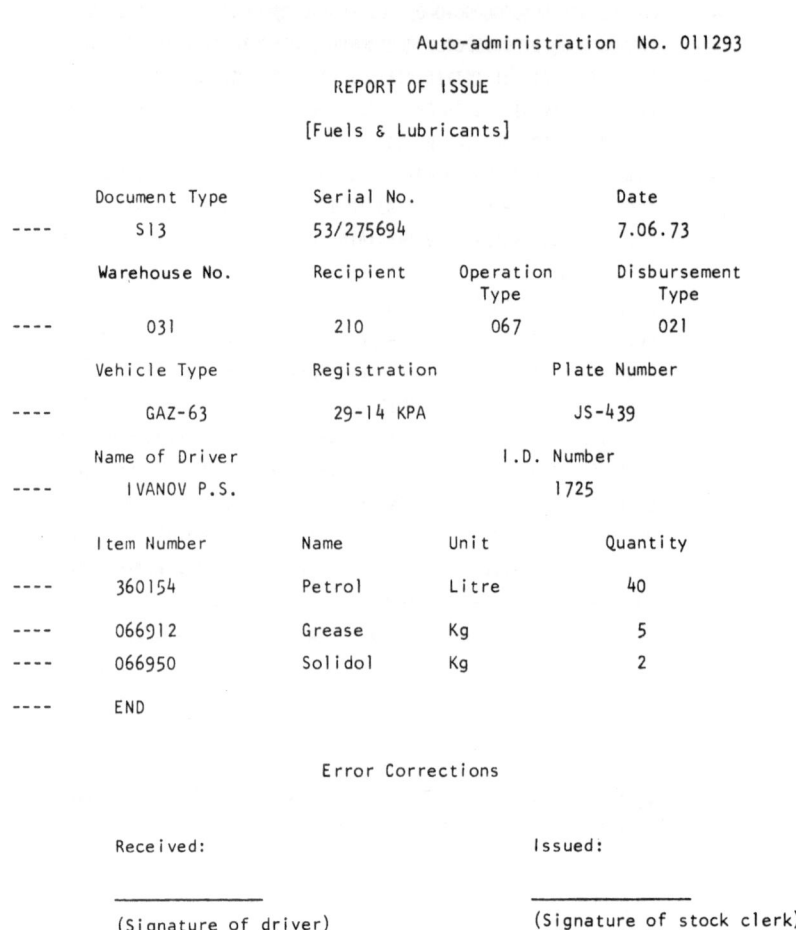

Auto-administration No. 011293

REPORT OF ISSUE

[Fuels & Lubricants]

	Document Type	Serial No.		Date
----	S13	53/275694		7.06.73

	Warehouse No.	Recipient	Operation Type	Disbursement Type
----	031	210	067	021

	Vehicle Type	Registration	Plate Number
----	GAZ-63	29-14 KPA	JS-439

	Name of Driver		I.D. Number
----	IVANOV P.S.		1725

	Item Number	Name	Unit	Quantity
----	360154	Petrol	Litre	40
----	066912	Grease	Kg	5
----	066950	Solidol	Kg	2
----	END			

Error Corrections

Received: Issued:

_____   _____
(Signature of driver)   (Signature of stock clerk)

Figure 9.13   Paraphrase of a sample of test document in the form of a table.

size (not conforming to the GOST standard) and would be improperly handled by the transfer mechanism.

The text material was also of three different types. Documents of the numerical array contained the digits from 0 to 9, with blanks, and two-digit numbers from 00 to 99 without blanks; in all, there were 40,920 characters. The documents of the mixed array contained all possible pairs of characters from the entire alphabet, totaling 39,060 characters. A sample document of this type is shown in Figure 9.12. The documents of the alphabetic array contained texts transcribed from newspapers or books. One such array contained 24,050 characters, and another, 16,200 characters. Each document (the paper measured 210×297 mm) contained 30 printed lines of 62 characters per line, i.e., 1860 characters in all, not counting blanks at the beginning and end of a line.

Table 9.1

Run No.	Type of test array and test conditions	Number of characters read	Errors				Rejected characters			
			Number	Frequency	Lower bound of probability	Upper bound of probability	Number	Frequency	Lower bound of probability	Upper bound of probability
1	Numerical array (3 readings)	$40,920 \times 3 = 122,760$	0	0	0	2.4×10^{-5}	3	2.4×10^{-5}	0.67×10^{-5}	6.3×10^{-5}
2	Alphabetic array (from *Pravda*, 3 readings)	48,600	3	6.2×10^{-5}	1.7×10^{-5}	1.6×10^{-4}	7	1.4×10^{-4}	0.68×10^{-4}	2.7×10^{-4}
3	Mixed array (3 readings)	117,180	22	1.9×10^{-4}	1.4×10^{-4}	2.7×10^{-4}	67	5.7×10^{-4}	4.6×10^{-4}	7.0×10^{-4}
4	Alpha array, normal voltage	24,050	5	2.1×10^{-4}	2.1×10^{-4}	4.3×10^{-4}	13	5.4×10^{-4}	3.2×10^{-4}	8.5×10^{-4}
5	Alpha array, high voltage (220 V + 10%)	24,050	6	2.5×10^{-4}	1.1×10^{-4}	4.9×10^{-4}	12	5.0×10^{-4}	2.9×10^{-4}	8.0×10^{-4}
6	Alpha array, low voltage (220 V − 10%)	24,050	2	8.3×10^{-5}	1.5×10^{-5}	2.6×10^{-4}	12	5.0×10^{-4}	2.9×10^{-4}	8.0×10^{-4}
7	Mixed array, low temperature (+6° C.)	39,060	9	2.3×10^{-4}	1.2×10^{-4}	4.0×10^{-4}	23	5.9×10^{-4}	4.0×10^{-4}	8.3×10^{-4}
8	Mixed array, high temperature (+40° C)	39,060	8	2.0×10^{-4}	1.0×10^{-4}	3.7×10^{-4}	22	5.6×10^{-4}	3.8×10^{-4}	8.0×10^{-4}

An automatic error count was obtained by storing sequences of codes corresponding to the documents in the memory of a BESM-6 electronic computer. At the end of the trial with an array of documents, the computer counted the errors and produced a printout with the results of the recognition. Texts produced at the time of the trials were read by the machine, fed to the computer, and then printed out on the line printer. The error count was made manually.

Table 9.1 shows the results of the ČARS trials under the various conditions. The trials showed that with an alphabet containing the 53 characters

$$\{0\,1\,2\,3\,4\,5\,6\,7\,8\,9 + \; - \; \times \; / \; = \; \% \,? \; \; .. \,(\,)$$

$$\S \; \textit{"blank"} \; А \; \textit{V} \; В \; Г \; д \; Е \; Ж \; З \; и \; К \; Л \; М \; Н \; П \; Р \; С \; Т \; У$$

$$Ф \; Х \; Ц \; Ч \; Ш \; Щ \; ы \; Ь \; Э \; Ю \; Я\}$$

and an average reading speed of 150 characters per second, the upper confidence limit for the error probability is 2.7×10^{-4}, with a fiducial probability of 95%. For purely numerical material, the corresponding confidence limit is 2.4×10^{-5}.

The occurrence of illegible characters bears only on the reading speed, since these characters are corrected by the operator. The values obtained in the trials yield a rejection probability of 8×10^{-4} for mixed text and 6×10^{-5} for purely numerical text. (These are upper confidence limits with a fiducial probability of 95%.) These relatively small rejection probabilities do not lower the reading speed significantly.

9.6 Conclusions. On the Use of Character Readers

The ČARS trials show that the recognition algorithms described here and the technical methods chosen to implement them yield rather high figures of merit: namely, the reading speed and the probability of correct recognition. However, the construction of a machine, even one with such high performance indices, does not in itself guarantee that automation of the input to electronic computers will be economically effective. Three principal requirements must be met:

1. The input to the machine should amount to something between one and ten million characters per day;
2. There must be a preplanned procedure for correcting misprints in the documents, convenient for the user;
3. a procedure must be developed for detecting and correcting misprints overlooked by the operator and recognition errors made by the reader.

A high input rate will occur if the input documents are typed concurrently by many operators. It is best if the document is typed by its originator and not retyped before submission to the machine.

To meet the second requirement we need a notation system by which an operator can indicate the location of a misprint in a document, and the correct character to replace it. Then the computer could be equipped with software for decoding the notation and correcting the misprint.

The third requirement is much harder to meet, since it demands the expense of extra work during the preparation of the documents. The automatic detection of errors is based on the redundancy of information. For numerical data the redundancy can be introduced by supplying a control total, for example. To produce the control total it is necessary to key all the digits to be controlled into some calculator, take the total, and print it in a specified place on the document. The input to the calculator is an additional manual task, comparable in difficulty to the original typing of the digits to be controlled.

Alphabetic information could be controlled by a similar method, using a special calculator with an alphanumeric keyboard and an automatic coding element that would associate each character with a definite code or number. A device of this sort, if it were constructed, would cost much more than a typewriter, and would increase the document preparation costs substantially. If we combine the device with a typewriter, and combine the computation of the control total with the typing, we cannot detect errors made by the operator through pressing the wrong key.

A satisfactory method of controlling information consists in typing the document twice. The cost of duplication does not exceed the cost of calculating a control total. We may surmise that there exists no control process costing less than duplication or the calculation of a control total. A defect of the duplication method is the high probability of repeating the same errors made in the original recognition, since the highest error probability is found in connection with certain definite characters in the alphabet. It would be desirable, on this account, to change the duplication method by changing the alphabet according to some definite substitution rule, so that some, or all, of the characters are replaced. This would greatly complicate the preparation of the document. No satisfactory solution of this problem has been discovered.

To sum up, we may conclude that successful exploitation of character readers will require the development of a carefully thought-out document preparation process, and computer software that will verify the input information and allow easy correction of misprints and recognition errors. The development of such a system is one of the most important and difficult tasks for the management of contemporary information processing.

References

(Transliterations of Russian text in *Mathematical Reviews* notation)

1. Braverman, E. M., ed.: *Avtomatičeskii Analiz Složnyh Izobraženiĭ*. Sb. perevodov pod red. E. M. Bravermana. Mir, 1969. (*Automatic Analysis of Complex Images*. Collection of translations.)

2. Aizerman, M. A., Braverman, E. M., Rozonoer, L. I.: *Metod Potencial'nyh Funkciĭ v Teorii Obučenija Mašin*. Nauka, 1970. (*The Method of Potential Functions in the Theory of Learning Machines*.)

3. Bagdonas, A. S., Žlabis, R. et al.: Čitajusčee ustroĭstvo RUTA-701. V sb. pod red. L. A. Tel'ksnisa *Avtomatizacija Vvoda Pis'mennyh Znakov v EVM*. RINTIP, Vilnius, 1965. (The RUTA-701 reading machine.)

4. Baraško, A. S., Kovalevskiĭ, V. A., Mazyra, Ju. S., Netrebenko, K. A., Semenovskiĭ, A. G.: Korrelacionnyĭ čitajuščiĭ avtomat so sdvigovym registrom ČARS. V sb. pod red. V. A. Kovalevskogo *Čitajuščie Avtomaty*. Naukova dumka, Kiev, 1965. (The CHARS correlative character reader. English translation in *Character Readers and Pattern Recognition*, Spartan Books, Washington D.C., 1968.)

5. Baraško, A. S., Kovalevskiĭ, V. A., Mazyra, Ju. S., Semenovskiĭ, A. G.: Sostojanie razrabotki i perspektivy vnedrenija čitajuščego avtomata ČARS. V sb. pod red. L. A. Tel'ksnisa *Avtomatizacija Vvoda Pis'mennyh Znakov v ÈVM*, RINTIP, Vilnius, 1965. (Current state of development and perspectives for the introduction of the ČARS character reader.)

6. Bellman, R., Dreyfus, S. E.: *Prikladnye zadači Dinamičeskogo Programmirovanija*. Nauka, 1965. (Translated from Bellman and Dreyfus, *Applied Dynamic Programming*, Princeton, 1962.)

7. Belobragina, L. S., Eliseev, V. K.: A statistical study of an algorithm for the recognition of typewritten characters. *Cybernetics*, 3 No. 6, 1967.

8. Blackwell, D., Giršik, M. A.: *Teorija Igr i Statističeskyh Rešenii*. IL, 1958. (Translation of Blackwell and Girshick, *Theory of Games and Statistical Decisions*. John Wiley, New York; Chapman and Hall, London.)

9. Bongard, M. M.: *Problema Uznavanija*. Nauka, 1967. (*The Recognition Problem*.)

10. Vapnik, V. N., Červonenkis, A. Ja.: *Teorija Raspoznavanija Obrazov— Statističeskie Problemy Obučenija*. Nauka, 1974. (*Theory of Image Recognition and Statistical Problems of Learning*.)

11. Vintsiuk, T. K., Generative grammars and dynamic programming in speech recognition with learning. Conference record of IEEE Int. Conf. on Acoustics, Speech, and Signal Processing, Philadelphia 1976, pp. 446–452.

12. Vozijanov, A. F.: Issledovanie adekvatnosti modeli izobraženii mašinopisnyh znakov. B sb. pod red. K. B. Starkusa *Avtomatizacija Vvoda Pis'mennyh Znakov v ÈVM*, t. I, izd. Kaunasskogo politehničeskogo in-ta, Kaunas, 1973. (A study of the adequacy of models of images of typewritten characters.)

13. Vozijanov, A. F., Galočkin V. G., Kalmykov, V. G., Kovalevskiï, V. A., Provalov, Ju. L., Šlezinger, M. I.: Sintez optimal'nyh ètalonov dlja čitajuščih avtomatov i issledovanie ih effecktivnosti. V sb. pod red. K. B. Starkusa *Avtomatizacija Vvoda Pis'mennyh Znakov v ÈVM*, t. I, izd. Kaunasskogo politehničeskogo in-ta, Kaunas, 1973. (The synthesis of optimal prototypes for character readers and a study of their effectiveness.)

14. Vozijanov, A. F., Denisov, V. A., Kovalevskiï, V. A.: Vybor parametrov algoritma predvaritel'noi obrabotki izobraženii. V sb. pod red. K. B. Starkusa *Avtomatizacija Vvoda Pis'mennyh Znakov v CVM*, t. I, izd. Kaunasskogo politehničeskogo in-ta, Kaunas, 1973. (The selection of parameters for the preprocessing of images.)

15. Vozijanov, A. F., Gimel'farb, G. L.: Sovremennye optičeskie avtomaty dlja čtenija pečatnogo i rukopisnogo teksta. *Upravljajuščie Sistemy i Mašiny*, No. 1, 1973. (Contemporary optical character readers for printed and handwritten text.)

16. Vozijanov, A. F., Kovalevskiï, V. A., Koršak, V. K., Provalov, Ju. L., Semenovskiï, A. G.: Rezul'taty modernizacii avtomata ČARS. V sb. pod red. K. B. Starkusa *Avtomatizacija Vvoda Pis'mennyh Znakov v ÈVM*, t. I, izd. Kaunasskogo politehničeskogo in-ta, Kaunas, 1973. (The results of modernizing the ČARS character reader.)

17. Vozijanov, A. F., Koršak, V. K., Niščenec, V. N.: Čitajuščiï avtomat. Avtorskoe svid. No. 413503, *Bjulleten' Izobretenii*, No. 4, 1974. (A character reader; a USSR patent.)

18. Gimel'farb, G. L., Eliseev, V. K., Moskanov, N. D., Curin, O. F.: Korreljacionnyï čitajuščiï avtomat s elektronno-optičeskim preobrazovatelem izobraženii. *Avtomatika i Telemehanika*, No. 2, 1968. (A correlating character reader with electron-optical image transducer.)

19. Ginzburg, S., *Matematičeskaja Teorija Kontekstnosvobodnyh Jazykov*. Mir, 1970. (*The Mathematical Theory of Context-Free Languages*.)

20. Gluškov, V. M.: *Sintez Cifrovyh Avtomatov.* Fizmatgiz, 1962. (*The Construction of Numerical Machines.*)

21. Gluškov, V. M., Kovalevskiĭ, V. A., Rybak, V. I.: Universal'naja ustanovka dlja issledovanija algoritmov raspoznavanija izobraženiĭ. V sb. *Principy Postroenija Samoobučajuščihsja Sistem.* Gostehizdat UkSSR, Kiev, 1962. (Principles of construction of self-learning systems.)

22. Grebnev, V. A., Šlezinger, M. I.: Samonastraivajuščiĭsja algoritm dlja raspoznavanija mašinopisnyh izobraženii. V trudah seminara *Raspoznavanie Obrazov i Konstruirovanie Čitajuščih Avtomatov.* vyp. 2, izd. IK AN UkSSR, Kiev, 1967. (A self-adjusting algorithm for the recognition of typewritten images.)

23. De Groot, M.: *Optimal'nye Statističeskie Rešenija.* Mir, 1974. (Translated from M. H. DeGroot, *Optimal Statistical Decisions,* New York: McGraw-hill, 1970.)

24. Eliseev, V. K., Kovalevskiĭ, V. A.: Issledovanie algoritma raspoznavanija mašinopisnyh cifr. *Žurnal Vyčislitel'noĭ Matematiki i Matematičeskoĭ Fiziki,* 2, No. 5., 1962. (Investigation of an algorithm for the recognition of typewritten numbers.)

25. Žuravlev, Ju. I.: Algoritmy raspoznavanija, osnovannye na vyčislenii ocenok. Soderžatel'nyi smysl parametrov, zadajuščih algoritm. V sb. *Raspoznavanie Obrazov. Trudy Meždunarodnogo Seminara 1971 G. po Praktičeskim Primenenijam Metodov Raspoznavanija Obrazov,* izd. Vyčislitel'nogo centra AN SSSR, M., 1973. (A recognition algorithm based on the computation of estimates. The meaning of the parameters defining the algorithm.)

26. Zagoruĭko, N. G.: Metody Raspoznavanija i ih Primenenija. Izd-vo Sovetskoe radio, 1972. (Recognition Methods and Their Applications.)

27. Zaĭcev, V. I., Savin, A. A.: Ob odnoĭ sisteme čitajuščego avtomata. V sb. *Čitajuščie Ustroĭstva,* Izd. VINITI, 1962. (On a system for a character reader.)

28. Zuhovickiĭ, S. I., Radčik, I. A.: *Matematičeskie Metody Setevogo Planirovanija.* Nauka, 1965. (Mathematical Methods of Network Planning.)

29. Kalmykov, V. G.: Avtomatičeskoe čtenie strok mašinopisnogo teksta. *Izvestija AN SSSR, Serija Tehničeskaya Kibernetika,* No. 3, 1973. (Automatic reading of lines of typewritten text.)

30. Kalmykov, V. G.: Sposob vydelenija znakov v stroke. Avtorskoe svid. No. 367434, *Bjulleten' Izobretenii,* No. 8, 1973. (A method for separating symbols into strokes; a USSR patent.)

31. Katinskiĭ, V. S., Tihomirov, B. D.: Avtomat dlja sčityvanija tipografičeskih tekstov. *Trudy III Vsesojuznoĭ Konferencii po Informacionno-Poiskovym Sistemam,* t. III. VINITI, 1967. (A machine for reading typographic text.)

32. Kovalevskiĭ, V. A.: Korreljacionnyĭ metod raspoznavanija izobraženiĭ. *Žurnal Vyčislitel'noĭ Matematiki i Matematičeskoĭ Fiziki,* 2, No. 4, 1962. (English translation available: Kovalevsky, V. A.: Correlation method of pattern recognition. U.S. Dept. of Commerce Joint Publication Research Service 17391, OTS 63-21024.)

33. Kovalevskiĭ, V. A.: Čitajuščee ustroĭstvo. Avtorskoe svid. No. 188153, *Bjulleten' Izobretenii* No. 21, 1966. (A reading apparatus; USSR patent.)

34. Kovalevskiĭ, V. A.: Statisticeskiĭ podhod k probleme obučenija raspoznavaniju obrazov. *Trudy III Vsesojuznogo Sovescanija po Avatmatičeskomu*

Upravleniju, Odessa, 1965. Nauka, 1967. (A statistical approach to the problem of learning pattern recognition.)

35. Kovalevsky, V. A.: An optimal algorithm for the recognition of some sequences. *Cybernetics,* **3,** No. 4, 1967.

36. Kovalevsky, V. A.: The state of the art in the problem of pattern recognition. *Cybernetics,* **3,** No. 5, 1967.

37. Kovalevskiĭ, V. A.: Optimal'nyĭ metod diskretizacii grafičeskih izobraženiĭ. V sb. pod red. V. A. Kovalevskogo *Kibernetika i Vyčislitel'naja Tehnika.* Naukova dumka, Kiev, 1969. (An optimal method for digitizing graphic images).

38. Kovalevsky, V. A.: Application of mathematical programming for character and pattern recognition. Fifth International Congress on Cybernetics, Namur, 1967.

39. Kovalevsky, V. A.: Recognition by imitating the process of pattern generation. In Watanabe, M. S. (ed.): *Methodologies of Pattern Recognition.* New York, Academic, 1969.

40. Kovalevsky, V. A.: Pattern recognition—heuristics or science? In *Advances in Information Systems Sciences.* New York, Plenum, 1970.

41. Kozinec, B. N.: Rekurrentnyĭ algoritm razdelenija vypuklyh oboloček dvuh množestv. V sb. pod red. V. N. Vapnika *Algoritmy Obučenija Raspoznavaniju Obrazov.* Izd-vo "Sovetskoe radio", 1973. (A recursive algorithm for separating the convex hulls of two sets.)

42. Kul'bak, S.: *Teorija Informacii i Statistika.* Mir, 1967. (Kullback, Solomon: Information theory and statistics, New York, John Wiley; London, Chapman & Hall.)

43. Kušner, E. F.: Opyty po primeneniju korreljacionnogo metoda dlja raspoznavanija cifr i bukv, napisannyh ot ruki. V trudah seminara *Raspoznavanie Obrazov i Konstruirovanie Čitajuščih Avtomatov.* IK AN UkSSR, Kiev, 1966. (Experimental application of the correlation method to the recognition of handwritten digits and letters.)

44. Leman, E.: *Proverka Statističeskih Gipotez.* Nauka, M., 1964. (Tr. from Lehmann, E. L.: *Testing Statistical Hypotheses,* New York, John Wiley; London, Chapman & Hall.)

45. Lindli, D. V.: O mere informacii, davaemoĭ eksperimentom. Sbornik perevodov *Matematika,* vyp. 3:3, IL, 1959. (Tr. from Lindley, D. V.: On a measure of the information provided by an experiment, *Ann. Math. Statistics,* **27,** 1965.)

46. Loginov, N. V.: Metody stohastičeskoĭ approksimacii. *Avtomatika i tele-mehanika,* **XXVII,** No. 14, 1966. (Stochastic approximation methods.)

47. Milen'kiĭ, A. V.: *Klassifikacija Signalov v Uslovijah Neopredelennosti.* Izd-vo "Sovetskoe radio", 1975. (*The Classification of Signals under Conditions of Indeterminacy.*)

48. Minskiĭ, M., Peĭpert, S.: *Perseptrony.* Mir, 1971. (Tr. from Minsky, M., and Papert, S.: *Perceptrons: An Introduction to Computational Geometry.* Cambridge, Mass., MIT Press, 1969.)

49. Mučnik, I. B.: Formirovanie jazyka opisanija zritel'nyh obrazov. V sb. pod

red. E. M. Bravermana *Avtomatičeskiĭ Analiz Složnyh Izobraženii*. Mir, 1969. (Construction of a language for describing visual patterns.)

50. Narasimhan, R. A.: Linguistic Approach to Pattern Recognition. Univ. of Illinois, Digital Computer Lab Report No. 121, July 1962.

51. Narasimhan, R. A.: Syntax-directed interpretation of classes of pictures. CACM, **9**, No. 3, 1966.

52. Našljunas, R. A., Jašinskas, P. P.: Issledovanie vlijanija diskretizacii izobrazenija na dostovernost' algoritmov opoznovanija. *Trudy III Vsesojuznoĭ Konferencii po Informacionno-poskovym Sistemam*, t. III. VINITI, 1967. (An investigation of the influence of digitization of images on the reliability of recognition algorithms.)

53. Neĭmark, Ju. I., Batalova, Z. S., et al.: Raspoznavanie Obrazov i Medicinskaja Diagnostika. Nauka, 1972. (*Pattern Recognition and Medical Diagnosis.*)

54. Netrebenko. K. A.: Ukazatel' ekstremuma. Avtorskoe svid. No. 181169. *Bjulleten' Izobretenii*, No. 9, 1966. (An extremum indicator; USSR patent.)

55. Netrebenko, K. A.: *Kompensacionnye Shemy Amplitudnyh Vol'tmetrov i Ukazateleĭ Ekstremuma*. Izd-vo "Energija", 1967. (*Compensating Circuits for Amplitude Voltmeters and Extremum Indicators.*)

56. Nil'son N.: *Obučajuščiesja Mašiny*. Mir, 1967. (Tr. from Nilson, N. J., *Learning Machines*, New York, McGraw-Hill, 1968.)

57. Pugačev, V. S.: Optimal'nye algoritmy obučenija avtomatičeskih sistem v slučae neideal'nogo ucitelja. *DAN AN SSSR*, **172**, No. 5, 1967. (Optimal algorithms for training automatic systems with a nonideal trainer.)

58. Rozenblatt, F.: *Principy Neĭrodinamiki. Perseptron i Teorija Mehanizmov Mozga*. Mir, 1965. (Tr. from Rosenblatt, Frank: *Principles of Neurodynamics. The Perceptron and the Theory of the Mechansims of the Brain.*)

59. Romanov, V. P.: O lingvističeskom metode interpretacii složnyh izobraženii. *Naučno-Tehničeskaja Informacija*, No. 11, 1965. (On a linguistic method for the interpretation of complex images.)

60. Romanov, V. P.: Sistema interpretacii, raspoznavanija izobraženiĭ i ustanovlenija sootvetstvija—SIRIUS, *Trudy III Vsesojuznoĭ Konferencii po Informacionno-Poiskovym Sistemam*. t. III. VINITI, 1967. (System for the interpretation and recognition of images and the establishment of correspondences—The SIRIUS.)

61. Svjatogor, L. A.: Ètalonnye oblasti v modeljah optičeskih izobraženiĭ. V sb. *Raspoznavanie Obrazov*. IK AN UkSSR, Kiev, 1973. (Prototype domains in models of optical images.)

62. Semenovskiĭ, A. G.: Cifrovoĭ analizator maksimal'nogo značenija amplitudy. Avtorskoe svid. No. 206901. *Bjulleten' Izobretenii*, No. 1, 1967. (A digital analyzer of maximum amplitude value; USSR patent.).

63. Faĭn, V. S.: *Opoznovanie Izobraženiĭ*. Nauka, 1970. (*Image Recognition.*)

64. Faĭnstein, A.: *Osnovy Teorii Informacii*. IL, 1962. (Tr. from Feinstein, Amiel: *Foundations of Information Theory*, New York, McGraw-Hill, 1965.)

65. Helstrom, K.: *Statističeskaja Teorija Obnaruženija Signalov*. IL, 1963. (*The Statistical Theory of Signal Detection.*)

66. Cypkin, Ja. Z.: Adaptacija, obučenie i samoobučenie v avtomatičeskih sistemah. *Avtomatika i Telemehanika*, **XXVII**, No. 1, 1966. (Adaptation, learning, and self-learning in automatic systems.)

67. Cypkin, Ja. Z., Kel'mans, G. K.: Rekurrentnye algoritmy samoobučenija. Izvestija AN SSSR, serija "Tehničeskaja kibernetika", No. 5, 1967. (Recursive algorithms for self-learning.)

68. Šarypanov, V. M., Šlezinger, M. I.: Algoritm raspoznavanija snimkov sobytiĭ v puzyr'kovyh kamerah. V sb. *Raspoznavanie Obrazov. Trudy Meždunarodnogo Seminara 1971 G. po Praktičeskim Primenenijam Metodov Raspoznavanija Obrazov*, izd. Vyčislitel'nogo centra AN SSSR, M., 1973. (An algorithm for recognizing photographs of events in bubble chambers.)

69. Schlesinger, M. I.: On spontaneous distinguishing of patterns, in *Character Readers and Pattern Recognition*, Spartan Books, Washington, D. C., 1968.

70. Schlesinger, M. I.: A correlation method for recognizing sequences of images. op. cit.

71. Šlezinger, M. I., Svjatogor, L. A.: O postroenija ètalonov dlja korreljacionnyh čitajuščih avtomatov. *Trudy III Vsesojuznoi Konferencii po Informacionno-Poiskovym Sistemam*, t. III. VINITI, 1967. (On the construction of prototypes for correlative character readers.)

72. Schlesinger, M. I.: The interconnection between learning and self-learning in pattern recognition. *Cybernetics*, **4**, No. 2, 1968.

73. Šlezinger, M. I.: Sintez lineĭnogo rešajuščego pravila dlja odnogo klassa zadač raspoznavanija obrazov. *Izvestija AN SSSR, Serija "Tehničeskaja kibernetika"*, No. 5, 1972. (Synthesis of a linear decision rule for a class of pattern recognition problems.)

74. Šlezinger, M. I.: Optimizacija raspoznajuščih ustroĭstv, realizujuščih kusočno-lineĭnye rešajuščie pravila. V sb. pod red. K. B. Starkusa *Avtomatizacija Vvoda Pis'mennyh Znakov v ÈVM*. Izd. Kaunasskogo politehničeskogo in-ta, Kaunas, 1973. (Optimization of recognizers implementing a piecewise linear decision rule.)

75. Shor, N. Z.: On the speed of convergence of the generalized gradient descent. *Cybernetics*, **4**, No. 3, 1968.

76. Alt, F.: Digital Pattern Recognition by Moments, Proceedings of Symposium on Optical Character Recognition, Washington, D. C., 1962.

77. Anderson, T. W., Bahadur R. P: Classification into two multivariate normal distributions with different covariance matrices. *The Annals of Mathematical Statistics*, June, vol. **133**, 1962.

78. Cooper, D. B., Cooper P. W.: Non-supervised adaptive signal detection and pattern recognition. *Information and Control*, vol. 7, Sept., 1960.

79. Evans, T. G.: A Formalism for the Description of Complex Objects and its Implementation. V International Congress on Cybernetics, Namur, 1967.

80. Görke, W.: Bestimmung von Strichelementen mittels dynamischer Optimierung. Institut für Nachrichtenverarbeitung Universität Karlsruhe (TH), Jahresbericht, 1969.

81. Huang, T., Fu, K. S.: Stochastic syntactic analysis for programmed grammars

and syntactic pattern recognition. *Computer Graphics and Image Processing*, vol. **1**, 1972.

82. Kirsch, R. A.: Computer interpretation of English text and picture patterns. *Trans. IEEE*, vol. **EC-13** 1964.

83. Kovalevsky, V. A.: *Present and Future of Pattern Recognition Theory*. Proceedings of IFIP Congress 65, Spartan Books, Washington D.C., 1965.

84. Kovalevsky, V. A.: *Sequential Optimization in Pattern Recognition and Pattern Description*. Proceedings of IFIP Congress 68, Academic Press, New York, 1969.

85. Martelli, A. and Montanari, U.: Optimal smoothing in picture processing: an application to fingerprints. *Information Processing* **71**, 1972.

86. Novikoff, A.: On Convergence Proofs for Perceptrons, *Proceedings of Symposium on Mathematical Theory of Automata*. Polytechnic Institute of Brooklyn, vol. XII, 1963.

87. Rosenblatt, F.: Two Theorems on Statistical Separability in the Perceptron. *Proceedings of the Symposium on the Mechanization of Thought Processes*, London, 1958.

88. Siromoney, G., Siromoney, R., Krithivasan, K.: Abstract families of matrices and picture languages, *Computer Graphics and Image Processing*, vol. **1**, 1972.

89. Schlesinger, M. I.: Syntactic analysis of two-dimensional visual signals in noise conditions. *Cybernetics,* **12**, No. 4, 1976.

90. Davis, L. S., Rosenfeld, A., Application of relaxation labeling, 2: spring-loaded template matching, *Proceedings of the Third International Joint Conference on Pattern Recognition*, Coronado, 1976, pp. 591–597.

91. Rosenfeld, A., Kak, A. C., *Digital Picture Processing*, Academic Press, New York, 1976.

List of Basic Notations

(With a brief definition and reference to the pages on which the notation is introduced.)

a	constant parameter in a probability distribution, p. 43
$\arg\max_x f(x)$	a value of x at which $f(x)$ attains its maximum, p. 6
$\text{Arg}\max_x f(x)$	the set of values $\{x : f(x) = \max_y f(y)\}$, p. 6
b	the nuisance parameter, p. 43
B, B_k	the set of values of b, p. 93
$\mathfrak{B}$	the alphabet of terminal symbols; the set $\{\beta_i\}$ of values of the components b_j of the parameter b, p. 147
c	a vector whose components are the coefficients of a linear discriminant function; in particular, a template, pp. 19, 53
c_i	the ith component of c, pp. 17, 53
$c(\dots)$	the vector c as a function depending on several parameters, p. 53
C	the set of templates c, p. 121
d	a decision arrived at in the course of recognition, p. 4
D	the set of values of d, p. 4

$\mathbf{D}_\theta x$	variance of the random variable x for a fixed value of the indicated parameter θ, p. 122
$e^{(k)}$	the archetype of the kth class, p. 47
$e(\dots)$	an elementary prototype depending on parameters, pp. 149, 158
$E(\dots)$	a prototype depending on parameters, p. 45
$\tilde{f}(v), \tilde{f}_k(v)$	discriminant functions, p. 6
$\mathscr{F}(v)$	decision function, p. 6
$g(v, E)$	similarity of image v with prototype E, p. 94
$g_i(\dots), g'(\dots),$ $g^*(\dots)$	various functions of parameters, whose values are interpreted as similarities, p. 152
$\hat{G}(\dots)$	a potentially optimal similarity, p. 154
$h(K\vert v)$	specific conditional entropy, p. 83
$H(K\vert V)$	conditional entropy, p. 75
$\mathscr{H}$	the Hamming distance, p. 51
k	the recognition parameter of a distribution, the designator of a class or abstract image, p. 2
$k(\dots)$	various functions of parameters, taking on values in the set K, p. 183
K	the set of values of k, p. 5
$\mathbf{K}$	covariance matrix of a signal (image) v, p. 123
$\mathscr{K}(\cdot, \cdot)$	potential function, p. 18
l	length of a training sample, p. 21
$\mathscr{L}$	a training sample, p. 18
$\mathbf{M}_\theta(x)$	mean value of a random variable x for a given value of the parameter θ, p. 122
n	the number of classes to be recognized, i.e., $n = \vert K \vert$, p. 27
N	the dimensionality of the space of features, the number of retinal cells, p. 4
$p(x\vert\theta)$	generalized probability density of the random variable x for a given value of the parameter or random variable θ, pp. 26, 70
$p_M(v)$	the specific error probability, i.e., the probability that the optimal decision for a given image v is wrong, p. 83
$\mathbf{P}_\theta(A)$	the probability of the event A for a given value of the parameter θ, p. 120
q	the width of a window and of an elementary prototype, p. 179
$q_e(k)$	the width of the elementary prototype of class k, p. 179
Q	the set of values of q, p. 182
r	a random vector, the noise, p. 7; in Chapter 7, a

	vector on the retina, indicating the location of a state, p. 158
R^m	m-dimensional Euclidean space, p. 98
$\mathcal{R}$	the recognition risk, p. 26
s	the state of a process, p. 149
$S(s,u)$	the function defining the next state to follow a given predecessor state s with the control u, pp. 59, 149
$\mathcal{S}$	the alphabet of nonterminal symbols, the set $\{\sigma_i\}$ of values assumed by the state s, p. 147
t	a component of the nuisance parameter b expressing the thickness of a stroke in the prototype, p. 133
$\mathcal{T}_b$	the image transformation operator, depending on a parameter, pp. 47, 93
u	the control, a variable defining the choice of one of the possible transitions from state to state, p. 149
$U(s)$	the set of admissible values of u for a given state s. p. 149
v	a multidimensional vector signal, or digitized image, p. 4
v_i	the ith component of v, having in particular the meaning of the brightness, or gray shade, of the ith cell of a digitized image, p. 4
v^j	the jth realization of v, p. 7
V	the set of values of v, p. 6
$w(k,d)$	the loss caused by the decision d when the signal belongs to class k, p. 26
W	a portion of the field of view, a window, p. 152
x, y	abscissa and ordinate of a point in the field of view; components of the nuisance parameter b, parametrizing horizontal and vertical displacements of a prototype, pp. 4, 133
z	the type of the state s, p. 159
$Z(\cdot)$	the function defining the type of the next state, p. 160
α, β	"optical" components of the nuisance parameter b. The pair (α, β) defines the contrast and uniform darkening of a prototype image, pp. 47, 99
β_i	terminal symbols which are at the same time values of the components of the parameter b, p. 147
$\Gamma(s)$	the rank of the vertex s in a network, p. 154
δ_{ik}	the Kronecker symbol, p. 27:

$$\delta_{ik} = \begin{cases} 1 & \text{if } i = k, \\ 0 & \text{if } i \neq k \end{cases}$$

ζ	a component of the nuisance parameter b, p. 98; or a discrete parameter of a decision rule, approximating a change in the nuisance parameter b (the discrete analogue of b), p. 132
$Z(\cdot)$	attachment function for ζ, p. 132
ξ, η	parameters of horizontal and vertical translations, p. 47
$\Xi(\cdot), H(\cdot)$	attachment functions for the parameters ξ and η, p. 133
ϑ	threshold of a linear threshold function, p. 14
$\bar{\theta}$	parameter of a family of distributions or more generally a family of functions, p. 51
μ	mean value of the difference between the similarities of an image with the prototypes of two different classes, p. 111
ρ	a vector on the retina, locating the origin of an elementary prototype. p.158
σ	standard deviation of a random variable, p. 111
σ_i	nonterminal symbols, or values of the variable s, p. 147
τ	a parameter denoting type of a template or elementary prototype, pp. 133, 178
$T(\cdot)$	a function defining the type of the next elementary prototype, p. 162; attachment function for the parameter τ, p. 133
$\varphi_j(v), \psi_j(v)$	secondary features, basis functions for the series expansion of discriminant functions, p. 14
$\Phi(x)$	the standard normal distribution function, p. 123
$\omega_i(x, y)$	weight functions for the image digitization process, p. 4
Ω_i	the ith cell of a grid or retina, p. 4
$[a, b] = \sum_{i=1}^{N} a_i b_i$	the scalar product of the vectors a and b, p. 19
$\ulcorner \quad \urcorner$	corners: take the value 1 or 0, corresponding respectively to the truth or falsehood of the enclosed predicate, p. 6

Index